מסורה

ArtScroll® Series

Rabbi Nosson Scherman / Rabbi Meir Zlotowitz

General Editors

הגדה של פסח

by Our Story

The Soul of the Seder
through stories and reflections

RABBI YECHIEL SPERO

Touched

Published by

ArtScroll®
Mesorah Publications ltd

FIRST EDITION
First Impression ... February 2015
Second Impression ... March 2015

Published and Distributed by
MESORAH PUBLICATIONS, LTD.
4401 Second Avenue / Brooklyn, N.Y 11232

Distributed in Europe by
LEHMANNS
Unit E, Viking Business Park
Rolling Mill Road
Jarow, Tyne & Wear, NE32 3DP
England

Distributed in Australia and New Zealand
by GOLDS WORLDS OF JUDAICA
3-13 William Street
Balaclava, Melbourne 3183
Victoria, Australia

Distributed in Israel by
SIFRIATI / A. GITLER — BOOKS
Moshav Magshimim
Israel

Distributed in South Africa by
KOLLEL BOOKSHOP
Northfield Centre, 17 Northfield Avenue
Glenhazel 2192, Johannesburg, South Africa

ARTSCROLL® SERIES
TOUCHED BY OUR STORY
© Copyright 2014, by MESORAH PUBLICATIONS, Ltd.
4401 Second Avenue / Brooklyn, N.Y. 11232 / (718) 921-9000 / www.artscroll.com

To contact the author with comments or stories, he can be reached via e-mail
at chiely1@gmail.com

ISBN 10: 1-4226-1563-4 / ISBN 13: 978-1-4226-1563-8

Typography by CompuScribe at ArtScroll Studios, Ltd.
Printed in the United States of America by Noble Book Press Corp.
Bound by Sefercraft, Quality Bookbinders, Ltd., Brooklyn N.Y. 11232

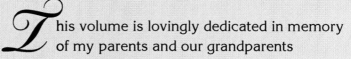

*T*his volume is lovingly dedicated in memory
of my parents and our grandparents

Menachem Mendel and Cyma Kirsch ז"ל

אבי מורי **מנחם מענדעל בן יוסף דוד הלוי** ז"ל
נפ' ב' סיון תשנ"ג

אמי מורתי **צימא בת קלונימוס קלמן** ע"ה
נפ' כ"ט אדר ב' תשס"ה

*H*e spent the War years in a Siberian labor camp.
She spent four years at hard labor in Auschwitz.
They never took the miracle of their survival lightly.

They came to America and settled on the Lower East Side.
Working hard all their lives — he as a merchant and she in
a factory — they were role models of Jews who maintained
their loyalty to Hashem and His Torah. He learned early
every morning and was kind to everyone, especially
his wife. She had a sense of beauty, had wonderful taste,
and always smiled and cared for others.

How fitting that this Haggadah — which symbolizes the
eternal Jew's privilege of passing on our heritage to future
generations — should be dedicated to a couple that
embodied this ideal, in times of both hardship and joy.

ולעלוי נשמות

פרומיט קירש ע"ה
פערל פרייגער ע"ה

Francine Kirsch Zweig

Feige Gittel and Yehuda Aryeh Lieberman
Klonimos Kalman Zweig
Blima Henna and Amir Chaim Nakash

Introduction

It is Seder night. There is so much to do, to learn, to accomplish, to experience. And so little time to do it.

The task seems daunting, perhaps even overwhelming. One may feel incapable of fulfilling the obligation of "*Ve'higadeta le'vincha ba'yom hahu* — You shall tell your son on that day" (*Shemos* 13:8), as Hashem intended. After all, the Seder has many aspects and angles. On which should we focus?

So if we were to simplify the message, what would it be?

Perhaps Rabbi Yehudah will help us along in our mission, as he was the one who sought a way to summarize the enormous lessons of the ten *makkos*. Thus, he came up with a mnemonic for the plagues: דצ"ך עד"ש באח"ב.

But does it really simplify or clarify anything? And do we need Rabbi Yehudah to put together the *makkos* into some sort of a code, which seems nothing more than a mumble-jumble of words?

For many years, I was bothered by this question. Then I came across a *vort* from the *Chasam Sofer*, which not only sheds light on this question, but also puts the lessons of the Seder night into focus.

The *Chasam Sofer* reads into the cryptic message and discovers the following: דצך — your joy (the word דִּיצָה means *joy,* and the כ' at the end of a word means *your*) should come from עֲדָשָׁה, *the lentil bean.* Mourners are given lentil beans to eat, since just as the lentil has no mouth, so, too, the mourner should work on having no complaints against the Almighty over his loss.

Rabbi Yehudah's message to us is: דצ"ך עד"ש. Even if the *tzaros* we encounter are as severe as those the Jews underwent in Mitzrayim, we must find joy in the silent and dignified manner in which we have reacted to those tragedies.

How? באח"ב. The letters 'ה and 'ח are interchangeable, so the word can be read as באהב — *with love,* we must accept everything Hashem does with love, be filled with happiness, and not have any complaints against Hashem.

This is a crucial and invaluable message for tonight. Through the generations, the Jewish people have suffered. There have been good times, but many harsh ones, as well. But we have survived, grown from those experiences, and accepted them all with love. We know that Hashem loves us, and that our suffering has a purpose; no pain or difficulty is for naught.

This theme is prevalent throughout the Seder. It is found in the *charoses,* a mixture of bitter memories — of children being slaughtered and backbreaking labor — yet sweetened with apples, to which Bnei Yisrael are lovingly compared. This can also represent our acknowledgment that Hashem sweetens our lives and mitigates our pain as much as possible. We can also find it in the *korech* sandwich, where we place our bitter herbs between two matzos, signifying that the bitter moments of our lives are sandwiched between happier ones.

It is found in our very existence, in the smiles and laughter of families shattered and fragmented by tragedy and loss, sitting together at the Seder, believing with every ounce of their being in the words: "*Le'shanah habaah biYerushalayim* — Next year in Jerusalem!"

It is found in the tickets placed on my Seder table, the ones I received from my mother, who received them from her mother, Rebbetzin Chana Leah Moses. These fragile and delicate reminders come from Buchenwald, where my Bubby spent nine months of her life; it is one of the three concentration camps she survived. She was awarded these tickets for good behavior. By using them, she could "purchase" soap in the camp. The Nazis had robbed her of all she held dear. Her family. Her friends. Everything.

Everything but her faith. Her battle cry was: "*Mir zol nahr blieben bie di emunah* — May we be able to endure all this with our faith intact."

After the war, she and her husband, my Zeidy Moses — who conducted a Seder in Auschwitz with no matzah, no wine, but plenty of *maror* — rebuilt their lives.

And now, their grandchildren and great-grandchildren sit around the Seder table, with those tickets as reminders of what has brought us to this moment:

Ironclad *emunah.*
Unshakeable.
Unbreakable.

How did they do it? What enabled them? The answer, and the key component and ingredient of tonight's Seder, is the variation of the third word of Rabbi Yehudah's phrase: באהב. With an indescribable love for *HaKadosh Baruch Hu,* which can best be transmitted on a night like this.

Dearest parents, this is your mission tonight. Bring the stories to life. Of Mitzrayim. Of Buchenwald. And the rich and memorable journey that connects the two. Our trials and tribulations and the redemption from both. Our survival. The *maror* and matzah, and also the *charoses.*

Whether you are a parent or a grandparent, you are a proud link in the *mesorah,* a chain that has lasted thousands of years.

Portray the difficulties we have endured, and the perseverance and commitment we have displayed. Many villains have tried to destroy us: Pharaoh and Nevuchadnetzar, Torquemada and Chmielnicki, Hitler and Hussein. But they have all failed, and we are still here. Describe the times of *kiddush Hashem,* the bloodcurdling cries of *Shema Yisrael,* the silent suffering and *mesirus nefesh* of Jews who held onto their love of Hashem in the darkest moments of Jewish history.

Teach them to be proud. Proud to carry the burden, mantra, and crown of *bnei Torah* and *bnos Yisrael.* Proud to be the next link in a chain that has spanned continents and millennia, that has stood fearlessly in the face of history's most infamous naysayers, and with unflinching strength has negated their cynicism and foiled their efforts.

Treasure the night. Treasure your children. Treasure the opportunity to share with them our story. Our successes, and perhaps more important, our failures. And how we have survived them all.

The Alexander Rebbe, Rav Yitzchak Menachem Danziger, who was killed in Treblinka in Elul, 1942, highlights the declaration we make at the beginning of the *Maggid* portion of the Seder. We say at the end of *Ha Lachma Anya,* "*Hashata hacha* — Now, we are here!" From the fact that we are here, mired in the current *tzarah,* we trust that soon we will merit the next step: "*le'shanah habaah be'ara de'Yisrael* — next year may we be in the Land of Israel." All the *tzaros* come from Hashem, and all the difficulties are for our good. Here, the *baal Haggadah* is encouraging us not to give up, even with all the tribulations that surround us from all sides. Rather, we should strengthen ourselves, because this is a sign that the time of the Final Redemption is coming soon.

All children come to the Seder tonight. The good ones, and the "bad" ones, as well. Cherish the so-called bad ones. They are not really bad; no children are. They are misled. Confused. Lost. But they are here. Let them hear that they are not the first to struggle. We, as individuals and as a people, have struggled. But no matter how lost we are, we find our way back home. This is what the *simanim* of the Seder are for. They are signs to help us find our way.

A story is told by Rav Dovid Rosenfeld. It is a story that breaks my heart, but warms it, as well. Rav Dovid was conducting a quiet, intimate Seder with a few other brave inmates in the barracks of the concentration camp, when suddenly, a kapo burst through the door. With an angry look on his face, he pointed to Rav Dovid and ordered him to follow him outside. Everyone knew what this meant. Rav Dovid would be beaten, perhaps to death, for the crime of conducting a Seder. As he walked out, he could be heard whispering a prayer that he was prepared to offer himself as a *korban pesach*, one that was slaughtered trying to observe Pesach.

But three hours later, he emerged, unharmed, with potatoes and eggs for himself and the others, as well.

What happened?

He was brought to a room where all the kapos sat. However, just this one night, they wanted to be good, too. But they had no idea how to conduct a Seder, so they went to bring someone to help them.

They cried the whole night, trying to remember what it meant to be free. To be a Jew. To be kind. To be merciful. To love and to be loved. To be connected to the Almighty and feel like part of the *am hanivchar*.

Tonight, everyone can find his way home. Tonight, we can accept our pain with joy and love. Tonight, we understand that we don't have to understand.

We will travel through the prism of time on this, the most special of nights, and at the end of the night, we will stand and sing and dance, "*Le'shanah habaah biYerushalayim* — Next year in Jerusalem!"

This is how my Zeidy's Seder ended in Auschwitz. I imagine there were tears; how could there not be? But somehow, he mustered up the strength to sing, "*Le'shanah habaah biYerushalayim.*"

This is the greatest story ever told.

For this is our story.

Acknowledgments

Odeh Hashem be'chol libi ...

Ribbono Shel Olam, I thank You with all my heart, and even that is insufficient. *Ein anachanu maspikim le'hodos lecha Hashem Elokeinu.*

Rabbi Meir Zlotowitz and **Rabbi Nosson Scherman** continue to inspire me and the rest of the world with their energy, drive, and commitment to make Torah more accessible to the masses. What a *zechus* it is to be part of their vision and dream.

My heartfelt thanks to the **ArtScroll staff:**

Gedaliah Zlotowitz — who never questions my unrealistic hopes, and instead makes them real and tangible. What a friend!

Avrohom Biderman — for his guidance and *eitzah tovah* on all delicate matters.

Mendy Herzberg — It is hard to imagine how someone with so much pressure on his plate manages to stay so calm.

Eli Kroen — who succeeded in capturing the striking beauty and elegance I imagined for the cover.

Mrs. Rivky Kapenstein — who did a masterful job on the graphics, and paid special attention to my unusual requests.

Mrs. Faygie Weinbaum — Thank you for your thorough proofreading.

A special note of thanks to **Mrs. Mindy Stern** for appreciating the stories and *divrei Torah,* while fine-tuning and tweaking each one. I cherish, and am humbled by, your praise.

The Pesach Seder of my dear parents, **Dr. and Mrs. Abba and Sarah Spero**, will always be the model for mine. My parents' Seder table is majestic and regal — with my mother's special touch. She sets the table days before, as it makes the house feel "*Yontufdik.*" My father's *divrei Torah,* some of which appear in this *Haggadah,* are etched in my memory. But most of all, the unforgettable manner in which he sings the words — with his inimitable *"she'neeeeemar"* — rings in the ears of my children now, and will, *iy"H,* continue for generations to come.

I remember my first Seder at the home of my in-laws, **Rabbi and Mrs. Yehuda and Nusy Lefkovitz.** It was warm and inviting, special in many ways. But perhaps what was most beautiful was the attention paid to each child. Each one had his chance to speak and perform. To shine. Many years have passed since that first Seder. Many of the children have moved on. And now, it is the grandchildren who share their *divrei Torah.* Yet my in-laws, who are as young as ever, listen to the grandchildren with wide-eyed excitement — as if they are hearing these *divrei Torah* for the very first time.

Rabbi Nachum and Mrs. Tova Salb are my editors. Reb Nachum is a *talmid chacham* who uses his wisdom to ensure the accuracy of my *divrei Torah.* Without Mrs. Salb's expertise and patience, my work would be drastically different. She makes each piece readable and enjoyable — quite an accomplishment.

Another *Haggadah*? Really? Is that necessary?

I asked myself these questions, as well. But after I wrote my first *Haggadah* nine years ago, the kids in my class were buying that *Haggadah* and stealing my thunder. I had to come up with new material; there is nothing like a *"mechayeiv."* So I began to collect new stories and *divrei Torah* for the Seder, which eventually turned into this volume. And that is why I thank those boys who refused to take notes, saying, "I can just buy the *Haggadah* and read it myself."

The following is a partial list of *Haggados* and *sefarim* I used in preparing this volume: *Asichah BeChukecha, Be'er HaChaim, Darash Mordechai, Derech Pikudecha, Doreish Tov, HaLekach VeHaLibuv, LeHa'ir LeHoros U'LeHaskil, Likkutei Av, MiPi Sefarim VeSofrim, Shaarei Leil HaSeder, Yeisei VeYifsach.*

To the hundreds of people who have shared their stories with me: Thank you! Although I am not able to use each and every story, I am grateful nonetheless. I hope to make use of them in some way in the future. For various reasons, it is often necessary to camouflage the identity of the individuals involved in a story. In many instances in this book, I have taken the liberty of doing so, in order to protect the identity of the characters.

I would like to express my gratitude to the many institutions that have invited me to speak on behalf of their organizations. Thank you for keeping me in mind.

To my children, **Tzvi, Avromi, Efraim, Miri, Shmueli, Chana Leah, Henni, and Chayala:** Our Sedarim are special, and you are the reason why. Never forget that.

And finally, to my wife, **Chumi,** making Pesach is a difficult chore. But somehow, you do it with humor and grace, and a smile that lights up our world.

May the Almighty continue to bless us with immeasurable *siyata d'Shmaya.*

Yechiel Spero

Adar 5775

Preface

ک۶ "Grow, Seeds, Grow!"

On the night of the Seder, we are instructed to occupy ourselves with the story of the Exodus, until sleep overtakes us. This seems to be an unusual time frame. Perhaps we can understand it better with a humorous but touching story.

A few weeks ago, I was reading my daughter a bedtime story. The book she chose was about a frog and a toad, two friends who learn about life together.

One day, the frog saw the toad planting some seeds. After he put the seeds in the ground, the toad bent down and whispered, "Grow, seeds, grow." However, despite his encouragement, the seeds did not grow. The next day, he called out to the seeds in a louder voice and commanded, "Grow, seeds, grow." Yet once again, the seeds did not grow. The next day, the toad screamed in his loudest voice, "Grow, seeds, grow!"

Hearing the noise, the frog ran over to the toad and asked him what he was doing. He told the frog that he wanted the seeds to grow. The frog explained to his friend that in order for seeds to grow, you must water them and nurture them; you must give them sunlight. The toad followed the instructions and watered his seeds and provided them with sunlight. He even played the violin for them. But no matter what he did, the seeds did not grow. Exhausted and overwhelmed after his long and unproductive day, the toad fell asleep.

A short while later, the frog tapped his friend on the shoulder. "Look! Look!" Startled, the toad jumped to his feet and looked. A huge smile spread across his face.

The seeds had begun to grow.

As I read the story, the thought occurred to me that this is the story of parents everywhere. Our seeds, our children, are planted in the ground. We want them to grow, so we whisper, instruct, demand, and sometimes, we may even scream. But despite all of our efforts, they may not grow in the manner we had envisioned.

Eventually, with some advice and guidance, we learn that our children need to be nurtured. They need to be watered and given sunlight. We must provide them with love and encouragement, and bring light into their lives. We need to make them feel good about themselves. Sometimes, even then, our efforts are for naught. Exhausted and overwhelmed, we fall asleep. We have done everything we can.

One day, we wake up. We look around and a big smile crosses our face. With *siyata d'Shmaya*, our children, our precious seeds, have grown. Our efforts were not in vain.

It could not happen overnight. It never does. But if our hearts are in the right place — if we do our utmost, and we pray and cry to Hashem for His guidance and assistance — our seeds will grow.

Tonight, we plant and water and give the necessary sunlight to our children. We hope that their faces will shine. We hope that they will be proud of their heritage, proud of where they come from, proud to be Jews. We do this until we are overcome by exhaustion and we fall asleep.

And soon, we will be able to see the beautiful trees we have planted.

Chodesh Nissan

ᴥ A Month of Mesirus Nefesh

A famous question is posed by the *Taz* (*Orach Chaim* 430:1). If the *korban pesach* was taken on the 10th of Nissan, why do we commemorate that event on Shabbos HaGadol, which occasionally falls on the 10th of Nissan, but not always? He explains, in the name of *Rav Moshe Charif*, that Bnei Yisrael also crossed the Yardein into Eretz Yisrael on the 10th of Nissan. In order not to diminish the focus from that miraculous incident, we commemorate the act of taking the *korban pesach* on Shabbos HaGadol.

We can often discover the secret to the *Arba Parashiyos* through the *piyut* recited on those Shabbasos. The *piyut* titled *Merimei Ol*, said on *Parashas HaChodesh*, which is the Shabbos before the month of Nissan (or on Rosh Chodesh itself), actually connects the above occurrences: "*Patz mi'be'asor le'asro be'avos, tzelichas Yardein bo le'hasvos* — He said that the *pesach* lamb should be bound from the 10th of Nissan, as a symbol of the future crossing of the Yardein on that date."

What is the connection between these two events?

The *sefer Lev Aharon* explains that as the Jewish people were ready to cross the Yardein into Eretz Yisrael after 40 years in the wilderness, the Satan protested, "In what merit should they be able to cross over?" The effects of the sin of the Golden Calf hung over them like a dark cloud, as they had repeated their sin of *avodah zarah* from their earlier days in Egypt. But Yehoshua knew of the great merit of the taking of the *korban pesach,* for which they had risked their lives in Mitzrayim, as they themselves had pulled away from *avodah zarah*. It was that merit that helped them overcome the repercussions of the sin of the Golden Calf when they entered Eretz Yisrael.

The *Alshich* elaborates with a magnificent essay on the sequence of the events of Chodesh Nissan, which is also alluded to in the *piyut*. He begins with two basic questions. First of all, why was the commandment to take the lamb given on Rosh Chodesh, if they were not to take it until the 10th? Second, why did the Jews have to watch it for four days while it was bound to their bedposts? Wouldn't one day have sufficed?

The answer is that by serving *avodah zarah* in Mitzrayim, the Yidden's sin consisted of three parts: 1, they caused a *chillul Hashem*, by serving the Egyptian gods in public; 2, they had even sacrificed to the Egyptian gods they had worshiped; and 3, they had gathered its blood. These three sins had to be rectified, and Hashem gave them the *korban pesach* with which to do that. Let's discuss each one.

When the Jews were told that they had to take the Egyptian god, the lamb, and tie it to their bedposts, they knew that the Egyptians would protest and threaten to kill them. The *nisayon* was great, as it required that they risk their lives. But they drew strength from the knowledge that Avraham Avinu endured his own 10 arduous tests, and thus they were able to persevere. So they waited 10 days, from Rosh Chodesh until the 10th day of Nissan. In essence, these 10 days were equivalent to the 10 tests of Avraham, as all 10 days they agonized over what would happen to them when they would take the sheep in view of the Egyptians.

Hence, the first of the sins was rectified. Bnei Yisrael caused a *chillul Hashem,* and now they were sanctifying His Name on the highest level. The Alshich adds that the Yidden sanctified His Name for the four days during which the sheep were tied to their beds, symbolizing the four letters of Hashem's Name, which had been desecrated through their worship of idols.

The second facet of the *korban pesach* was tying it to the bedpost, paralleling the second sin, which was bringing offerings to other gods. The Jews were deserving of death by the sword on account of this sin. However, just as at the *Akeidah,* the Almighty had sent a ram to replace Yitzchak, so, too, He exchanged the lamb for Bnei Yisrael. It was in Yitzchak's merit, who was tied during the *Akeidah,* that they were given this atonement.

The final sin, the gathering of the blood, was rectified when the Yidden took the blood of the slaughtered lamb, dipped a hyssop branch into it, and then smeared it on the two doorposts and the lintel. Yaakov Avinu suffered greatly when his son Yosef's tunic was dipped into goat's blood and he was told Yosef was dead. The Jews smeared the blood of the *korban pesach* onto their doorposts, to conjure up the merit of Yaakov.

The Midrash (*Shemos Rabbah* 17:3) tells us that the two doorposts that were smeared with blood alluded to Yitzchak and Yaakov, and the lintel alluded to Avraham.

These demonstrations on the 1st, 10th, and 14th of the month are a declaration that we are prepared to die for the Almighty. However, it is one thing to die for the Almighty, but an entirely different challenge to *live* for Him. In the second half of the month, we proclaim that we are ready to live for *HaKadosh Baruch Hu,* and to subjugate our desires to His will.

The second half of the month begins with the *korban omer.* Although small in size, it represents a major concept. The Gemara in *Megillah* (16a) informs us that when Haman saw that the Yidden were learning about the *korban omer,* he lamented that the small measure of the *omer* would offset his 10,000 talents of silver. The Maharal (*Ohr Chadash, Esther* 6:10) asks: Why was it specifically this *zechus* that helped to defeat Haman's plan? He answers that the *omer* is brought on the first day of a period of 50, which culminates with Shavuos. When the Jews bring the *omer* before Hashem, they ascend the ladder until the 50th rung, upon which the Torah was given, and that is how they can overcome Haman, the descendant of Amalek.

It is the Jews' commitment to live with the Torah that destroys the seed of Amalek. Haman knew precisely where the strength of the Jewish people lay. With the *omer,* Bnei Yisrael symbolically stepped onto that first rung. Knowing they would continue to ascend, Haman bemoaned his fate.

The *siddur Iyun Tefillah* (322) finds that the word *omer* shares the same root as the word *me'amer* (of the 39 *melachos* of Shabbos), which means *to bundle together.* During the days of *Sefirah,* we bundle together our desires and channel them toward *avodas Hashem.* In fact, he posits that the word שָׁבוּעוֹת has within it the word שְׁבִי, *captive.* By the time Shavuos arrives, the 50th day since the bringing of the *omer,* our evil inclination has been captured, and the victory against Amalek and the evil it represents is complete.

Thus, we are prepared to live for His Name, just as we are prepared to die for Him!

The *Pesikta DeRav Kahana* (*Parashas HaChodesh*) writes that it says the words "*Be'asor la'chodesh* — On the tenth of the month," when the *pasuk* speaks about the *korban pesach* (*Shemos* 12:3), and it says those words again in *Yehoshua* (4:19). Rav Yochanan says that the *lekichah,* taking of the lamb, worked as a merit at the Yardein, while the eating of the *korban pesach* worked as a merit for the Jews in the days of Haman. We see this from the word *ba'lailah,* which is employed when the Torah speaks of the meat of the *korban pesach,* which was consumed at night (*Shemos* 12:8); the word is also found in *Megillas Esther* (6:1), where it says *ba'lailah* regarding the king's sleep that was disturbed, which was the beginning of Haman's downfall.

This is the meaning of another beautiful *pizmon* we read in the *Yotzer* of *Parashas HaChodesh, Adon MiKedem*: *"Kudash be'rosho u'shelisho chetzio ve'rubo lishmor* — It was sanctified at its beginning, after a third [the 10th of Nissan], in its middle. And the rest of the month, and after its majority, to observe." We sanctify His Name by preparing ourselves to die for Him. This is the first half of the month. Then we actualize that conviction by living to sanctify His Name.

We have an important month ahead of us. There is much work to be done.

Cleaning.

Cooking.

But most of all ... sacrificing. For Torah. For mitzvos.

For Him.

The Bluzhever Rebbe and the Beast of Belsen

The year was 1945; liberation was just around the corner. In the meantime, the inmates in the Bergen-Belsen concentration camp were struggling to survive. Their skeletal bodies yearned for another morsel of bread to still their hunger. Their minds, muddled and twisted after years of war and persecution, wanted nothing but freedom. But one man, Rav Yisrael Spira, the Bluzhever Rebbe, wanted something more. His neshamah was starved for ruchniyus. Longing for a taste of the cheirus that comes along with eating unleavened bread, the Rebbe made an announcement in the barracks that he was planning on baking matzos for Pesach.

His fellow inmates respected the Rebbe immensely, yet could not help but question his decision, not only to bake matzos, but to proclaim it publicly. But the Rebbe would not relent; his mind was set on having matzos. One by one, the 40 other inmates in the barracks expressed their wish to join him.

The Rebbe decided that he was going to bake the matzos with the permission of the cursed Nazis. The commandant of the camp, the notorious murderer named Josef Kramer, was known as the Beast of Belsen. Although the Rebbe knew that he was risking his life by merely placing the request, he walked valiantly toward the commandant's office. After the Rebbe entered, the steely eyed barbarian shocked the Rebbe by listening to his request, and even responding that he would submit the request to headquarters in Berlin, and they would decide on the procedure and policy.

After a short while, the call arrived: Berlin agreed! They would supply 40 Jews with enough flour for matzah for eight days, which would be baked in a makeshift oven. The flour would be given to them in place of their daily ration of bread.

As surreal as it seemed, the Jews erected a makeshift oven. After obtaining a sack of flour, an assembly line was formed. Humming the words of Hallel, a large group baked enough matzos for all eight days of Yom Tov. They could hardly believe their good fortune. It was a nearly miraculous opportunity, and they had done it with permission. Although they were still imprisoned, for the first time in a very long while they tasted freedom. But that taste did not last very long.

After they finished baking, the commandant stormed into their barracks and began destroying their oven. He grabbed the round matzos he had permitted them to bake and crushed them, driving his metal-tipped boots into the defenseless pile of matzos. The inmates cowered in fear, trembling at the thought of what he may do next.

After he finished smashing the pile of matzos, he turned his attention toward the Rebbe. Without any explanation, he took a metal truncheon and beat the Rebbe mercilessly. Then he marched out. The Rebbe lay there in a pool of blood, until the other inmates came to help him stand up and clean himself off.

At first, no one knew why the commandant had a sudden change of mind. Eventually, they found out that one inmate who had escaped had communicated with the Red Cross and charged the Nazis with inhumane behavior. Upon receiving a phone call concerning this charge, the infuriated commandant came to share his displeasure with the inmates. The Beast of Belsen exclaimed, "After treating them the way I did and extending my kindness to enable them to bake their religious wafers, this is how they repay me?"

After they sifted through the rubble of what used to be matzos, the men were able to salvage one matzah. The question was: Who should be the one to eat it? Some suggested that the oldest member of the group be given the matzah. But the overwhelming majority felt that since the Rebbe had risked his life to ask permission, had arranged the entire affair, and had endured the senseless beating, he should be the one to eat the matzah.

Suddenly, one woman named Bronia spoke up. She explained that she had a child in the camp who had somehow survived. "He should be the one to eat the matzah. One day soon, he will be free, and he will rebuild his life and conduct a Seder of his own. I want him to be able to say that he ate matzah in the concentration camp. He will tell the world that even though we were entrenched in the most bitter of exiles, we tasted freedom in Bergen-Belsen. He should eat it because he represents the future."

She spoke with passion and with tears. Everyone agreed with her that her child should eat the matzah. And so, the Rebbe handed her the matzah for her child.

Shortly thereafter, Bergen-Belsen was liberated. Unfortunately, by then hundreds of thousands had lost their lives. Even after liberation, despondency set in. As the Klausenberger Rebbe once said, the inmates of the camps had hoped that somehow they would be liberated not by the Allied soldiers, but by the Shivtei Kah.

Bronia approached the Rebbe and asked if he felt she should rebuild her life. He assured her that the time was right and blessed her to find her shidduch and rebuild her family. She did.

With him.

The Bluzhever Rebbe married her; the child who received the matzah became his stepson and his heir.

Little did the Rebbe know that when he gave the matzah to her child, it would be his child, as well.

His child.

His future.

A Portion for a Potato

Rav Yeshayah Steiner, the Rebbe of Kerestir, who was known affectionately as Rav Shaya'le, dedicated his life to helping others and making their lives easier. Reb Hillel Rothstein came from the town of Kerestir. Reb Hillel's mother had been the cook in Rav Shaya'le's home for an eight-year period and was privy to his greatness and the responsibility he felt toward his fellow Jews. Reb Hillel related the following story.

The inhabitants of the city were cleaning and preparing for the upcoming Pesach holiday. The men spent much time at the matzah bakery, ensuring that they would receive the best matzos. In the home of Rav Shaya'le, where many guests were always hosted, the preparations reached a feverish pace.

Yet, there was one problem. There were no potatoes in the entire area. A harsh and unforgiving winter had caused irreparable damage to the potato crop, and all the potato fields were destroyed. In those days, the Jews' primary source of sustenance during Pesach was from potatoes. And now, there weren't any.

As Pesach drew near, the heads of the city reached out to the adjacent towns and villages to ask if they could supply any potatoes. But they hardly had enough for themselves, and definitely none to spare. Rav Shaya'le, who felt a personal sense of responsibility for the townspeople, was very worried — until he was informed of a non-Jewish landowner in a faraway city, who had silos full of extra potatoes.

Unwilling to trust a messenger, Rav Shaya'le decided to go by himself, with two of his trustworthy attendants. They hired a wagon driver and filled the back of the wagon with empty sacks. They also brought along a suitcase filled with money. Who knew how much the non-Jewish landowner would charge? They had to be prepared for anything.

The wagon driver hurried along, knowing that time was of the essence. After a day of travel, Rav Shaya'le descended from the wagon along with his assistants and knocked on the door of the landowner's home. When the man answered the door, Rav Shaya'le introduced himself as the rabbi of a faraway village. After explaining the situation, he asked if he could purchase potatoes at a fair price. The man let out a hearty chuckle and explained that money was not the issue. He was not willing to sell, no matter what the price. But Rav Shaya'le would not take no for an answer. He told the stubborn fellow that he was willing to pay whatever he asked. But for some reason, the man was not willing to budge: the potatoes were not for sale. Even when Rav Shaya'le doubled and then tripled his offer, the man still did not change his stance.

Finally, after some thought, the landowner said, "I will sell you whatever you ask, but my price will be very high." Excited that he had finally made a breakthrough, Rav Shaya'le quickly asked, "What is it? What do you want?"

The non-Jewish man then asked for the unthinkable. "I will give you the potatoes on the condition that you give me your portion in the World to Come."

Rav Shaya'le's attendants turned to leave. The mere notion of such a demand seemed ludicrous. As they turned to go, however, Rav Shaya'le responded emphatically, "It's a deal."

The attendants could not believe what they were hearing. They looked at their Rebbe and said, "You can't possibly be serious, right? Are you really going to give away your portion in the World to Come for a few measly potatoes?"

But there was no time to waste. The landowner was pleased that the rabbi had agreed, but he immediately asked for a quill and some parchment; he wanted a signed document to prove that the sale was for real. Rav Shaya'le signed on the dotted line and filled his wagon with the potatoes. As they prepared to leave, Rav Shaya'le turned to his assistants and explained that no one was to find out what he had sacrificed to provide potatoes for the townspeople. They both agreed, and soon they were on their way. Within a day, they reached their hometown, and the people of the city were ecstatic: they had food for Pesach. That year, Rav Shaya'le hosted 60 people in his home for the meals.

Although his attendants had promised to keep it a secret, as is most often the case, word began to spread of the sacrifice Rav Shaya'le had made. Within a few days after Pesach, everybody knew the true story. A group of individuals approached Rav Shaya'le and asked him why he had sold his portion in the World to Come for a few spuds.

Rav Shaya'le's response speaks to his extraordinary love for his fellow man. "My portion in the World to Come is worthless as long as there is one Yid in Kerestir who doesn't have potatoes to feed himself and his family."

Pesach Preparations

A Time and Place for Everything

The Tepliker Rav, Rav Shimshon Aharon Polansky, entered the beis midrash a few days before Pesach. A number of married individuals, each of whom had a large family at home, were learning studiously. He walked up to the front of the beis midrash, stood at the podium, and banged three times to grab everyone's attention. As the Rav proclaimed that he had a very important message, each man perked up and got ready to listen.

"Rabbosai, I am holding in my hand a paper that contains a list of women in town who need assistance in preparing for Yom Tov. They are overwhelmed and have no husband to help them. Anyone who can should please come forward and take part in this very important mitzvah. I promise that there will be immeasurable reward awaiting each of you."

Without a moment's hesitation, all of the men closed their Gemaras and approached the Rav to offer their services. He thanked them for their help and told them to please form a line so that he could hand each one a paper with the name and address of the woman who needs his help. They readily got into line and awaited their marching orders.

One by one, he handed them a small paper with an address on it. As each one opened his paper, he was shocked to discover that the address was none other than his own. The Rav smiled and nodded to each of them.

The message was loud and clear.

In each of their cases, their wives had, in all probability, encouraged them to go and learn. But the Rav knew each of their situations and understood that even when one's wife encourages him to learn, he must know that there are times when he must thank her for her selflessness — and help anyway.

He had determined that this was one of those times.

Just Like Your Mother

It had been a terribly painful ordeal for the young family; their mother had lost her battle with cancer and had passed away. The father had tried desperately to keep the family together. However, he himself was in so much pain that it was difficult for him to keep everyone else united and strong. To top it all off, Pesach was just around the corner. What was a Yiddishe shtub — a Jewish home — without a mother around?

The recently orphaned young sisters tried their best to recall the way their mother used to prepare for Pesach. Although they had always helped around the house and had done everything their mother had asked them to do, the task of "changing over" from a chametzdik kitchen to a Pesachdik one was a monumental ordeal, especially for three young girls.

Despite their reservations, the girls got down to work. The sisters removed the dishes from the cabinet and exchanged them for the

Pesach plates, bowls, and saucers. They switched the cutlery and silverware with relative ease. The glasses were noticeably different and also easy to substitute. As the bulk of the kitchen utensils were swapped with their Pesach counterparts, the Pesach kitchen started to take form.

They really wanted to accomplish the feat of transforming the kitchen by themselves before their father returned from work. What a surprise it would be for him! They tried to imagine his excitement and happiness when he would walk through the door.

Covering every revealed surface with aluminum foil is a ritual that has become customary, along with the required obligation to kasher the rest of the kitchen. This, though, was easier said than done. Nevertheless, the girls rallied together to finish this task, too. As they surveyed their handiwork, the young women, for the most part, were pleased with what they had accomplished. Even though it was not perfect, they had done their best. Alas, there was still something missing.

It was just not the way their mother had done it. That missing ingredient of a mother's love that is infused into every inch of a Yiddishe home was still sorely lacking. Perhaps it was not tangible, but it was there. They all could sense it; all could feel it. And it caused a measure of sadness.

A long-lasting moment of silence filled the air, as they were all thinking the same thing. They missed their mother terribly. If only she were here, she would have given the Pesach kitchen her motherly touch. The emotional trauma of a home without a mother was never more evident. Just then, there was a soft knock at the door.

Gitty, the eldest daughter, opened the door, and was completely taken aback. It was the Belzer Rebbe. Their family was quite close to the Rebbe; their mother, in fact, had had a special relationship with the Belzer Rebbetzin. Still, Rebbes by and large do not visit people. When a Rebbe wants to see someone, he calls for him to come. This visit was considered highly unusual.

After a moment, Gitty recovered from her shock and asked the Rebbe what she could do for him.

"Ken ich areinkumin — Can I please come in?"

Though she could not imagine what the Rebbe could possibly want from them, she graciously invited him in. As he headed from one room to the other, he smiled and nodded his head in satisfaction. Finally, he made his way into the kitchen.

Although the kitchen had been transformed, it certainly had not been professionally done. It was an adequate job at best. The aluminum foil was not perfectly cut; there were areas in the room that still needed some work before they could be declared completely kosher for Pesach use.

The Rebbe examined the room; he checked the countertops and the kitchen sink. Finally, he turned to leave. "Kinderlach," he declared, "mamash azoi vi di mamma hut getun — Children, this is just like your mother used to do it." And with that, he wished them a gut Yom Tov and turned to leave.

The children smiled. The tears that formed in their eyes were now tears of relief, tears of bittersweet joy. True, their mother was no longer alive. Yet now, perhaps more than ever since she had passed away, they were able to feel her love, her presence, her aura. For they knew that others were thinking of them and were looking out for their welfare.

They continued making their last, finishing touches. They had to prepare for the special guest who would be spending Yom Tov with them; their mother was going to be with them for Pesach, after all.

Pesach Stringencies

Beginning Anew

We are extra careful and extra strict about our observance of *hilchos Pesach*. This manifests itself before the holiday, as well. We make sure to clean our homes and check them with extra scrutiny. We are careful that the measurements of matzah and *maror* are precise and go well beyond the call of halachah. In areas of kashrus of Pesach foods, we extend beyond the norm. Why? In order to answer this question, we will cite two separate stories, which bring home the same point.

It was a beautiful bar mitzvah, and in attendance were two very great individuals. One of them was the Tchebiner Rav, Rav Dov Berish Weidenfeld, and the other was the Belzer Rebbe, Rav Aharon Rokeach. They sat on either side of the bar mitzvah boy, and they watched as he bentched on a cup of wine. When he finished, he drank most of the contents of the cup and then put it down. The Belzer Rebbe saw that the boy had put the cup down and encouraged him to finish all the wine that remained. The bar mitzvah boy did as he was told. The Tchebiner Rav could not help but wonder why the Rebbe was so insistent that the boy finish the cup of wine. The halachah clearly states that drinking the majority of the cup is sufficient.

Since he held the tzaddik in great regard, he did not dare question him. Yet a moment or two later, the Rebbe turned to the Tchebiner Rav and brought up the question himself. "Nu . . . Don't you want to know why I asked the bar mitzvah boy to drink the entire cup?

"In the story of Chanukah, the Chashmonaim found one pure flask of oil, which was enough for one day. They used only that flask to light the Menorah, which miraculously burned for eight days. That is why we celebrate the eight-day holiday.

"A question arises: Although the other flasks were impure, the halachah is that impurity is permitted in a communal setting — 'tumah hutrah be'tzibbur.' So why didn't they use those other flasks? The answer is that since they were consecrating the Beis HaMikdash and beginning anew, they wanted to perform the mitzvah in the best way possible. Second best was not an option.

"The same holds true with our bar mitzvah boy. You are right. He does not need to finish the entire cup. The majority of a cup suffices and is more than enough. But tonight, when he is beginning his career as a bar mitzvah, I wanted him to fulfill all his obligations in the best possible way, lechatchilah, and not bedi'eved. This is why I encouraged him to finish the entire cup."

As Rav Shmuel Salant, the elderly Rav of Yerushalayim, began losing his strength, Rav Eliyahu Dovid Rabinowitz Teomim, who was better known as the Aderes (the acronym of his name), was invited to Yerushalayim to become his successor. When he arrived, the entire city, led by Rav Shmuel, came out to greet him. After reciting the berachah of "She'chalak Mei'chochmaso Li'rei'av — Who has apportioned of His knowledge to those who fear Him," Rav Shmuel informed the Aderes that he wanted him to begin serving as the Rav right away, by acting as the mesader kiddushin at a chasunah.

Although he was thoroughly exhausted from the journey, the Aderes acquiesced and went straight to the wedding. But because of his fatigue, when he said the blessings under the chuppah, he *inadvertently made a Shehakol instead of a Borei Pri Hagafen, and he quickly corrected himself by making a new berachah, a Borei Pri Hagafen.*

After the chuppah, the rabbanim asked him why he had made a Hagafen, since he could have been yotzei with the Shehakol he had originally recited. The Aderes explained that the mesader kiddushin is only the agent for the chassan, in order not to embarrass a chassan who can't make the berachos on his own. But the chassan designates the mesader kiddushin to be his shaliach only if he is fulfilling the mitzvah lechatchilah, not if he is doing it bedi'eved.

When starting a Yiddishe shtub, second best is not an option.

On Pesach, the Jewish nation was born. By reliving the Exodus at the Seder, we, too, are beginning anew, and we want to begin our existence as a people in the best possible manner. Although the story of the Jewish people and the Exodus took place over 3,300 years ago, every Pesach night we relive it again. We are born again as a nation. Fresh and new and ready to accomplish.

Why settle for second best?

The Power of a Mitzvah

In December 2001, Rabbi Yosef Zaretzky spoke at a seminary in Bnei Brak. He discussed the concept of keeping the highest standard of kosher. While many of the girls already kept that standard, one young lady named Leah came from a family that did not. She was moved and inspired by his speech and decided to do something about it.

When she called home that day, she informed her parents that she wanted to start buying food that had a higher standard of kashrus. While her mother was willing to do so, her father would not hear of it. He insisted that what was kosher enough for him should be kosher enough for his daughter.

Leah begged her father and explained that she very much wanted to elevate her standards. When he still refused, Leah told him that if that was the case, she would not be coming home from seminary for Shabbos. Her father was furious and insisted she come home. He told her that she was overreacting and needed to come to her senses. But she was adamant.

The next day, Friday, she pretended to be like all the other girls. She made it look like she was packing a suitcase. However, when the bus arrived, she turned back and told them not to wait for her. She would catch a later ride back to Emmanuel, where she lived.

That afternoon, she bought two rolls and some chocolate spread. It was a lonely Shabbos meal, the loneliest one of her life. But she was proud that she had stuck to her guns. She cried to the Almighty that she should be able to withstand all the pressure that would come her way. After Shabbos, when the girls came back to the dormitory, she also pretended to unpack her suitcase. The girls spoke about what a wonderful Shabbos they had had, and she told them that she had also had a beautiful Shabbos. Yet inside, she was crying. Her heart was broken. But she would not let that break her spirit. The next Shabbos, after not hearing from her father all week, she stayed in the dormitory again. Once more, she was lonely and heartbroken. But she was proud that she was able to withstand the pressure.

In the middle of the next week, her father finally gave in. He called her up and asked her if she was angry. She told him that she was not angry, but she was not going to change her mind. He said he would visit her during the week, and they would shop together for all the foods that required a higher stamp of approval. Although he was not happy about it, he had agreed to help her, and that was a step in the right direction.

When he came, she directed him to the store that carried the groceries they were looking for. She walked up and down the aisles and filled her shopping cart with all types of foods. After a while, her father grew impatient. He commented that he needed the wealth of Rothschild to be able to afford all these expensive items. She knew better than to argue with him. But soon, he mentioned to her that the last bus to Emmanuel from Bnei Brak was scheduled to leave shortly. She had no choice but to quickly check out. Loaded down with packages, they made their way to the bus. But by the time they arrived, the Dan bus Number 189 was pulling away.

Leah's father was furious. He threw down the many bags of groceries he had been carrying and unleashed a verbal assault on his daughter. Feeling extremely guilty about the unfortunate inconvenience to her father, she called her teacher, who graciously invited them to her home for supper and to stay the night.

The taxi to her teacher's home brought them there in no time at all. They walked up the steps and were surprised to see that the house was bustling and lively. Nonetheless, there were two place settings with a beautiful supper prepared for them. By that point, Leah's father was embarrassed about his earlier behavior.

After an hour, Leah's father decided to call his wife to inform her that he would not be returning that night to Emmanuel. When his wife answered the phone, he could barely make out her words because she was crying so hard. After he managed to calm her down, she repeated the news, but more coherently. In a horrific attack, Dan bus Number 189 was struck by terrorists, just outside of Emmanuel. After setting off several roadside bombs, the three terrorists shot at the passengers and threw grenades, inflicting further damage. In the end, 11 people were killed and about 30 injured.

Leah's extended kashrus shopping spree had saved their lives.

Priorities ... Priorities ...

At times, as we try to perform mitzvos with a high level of stringency, we fail to recognize the importance of other people's feelings. This is especially true when it comes to baking matzos. Often, there will be people in the factory who are either young *yesomim* or older *almanos* who are looking to make some extra money to support their families. This does not necessarily mean that one should compromise his standards. Rather, it means that one must be thoughtful, clever, and considerate in his dealings with these people.

A present-day rosh yeshivah told the following personal story, which happened over 40 years ago, when he was one of those young orphan boys looking to help out his family and make some extra money before Pesach. He was given the job of checking the matzah after it came out of the oven, to make sure that it was not doubled over, which would invalidate it. Early on in the process, a man asked him to teach him how to check the matzah. Proud to be one of the expert checkers, he patiently showed the man how he checked the matzah. The man nodded and thanked the boy for his patience in explaining it. Then he came over with another matzah and asked him if it was kosher. This process repeated itself three times. The young checker thought that the man who kept on coming over to him must have something wrong with him. Which normal person would keep on asking him the same thing, over and over again?

The truth is that that man was not a regular man. He was none other than the rosh yeshivah of Tchebin, Rav Avrohom Ganochofsky. In his humility, he did not want anyone to know who he was. Furthermore, he was concerned that the boy would feel uncomfortable that he was in the room. But he still wanted to make sure that the boy knew what he was doing. So instead of testing him, he made himself appear to be a simpleton who did not know even the most basic rules of checking a matzah. In truth, he was just making sure that the boy did know the various rules.

When one is faced with such situations, one must be clever to figure out how to do the mitzvah properly, while not causing discomfort and embarrassment to others.

Rav Avrohom recorded a beautiful story that he heard about Rav Yosef Liss. Rav Yosef noticed a young boy who was about to cross a busy street, with many cars whizzing by. Rav Yosef wanted to hold his hand to make sure he crossed safely, but he knew that the boy would not want to be treated like a baby. He thought of a clever idea. He called the boy over and asked him if he could do him a favor and help him cross the street. The boy smiled proudly, eager to help out another individual.

One of the earlier Rebbes of the Belz dynasty was very careful not to eat gebrokts on Pesach. But one Seder night, his custom changed. His mother, an old woman who had become very forgetful, sat right next to him. When it came time to serve the soup at the meal, she took her matzah and crumbled it up into the bowl of boiling hot soup they were sharing. Those around her gasped, horrified at what she had done. But their shock paled in comparison to what they witnessed next. Her son pushed the matzah to the other side of the bowl and ate the hot soup.

Noticing the stares, he immediately explained, "To embarrass my mother would be a much more grievous sin than breaking the custom of not eating gebrokts."

On the nights when we can elevate ourselves to unimaginable heights by doing the proper thing, we can reach even greater heights by doing the seemingly improper.

ערב פסח
EREV PESACH

Laws of the Search for Chametz

1. One must begin the search immediately at the beginning of the night of the 14th of Nissan. It is proper for one to begin just after *tzeis hakochavim*, even before the light of day has completely subsided, so that he not delay the search or forget about it (*Orach Chayim* 431:1 and *Mishnah Berurah* 1).

2. It is forbidden to begin a meal or to begin a bath or to do any kind of work starting from a half-hour before nighttime. However, a snack — that is, a *k'beitzah* or less of bread, or fruit in any amount — is permitted at this time. When the actual time for the search arrives one should not spend much time eating even a snack, as this would cause a delay in the start of the search (432:2 and *Mishnah Berurah* 2, 5-6).

3. It is also forbidden to engage in Torah study once the time for the search has arrived. (There are those who forbid this also during the half-hour before nightfall. This applies only in private, however, and not, for instance, to someone who gives a short *shiur* in a *beis midrash* after *Ma'ariv*. If someone asks a person who is not learning to remind him about the search when the proper time comes, he may also learn during this half-hour interval) (ibid. *Mishnah Berurah* 7).

4. Any place into which it is possible that *chametz* might have been brought must be searched. Even places not normally used for *chametz*, but where there is a reasonable possibility that *chametz* may happen to have been brought there, require a search. This includes houses, yards (except in cases where one can assume that leftover food is eaten by animals or birds), nooks and crevices as far as the hand can reach, and whatever containers might have once been used for holding *chametz*. In a situation where a search in a particular place would entail great difficulty, it is possible to be lenient and sell that place to a non-Jew, so that it would not require a search. The details of these rules may be found in *Orach Chayim* 433:3,5 and *Mishnah Berurah* 23.

5. Pockets of garments must be searched, even if one feels confident that he has never put any *chametz* in them, because one often does so without realizing it (433:11 and *Mishnah Berurah* 47).

Note: Source references within the laws refer to *Shulchan Aruch Orach Chayim*, unless otherwise noted.

6. One should clean up the house before the search is begun. It is customary to clean the whole house on or before the 13th of Nissan, so that the search can be started without delay at nightfall of the 14th. It is also customary to take a feather with which to dust out the *chametz* from holes and crevices (ibid. and *Mishnah Berurah* 46).

7. It is preferable to use a single wax candle for the search. A search done by the light of a torch is not valid at all, but one done using a candle made of tallow is valid. The validity of a search done by the light of an oil candle is a matter of dispute between halachic authorities (433:2 and *Mishnah Berurah* 10). Contemporary authorities rule that one may use a flashlight for the search.

8. It is customary to place several pieces of bread (taking care that they should not crumble) in safe places around the house, where they may be found by the person conducting the search. (The *Arizal* wrote that 10 pieces should be used.) Some halachic authorities write that this practice is not obligatory, and the *Taz* in fact advises against it, lest the pieces become lost. (The *Pischei Teshuvah*, however, notes that nowadays, when the entire house is rid of *chametz* before the search, there is a sound halachic basis for the practice of placing some *chametz* around the house to provide something for which to search.) (432:2, *Mishnah Berurah* 13 and *Shaar HaTziun* ad loc.)

9. There is a controversy as to whether one must search those rooms which are to be sold to a non-Jew with the *chametz*. The custom is to be lenient in this regard, although it would be preferable that in this circumstance the *chametz* be sold before the search (436, *Mishnah Berurah* 32).

Laws of the Berachah over the Search

1. Some say that it is proper to wash the hands before reciting the *berachah* for the search, but this is only for the sake of cleanliness (432, *Mishnah Berurah* 1).

2. One must not speak between the *berachah* and the onset of the search. If he spoke about matters unrelated to the search, he must repeat the *berachah* (432:1, *Mishnah Berurah* 5).

3. One should not speak about matters unrelated to the search until he completes the search, so that one may devote his entire concentration to the task at hand. If he did, however, speak about

unrelated matters after beginning the search, he need not repeat the *berachah*. Furthermore, it is altogether permitted to speak about any matters related to the search at this point (ibid.).

4. Immediately after the search one should recite the כָּל חֲמִירָא declaration, annulling all the unknown *chametz* in his possession. If one does not understand the Aramaic content of this declaration, he should say it in Hebrew or English or whatever language he does understand. If one said it in Aramaic, so long as he has a basic understanding of what the declaration means, though he may not understand the translation of every word, the annulment is valid. One who does not understand the content at all, and thinks he is reciting a prayer of some sort, has not annulled his *chametz* (434:2 and *Mishnah Berurah* 8).

Laws of Erev Pesach

1. Prayers are held early on Erev Pesach in order to allow people to finish eating before the end of the fourth hour of the day (*Mishnah Berurah* 429:13).

2. מִזְמוֹר לְתוֹדָה and ,לַמְנַצֵּחַ, אֵל אֶרֶךְ אַפַּיִם are not said on Erev Pesach (*Orach Chayim* 429:2).

3. It is forbidden to eat *chametz* after a third of the halachic day has passed. The duration of the day can be calculated in various ways. One should consult a competent halachic authority or a reliable Jewish calendar (443:1 and *Mishnah Berurah* 8).

4. The deadline for ridding one's property of *chametz* and deriving benefit from the *chametz* is at the end of the fifth hour of the halachic day (*Mishnah Berurah* 9).

5. Immediately after a third of the day has passed, one should burn the remaining *chametz* and then recite the second כָּל חֲמִירָא declaration, annulling all the *chametz* in his possession. This declaration must not be delayed past the start of the sixth hour, for at that time the annulment no longer has any validity (434:2). See "Burning the *Chametz*" below.

6. If Erev Pesach falls on a Shabbos, the *chametz* should be burned on the day before Erev Pesach (Friday) in the morning, at the same time as other years. However, the כָּל חֲמִירָא declaration should not be said until the 14th of Nissan, i.e., Shabbos morning, after the last *chametz* meal has been eaten (444:2).

7. One should take care that all food utensils not *kashered* for Pesach have been thoroughly cleaned, so that they do not contain any *chametz* residue, and they should be placed out of reach for the duration of Pesach (440:2; end of 442, *Mishnah Berurah* 433:23).

8. Those utensils too hard to clean from *chametz* residue should be sold together with the *chametz*. (Only the residue itself should be sold, not the utensil, so as to avoid the necessity of immersing the utensil in a *mikveh* when it is repurchased from the non-Jew.) These utensils should also be placed in a room where they are out of reach, or together with the *chametz* that is being sold (ibid.).

9. After halachic noon it is forbidden to do any work (מְלָאכָה). If someone's clothing tore at that time, and he needs that article of clothing for Yom Tov, he may make a minor repair for himself, even if it involves expert workmanship. Someone else may also do it for him at no charge (*Orach Chayim* 468, *Mishnah Berurah* 5).

10. Any manner of work which is forbidden on Chol HaMoed is also forbidden on Erev Pesach afternoon, although it is permissible for one to have a non-Jew do these things for him (*Mishnah Berurah* 7).

11. One should cut his nails and have his hair cut before noon. If, however, he neglected to do so, he may have his hair cut by a non-Jew even after noon, and he may cut his own nails (*Mishnah Berurah* 5).

12. Any matzah which one could use for fulfilling the mitzvah of matzah at the Seder may not be eaten all day on Erev Pesach, even if that matzah has been crumbled or ground into flour and mixed with water or juices. Some people have a custom not to eat matzah from Rosh Chodesh Nissan (471:2, *Mishnah Berurah* 10).

13. A child who is too young to understand the story of the Exodus may be fed matzah on Erev Pesach (471:2 and *Mishnah Berurah* 13).

14. Although we consider matzah with folds or bubbles to be unfit for Pesach use, these may also not be eaten on Erev Pesach (*Mishnah Berurah* 12).

15. Matzah that has been prepared by adding juices into the dough (such as egg matzah or fruit-juice matzah) may be eaten on Erev Pesach. (Note: It is the Ashkenazi practice to avoid such matzos whenever the eating of *chametz* is forbidden, except for the sick or elderly.)

16. From the beginning of the halachic 10th hour of the day, only snacks such as fruits and vegetables may be eaten. One should be careful, however, not to fill himself up on these either, to preserve one's appetite for the matzah at the Seder (471:1 and *Mishnah Berurah* 7).

17. The Gemara says that a small amount of wine can also cause satiety, but a large amount stimulates the appetite. *Be'ur Halachah* concludes that the amount of wine one may drink depends on his individual nature, and that a person should not drink (after the 10th hour) an amount of wine that he feels may make him feel sated (471:1 and *Be'ur Halachah* ad loc.).

Fast of the Firstborn

1. There is a custom for firstborn males to fast on Erev Pesach, even if they are firstborn to only one of their parents. If the firstborn son is a minor, the father fasts in his place. If the father is a firstborn himself (and thus has to fast in his own right), the mother fasts for the child. (See *Orach Chayim* 270 and *Mishnah Berurah* ad loc. for the details of this law.)

2. If the firstborn has a headache or similar infirmity he does not have to fast. Similarly, if the fast is likely to cause him to be unable to fulfill the evening's mitzvos of matzah, *maror*, and the four cups of wine properly, it is better for him not to fast. In either of these cases, however, he should limit his eating to small amounts rather than eating full meals (470 and *Mishnah Berurah* ad loc.).

3. There is a controversy among the halachic authorities as to whether a firstborn may eat at a meal served in honor of a mitzvah, and this issue depends on the local custom. The generally accepted practice is to permit eating at a festive meal at the completion of a *mesechta*, even if the firstborn himself did not participate in the learning (*Mishnah Berurah* 10).

Burning the Chametz

1. The *chametz* should preferably not be burned until the day of the 14th of Nissan, after the last *chametz* meal has been eaten. If someone is concerned that the *chametz* found in the search may become lost or find its way back into the rest of the house if it is left too long, he should burn it at night, and he is considered to have fulfilled the Torah commandment to destroy *chametz* on Erev Pesach (תַּשְׁבִּיתוּ) (*Orach Chayim* 445:1, *Mishnah Berurah* 6).

2. If one has *hoshanos* which had been used on Succos, he should use them to feed the flame burning the *chametz,* so that they may be used for yet another mitzvah (*Mishnah Berurah* 7).

3. The *chametz* must be burned (until it is completely charred) before the beginning of the sixth hour, and thereupon the declaration of annulment (כָּל חֲמִירָא) is recited. The annulment is ineffective if it is recited once the sixth hour has begun (*Mishnah Berurah* 1,6).

4. One should not recite the annulment declaration before his *chametz* has been fully burned, so that he will be able to fulfill the mitzvah of תַּשְׁבִּיתוּ (burning the *chametz*) with *chametz* that still belongs to him (443:2).

בדיקת חמץ

Some say this declaration of intent before searching for *chametz*:

הִנְנִי מוּכָן וּמְזוּמָן לְקַיֵּם מִצְוַת עֲשֵׂה וְלֹא תַעֲשֶׂה שֶׁל בְּדִיקַת חָמֵץ. לְשֵׁם יְחוּד קוּדְשָׁא בְּרִיךְ הוּא וּשְׁכִינְתֵּיהּ, עַל יְדֵי הַהוּא טָמִיר וְנֶעְלָם, בְּשֵׁם כָּל יִשְׂרָאֵל: וִיהִי נֹעַם אֲדֹנָי אֱלֹהֵינוּ עָלֵינוּ, וּמַעֲשֵׂה יָדֵינוּ כּוֹנְנָה עָלֵינוּ, וּמַעֲשֵׂה יָדֵינוּ כּוֹנְנֵהוּ:

The *chametz* search is initiated with the recitation of the
following blessing:

בָּרוּךְ אַתָּה יהוה אֱלֹהֵינוּ מֶלֶךְ הָעוֹלָם, אֲשֶׁר קִדְּשָׁנוּ בְּמִצְוֹתָיו, וְצִוָּנוּ עַל בִּעוּר חָמֵץ.

Bedikas Chametz / בדיקת חמץ

◆§ Our Homes and Our Hearts

When one searches for the unleavened bread around his home, he is searching not merely for physical *chametz,* but he should be searching for the evil inclination, which is called the *se'or she'be'issah,* within his home and his heart. This search must begin weeks before Pesach. The Kozhnitzer Maggid adds that just as when we physically rid our homes of *chametz* we prepare weeks beforehand, the same must be true when excising our sins and faults from within our hearts.

When a person walks around his home checking for *chametz,* he should also search for items in his home that may be destructive to his family's *neshamos.* Additionally, each person must do some serious introspection to make sure that he is acting properly toward others, especially family members. And when he burns the *chametz,* he should have in mind that he is destroying, along with the *chametz,* any bad character trait that he managed to find.

There is a law pertaining to *bedikas chametz,* which states that a person is required to search for *chametz* only "*kamah she'yado magaas* — as far as his hand reaches." The *Beis Aharon* interprets this homiletically and tells us that this law can also refer to a person's intellect. The halachah states: "*Ve'hashe'ar mevatlo be'libo* — The rest [meaning any *chametz* that a person cannot reach], he can nullify in his heart." Similarly, any negative traits that cannot be destroyed

THE SEARCH FOR CHAMETZ

Some say this declaration of intent before searching for *chametz:*

Behold, I am prepared and ready to fulfill the positive and prohibitive mitzvos of searching for *chametz.* For the sake of the unification of the Holy One, Blessed is He, and His presence, through Him Who is hidden and inscrutable — [I pray] in the name of all Israel. May the pleasantness of the Lord, our God, be upon us, and may He establish our handiwork for us; our handiwork may He establish.

The *chametz* search is initiated with the recitation of the following blessing:

Blessed are You, HASHEM, our God, King of the universe, Who has sanctified us with His commandments, and commanded us concerning the removal of *chametz.*

---

through his intellect can be nullified in his heart, or, as the *Beis Aharon* says in Yiddish: *"Mit ah shtik hartz* — With a piece of heart."

Along with other men, Rav Mordechai of Vizhnitz once accompanied his grandfather, the Ahavas Yisrael, as he performed the search for chametz. As his grandfather walked around his home and searched the nooks and crannies, he periodically let out a krechtz, "Oy! Oy!" He was clearly distraught and taking the search very much to heart. It was obvious that he was not only searching for the crumbs of bread, but that he was navigating the crevices of his heart to find his sins and faults. When he concluded his search, he turned to his grandson and handed him the candle.

Then the Ahavas Yisrael pulled aside his bekeshe and pointed to his heart. "Now I want you to check for the chametz inside of my heart." The small crowd turned toward Rav Mordechai to see his reaction. Without hesitation, he responded, "Rebbe, a makom she'ein machnisin bo chametz , a place where chametz is generally not brought does not need to be checked." His grandson was telling the Rebbe that no sin had ever entered his heart, so it need not be searched.

Often, it is the people who do not need much improvement who work the hardest to find ways to improve. Most of us, however, must check our homes and our hearts to make sure that we are cleaning them properly and ridding them of anything that is improper. This way, when the Seder begins, we can be confident that our homes — and our hearts — are *chametz*-free.

Upon completion of the *chametz* search, the *chametz* is wrapped well and set aside to be burned the next morning and the following declaration is made. The declaration must be understood in order to take effect; one who does not understand the Aramaic text may recite it in English, Yiddish, or any other language. Any *chametz* that will be used for that evening's supper or the next day's breakfast or for any other purpose prior to the final removal of *chametz* the next morning is not included in this declaration.

כָּל חֲמִירָא וַחֲמִיעָא דְּאִכָּא בִרְשׁוּתִי, דְּלָא חֲמִתֵּהּ וּדְלָא בְעַרְתֵּהּ וּדְלָא יָדַעְנָא לֵהּ, לִבָּטֵל וְלֶהֱוֵי הֶפְקֵר כְּעַפְרָא דְּאַרְעָא.

בִּיעוּר חָמֵץ

The following declaration, which includes all *chametz* without exception, is to be made after the burning of leftover *chametz*. It should be recited in a language which one understands. When Pesach begins on Motza'ei Shabbos, this declaration is made on Shabbos morning. Any *chametz* remaining from the Shabbos morning meal is flushed down the drain before the declaration is made.

Some have the custom to recite the following declaration of intent:

הִנְנִי מוּכָן וּמְזוּמָן לְקַיֵּם מִצְוַת עֲשֵׂה וְלֹא תַעֲשֶׂה שֶׁל שְׂרֵיפַת חָמֵץ, לְשֵׁם יִחוּד קוּדְשָׁא בְּרִיךְ הוּא וּשְׁכִינְתֵּיהּ עַל יְדֵי הַהוּא טָמִיר וְנֶעְלָם בְּשֵׁם כָּל יִשְׂרָאֵל: וִיהִי נֹעַם אֲדֹנָי אֱלֹהֵינוּ עָלֵינוּ, וּמַעֲשֵׂה יָדֵינוּ כּוֹנְנָה עָלֵינוּ, וּמַעֲשֵׂה יָדֵינוּ כּוֹנְנֵהוּ:

כָּל חֲמִירָא וַחֲמִיעָא דְּאִכָּא בִרְשׁוּתִי, דַּחֲזִתֵּהּ וּדְלָא חֲזִתֵּהּ, דַּחֲמִתֵּהּ וּדְלָא חֲמִתֵּהּ, דְּבַעַרְתֵּהּ וּדְלָא בְעַרְתֵּהּ, לִבָּטֵל וְלֶהֱוֵי הֶפְקֵר כְּעַפְרָא דְּאַרְעָא.

עֵירוּב תַּבְשִׁילִין

It is forbidden to prepare on Yom Tov for the next day even if that day is Shabbos. If, however, Shabbos preparations were started before Yom Tov began, they may be continued on Yom Tov. The *eruv tavshilin* constitutes this preparation. A matzah and any cooked food (such as fish, meat, or an egg) are set aside on the day before Yom Tov to be used on Shabbos and the blessing is recited followed by the declaration [made in a language understood by the one making the *eruv*]. If the first days of Pesach fall on Thursday and Friday, an *eruv tavshilin* must be made on Wednesday.

In Eretz Yisrael, where only one day Yom Tov is in effect, the *eruv* is omitted.

Upon completion of the *chametz* search, the *chametz* is wrapped well and set aside to be burned the next morning and the following declaration is made. The declaration must be understood in order to take effect; one who does not understand the Aramaic text may recite it in English, Yiddish, or any other language. Any *chametz* that will be used for that evening's supper or the next day's breakfast or for any other purpose prior to the final removal of *chametz* the next morning is not included in this declaration.

Any *chametz* which is in my possession which I did not see, and remove, nor know about, shall be nullified and become ownerless, like the dust of the earth.

BURNING THE CHAMETZ

The following declaration, which includes all *chametz* without exception, is to be made after the burning of leftover *chametz*. It should be recited in a language which one understands. When Pesach begins on Motza'ei Shabbos, this declaration is made on Shabbos morning. Any *chametz* remaining from the Shabbos morning meal is flushed down the drain before the declaration is made.

Some have the custom to recite the following declaration of intent:

Behold, I am prepared and ready to fulfill the positive and prohibitive mitzvos of burning *chametz*. For the sake of the unification of the Holy One, Blessed is He, and His presence, through Him Who is hidden and inscrutable — [I pray] in the name of all Israel. May the pleasantness of the Lord, our God, be upon us, and may He establish our handiwork for us; our handiwork may He establish.

Any *chametz* which is in my possession which I did or did not see, which I did or did not remove, shall be nullified and become ownerless, like the dust of the earth.

THE ERUV TAVSHILIN

It is forbidden to prepare on Yom Tov for the next day even if that day is Shabbos. If, however, Shabbos preparations were started before Yom Tov began, they may be continued on Yom Tov. The *eruv tavshilin* constitutes this preparation. A matzah and any cooked food (such as fish, meat, or an egg) are set aside on the day before Yom Tov to be used on Shabbos and the blessing is recited followed by the declaration [made in a language understood by the one making the *eruv*]. If the first days of Pesach fall on Thursday and Friday, an *eruv tavshilin* must be made on Wednesday.

In Eretz Yisrael, where only one day Yom Tov is in effect, the *eruv* is omitted.

The *eruv* foods are held while the following blessing and declaration are recited.

בָּרוּךְ אַתָּה יהוה אֱלֹהֵינוּ מֶלֶךְ הָעוֹלָם, אֲשֶׁר קִדְּשָׁנוּ בְּמִצְוֺתָיו, וְצִוָּנוּ עַל מִצְוַת עֵרוּב.

בְּהָדֵין עֵרוּבָא יְהֵא שָׁרֵא לָנָא לַאֲפוּיֵי לְבַשּׁוּלֵי וּלְאַצְלוּיֵי וּלְאַטְמוּנֵי וּלְאַדְלוּקֵי שְׁרָגָא וּלְתַקָּנָא וּלְמֶעֱבַד כָּל צָרְכָּנָא, מִיּוֹמָא טָבָא לְשַׁבַּתָּא לָנָא וּלְכָל יִשְׂרָאֵל הַדָּרִים בָּעִיר הַזֹּאת.

הדלקת נרות

The candles are lit and the following blessings are recited. When Yom Tov falls on Shabbos, the words in parentheses are added.

בָּרוּךְ אַתָּה יהוה אֱלֹהֵינוּ מֶלֶךְ הָעוֹלָם, אֲשֶׁר קִדְּשָׁנוּ בְּמִצְוֺתָיו, וְצִוָּנוּ לְהַדְלִיק נֵר שֶׁל (שַׁבָּת וְשֶׁל) יוֹם טוֹב.

בָּרוּךְ אַתָּה יהוה אֱלֹהֵינוּ מֶלֶךְ הָעוֹלָם, שֶׁהֶחֱיָנוּ וְקִיְּמָנוּ וְהִגִּיעָנוּ לַזְּמַן הַזֶּה.

It is customary to recite the following prayer after the kindling.
The words in brackets are included as they apply.

יְהִי רָצוֹן לְפָנֶיךָ, יהוה אֱלֹהַי וֵאלֹהֵי אֲבוֹתַי, שֶׁתְּחוֹנֵן אוֹתִי [וְאֶת אִישִׁי, וְאֶת בָּנַי, וְאֶת בְּנוֹתַי, וְאֶת אָבִי, וְאֶת אִמִּי] וְאֶת כָּל קְרוֹבַי; וְתִתֶּן לָנוּ וּלְכָל יִשְׂרָאֵל חַיִּים טוֹבִים וַאֲרוּכִים; וְתִזְכְּרֵנוּ בְּזִכְרוֹן טוֹבָה וּבְרָכָה; וְתִפְקְדֵנוּ בִּפְקֻדַּת יְשׁוּעָה וְרַחֲמִים; וּתְבָרְכֵנוּ בְּרָכוֹת גְּדוֹלוֹת; וְתַשְׁלִים בָּתֵּינוּ; וְתַשְׁכֵּן שְׁכִינָתְךָ בֵּינֵינוּ. וְזַכֵּנִי לְגַדֵּל בָּנִים וּבְנֵי בָנִים חֲכָמִים וּנְבוֹנִים, אוֹהֲבֵי יהוה, יִרְאֵי אֱלֹהִים, אַנְשֵׁי אֱמֶת, זֶרַע קֹדֶשׁ, בַּיהוה דְּבֵקִים, וּמְאִירִים אֶת הָעוֹלָם בַּתּוֹרָה וּבְמַעֲשִׂים טוֹבִים, וּבְכָל מְלֶאכֶת עֲבוֹדַת הַבּוֹרֵא. אָנָּא שְׁמַע אֶת תְּחִנָּתִי בָּעֵת הַזֹּאת, בִּזְכוּת שָׂרָה וְרִבְקָה וְרָחֵל וְלֵאָה אִמּוֹתֵינוּ, וְהָאֵר נֵרֵנוּ שֶׁלֹּא יִכְבֶּה לְעוֹלָם וָעֶד, וְהָאֵר פָּנֶיךָ וְנִוָּשֵׁעָה. אָמֵן.

The *eruv* foods are held while the following blessing and declaration are recited.

Blessed are You, HASHEM, our God, King of the universe, Who sanctified us by His commandments and commanded us concerning the commandment of *eruv*.

Through this *eruv* may we be permitted to bake, cook, fry, insulate, kindle flame, prepare for, and do anything necessary on the Festival for the sake of the Shabbos — for ourselves and for all Jews who live in this city.

LIGHTING THE CANDLES

The candles are lit and the following blessings are recited. When Yom Tov falls on Shabbos, the words in parentheses are added.

Blessed are You, HASHEM, our God, King of the universe, Who has sanctified us through His commandments, and commanded us to kindle the flame of the (Shabbos and the) Festival.

Blessed are You, HASHEM, our God, King of the universe, Who has kept us alive, sustained us, and brought us to this season.

It is customary to recite the following prayer after the kindling.
The words in brackets are included as they apply.

May it be Your will, HASHEM, my God and God of my forefathers, that You show favor to me [my husband, my sons, my daughters, my father, my mother] and all my relatives; and that You grant us and all Israel a good and long life; that You remember us with a beneficent memory and blessing; that You consider us with a consideration of salvation and compassion; that You bless us with great blessings; that You make our households complete; that You cause Your Presence to dwell among us. Privilege me to raise children and grandchildren who are wise and understanding, who love HASHEM and fear God, people of truth, holy offspring, attached to HASHEM, who illuminate the world with Torah and good deeds and with every labor in the service of the Creator. Please, hear my plea at this time, in the merit of Sarah, Rivkah, Rachel, and Leah, our mothers, and cause our light to illuminate that it not be extinguished forever, and let Your countenance shine so that we are saved. Amen.

ההכנות לסדר
PREPARING FOR THE SEDER

Wine for the Four Cups

1. It is preferable to use red wine, if it is not inferior in quality to the white wine available (472:11).

2. One may use boiled wine or wine to which flavoring has been added, although it is preferable to use pure, unboiled wine so long as it is not of inferior quality (472:2 and *Mishnah Berurah* 39-40).

Karpas

1. One should use the vegetable called *karpas*, because this word is an anagram of the words 'ס, *60* (referring to the 600,000 Jews), and פֶּרֶךְ, *worked hard*. However, any vegetable may be used other than those which may be used for *maror*.

2. One should prepare salt water or Kosher for Pesach vinegar in which to dip the *karpas*. (If the Seder night falls on Shabbos, the salt water should be made beforehand. If one forgot to do so, he may prepare the minimum amount of salt water on Shabbos, immediately prior to the meal, making sure that he puts less than 66 percent salt in the mixture.) (473:4 and *Mishnah Berurah* 19, 21).

Wearing a Kittel

≈§ The Time Machine

It is customary for married men to wear a *kittel*, a white robe, at the Seder. One reason is to remind each person of his upcoming death, since a man is buried in a *kittel*. Why would a man wear such a depressing garment on such a festive evening? Why would he want to remind himself of his demise?

In truth, by remembering that he is not immortal, a person will take heed not to get carried away, even in the midst of his celebrations.

But the Chassidim have another interpretation. Wearing the *kittel* is not meant to remind the person of his death, but to bring to mind our ancestors who come to visit us on this night and join us for the Seder.

At times, we may not feel connected to our past. However, even if our ancestors lived in Europe and we live in North America, or

Maror

1. There are five vegetables which the Mishnah (*Pesachim* 2:6) mentions which may be used for *maror: chazeres* (lettuce), *ulshin* (endives), *tamcha* (horseradish), *charchavinah*, and *maror.* One may use either the leaves or the stalks of these species. While one may not use their roots, the thick, hard part of the root (as the horseradish root) has the same status as the stalk. The leaves may not be used after they have dried out, but the stalk may be used when dry. Neither may be used if it has been soaked in water or any other liquid for 24 hours.

   Since the Mishnah lists the varieties in order of preference, and *chazeres* precedes *tamcha*, it should be more preferable to use lettuce than horseradish. However, since lettuce is extremely hard to rid of all the bugs that infest it, if one is unable to check and cleanse the lettuce thoroughly he should use horseradish instead (473:5, *Mishnah Berurah* ad loc.).

2. The horseradish should be ground, as eating a whole piece of horseradish constitutes a danger to one's well-being and is not

---

they lived in Asia and we live in South America, we are connected to them.

One Friday afternoon, I took my children to Rita's Italian Ice to buy them some frozen treats for Shabbos. As I helped my children decide which flavor to buy, a Hispanic woman asked me if I was a rabbi. After I answered in the affirmative, she told me that she was going to an Orthodox family for the Shabbos meal, and she wanted to know if it was appropriate to give the children of the family some "Rita dollars" as a gift. I told her that if she was going to an Orthodox family for the Shabbos meal, it would be best if she gave them the gift either before or after Shabbos. Although she did not appear to be Jewish, I asked her if she was. She told me that seven years ago, she had undergone a Reform conversion. However, by now she was aware that such a conversion would not be accepted by all, so she was pursuing further Jewish education, and was in the midst of arranging an Orthodox conversion.

Indeed, she was attending the Shabbos meal of an Orthodox rabbi. She said that she felt an innate attachment to Judaism and wanted to become a Jew. When she will become a mother, she told me, she only wants to be a Jewish mother. She had seen the way

a fulfillment of the mitzvah. However, the ground horseradish should not be left open for a long time after, as this causes all its bitterness to dissipate (ibid.).

3. The *Mishnah Berurah* records that the *Gra* used to leave the grinding of the horseradish until after he came home from shul on the Seder night, and then left it covered until the beginning of the Seder. (Note: The grinding of these vegetables on Yom Tov should be done differently than usual. See *Orach Chayim* 504.) When the Seder night comes out on Shabbos, when such grinding is forbidden, the horseradish should be prepared before Shabbos and left covered until the beginning of the Seder. (Nowadays many people prepare the horseradish before Yom Tov even when it is not Shabbos, since its sharpness can be preserved quite well in a closed container.

4. If someone is too ill or delicate to eat the entire *k'zayis* of horseradish at one time, he may spread it out over a period of *k'dei achilas peras* (approx. 2-9 minutes).

Jewish mothers care for and raise their children and believes that this type of life was meant for her, as well.

Her story and her passion seemed real. I pressed further and asked her where her love for Judaism came from. She told me that something fascinating had recently been unearthed. She was looking into her family ancestry, and she discovered that her great-great-grandfather originally came from Poland and had been a religious Jew. Incarcerated for his beliefs, he escaped and fled the country. Along with a few others, he came across the Atlantic Ocean and arrived in Cuba. At the time, there were very few options for a Jewish man in Cuba. He married a Cuban girl, and she immediately bought into his beliefs. She kept Shabbos, lit candles, and kept a strictly kosher home. In fact, this young woman told me that her grandmother remembers seeing her grandmother light Shabbos candles.

Although the woman was aware that Orthodox Judaism follows maternal descent, she felt a deep attachment to her great-great-grandfather and knew that she wanted to reconnect to him somehow.

The next week, I received the following message in my inbox:

Hello, Rabbi Spero,

We met last week at Rita's. I wanted to read your books before I emailed you back. I read two of them, and I'm deeply fascinated. I

Charoses

1. *Charoses* should be prepared with fruits which are used in *Tanach* as metaphors for Israel — such as figs (see *Shir HaShirim* 2:13), nuts (ibid., 6:11), and apples (ibid., 8:5). It is also customary to use almonds, because the Hebrew word for almond (שָׁקֵד) also means swift, and is thus a reminder of God's speedy deliverance of the Jews from Egypt. One should also put in pieces of ginger and cinnamon, to symbolize the straw that was used by the Jewish slaves to prepare bricks. The *charoses* should have a thick consistency, as a reminder of the mortar that the Egyptians forced the Jews to prepare. However, just before it is used (to dip the *maror*) some wine should be poured into it, as a remembrance of the blood that played an important role in the Exodus (and also to make it more usable as a dip). When the Seder is held on Shabbos the wine should be put into the *charoses* before Shabbos. If one forgot to do so, he may do it differently than usual, and should add enough wine to make a loose consistency (504).

---

find myself looking for more meaningful experiences in Judaism, and I need more than what I'm getting in my Conservative shul, but I'm not sure exactly what it is. Your books were a much needed influence for me. What a beautiful gift of storytelling!

Thanks for your generous advice!

Marie

The last chapter of this young woman's life has yet to be written. However, I was very inspired by the desire she had to reconnect to her past.

On Seder night, we have that unique and cherished opportunity. Don't let this treasure pass you by. If you are privileged to have a grandparent or a great-grandparent who is alive and well, ask him what it was like when he was at his grandparents' and great-grandparents' Seder. You will be amazed by what you hear. For as different as their environment and culture may have been, certain traditions remain exactly the same.

Rav Chaim Palagi brings another reason for donning a *kittel*. The *Maharal* explains that on the night of the Seder, a person is similar to the Kohen Gadol, who wore white linen garments. This is

Two Cooked Foods

1. After the destruction of the *Beis HaMikdash* the Sages instituted
   the practice of placing two kinds of cooked foods on the Seder
   table: one to commemorate the meat of the *pesach*-offering and
   the other to commemorate the meat of the *chagigah*-offering —
   both of which were sacrificed in the *Beis HaMikdash* on the 14
   of Nissan and eaten at the Seder. The custom has developed that
   one of the two foods should be meat, customarily a shankbone
   (corresponding to the human arm, symbolizing the "outstretched
   arm" of Hashem) that has been roasted on the fire (as the *pesach*
   meat was). The second food is customarily an egg, because
   the Aramaic word for egg (בֵּיעָא) is related to the Aramaic word
   for desire; God desired (בְּעָא) to take us out of Egypt with an

---

because on the night of the Seder every home is enveloped in the
holiness of the *Beis HaMikdash*. Hence, each person's home is also
like a *Beis HaMikdash*.

In this regard, Rav Chaim mentions another custom; some people
whitewash their homes before Pesach. This is similar to the practice
they had in the times of the *Beis HaMikdash*, where they would
whitewash its walls before Pesach, since the walls had become
blackened from the smoke of the offerings.

Unfortunately, not every home is capable of receiving Hashem's
holiness, and each person must try hard to build a home in which
the *Shechinah* dwells. However, on the night of the Seder, there
is a special holiness similar to the night of the Exodus, for that is
when the Jews were lifted from the furnace of impurity — for they
were among the Egyptians who were the most corrupt of nations —
to the highest level of holiness. Each Yid was able to begin anew,
with a newly whitewashed home that was comparable to the *Beis
HaMikdash*. In the same vein, explains Rav Palagi, the one who
leads the Seder dons a white garment, like the Kohen who serves
in the *Beis HaMikdash,* and merits Hashem's Presence in his home.

This understanding dovetails with the first one. We are not merely
remembering the past; we are reliving it. This echoes the theme of
the evening, which is to relive the experience of our Exodus from
Egypt. It is as if we enter a spiritual "time machine," where we re-
experience — and reenact — the miracles of yesteryear.

outstretched arm. The egg can be cooked or roasted in any way (as the *chagigah* was), although some have the custom to roast it specifically.

The *Rema* writes that many have the custom to eat eggs at the Seder. He explains that eggs are traditionally eaten by mourners, and they are eaten at this time as a commemoration of the destruction of the *Beis HaMikdash*. The *Mishnah Berurah*, citing *Gra*, says that we eat the egg of the Seder plate, since, as noted above, it symbolizes the *chagigah*-offering. (According to this explanation, only the egg on the Seder plate needs to be eaten, but this custom subsequently became popularly extended to include the eating of eggs in general.) (473:4, *Mishnah Berurah* ad loc.; 470:2, *Mishnah Berurah* 11.)

Itche, the Hero of Ger

Throughout his life, the Imrei Emes, Rav Avraham Mordechai Alter of Ger, was particular that no one should touch his clothing. He was so concerned that his clothes not be affected by impurity that he even chose his tailor very carefully. There was one person, however, who was allowed to touch his clothing. He was neither a Rebbe nor a learned individual, nor did he come from a prestigious background. Itche Greinemous was a rather simple fellow. However, because of one amazing day in his life, he had the privilege of helping the Rebbe don his kittel on Pesach night.

At the time of the story, the Sfas Emes, Rav Yehudah Aryeh Leib, stood at the helm of Ger Chassidus. One day, word began to spread that a plague had broken out in the city. Immediately, everyone ran to their homes and tried to protect themselves against the deadly plague. But it was too late; the plague spread quickly and mercilessly, claiming the lives of many, especially children. By the time daybreak had arrived, the streets were littered with the bodies of lifeless children. The authorities, desperate to get the situation under control, decreed that these bodies should be cremated to prevent the plague from spreading any further. The heartbroken families, who wanted so badly to give their children a proper final farewell, watched helplessly from inside their homes, since they knew that they were risking their lives by going outside.

The Sfas Emes was beside himself. There was really nothing anyone could do, as no one was prepared to risk his own life.

2. It is best to boil or roast these two foods before Yom Tov. If this was neglected, they may be prepared on Yom Tov. If they were prepared on Yom Tov, the foods must be eaten on that day of Yom Tov, as one may only cook food on Yom Tov if it will be eaten that same day. The two foods will thus have to be prepared anew for the second Seder (ibid.).

Making Arrangements for Reclining

1. The seats of those who must recline while drinking the wine and eating the matzah should be prepared in a manner that will enable comfortable reclining on one's left side (472:2).

Preparing the Cups

1. The cups should be whole (not chipped or broken) and clean, and should be able to hold at least a *revi'is*. Since it is preferable to drink a majority of the wine in the cup for each of the four cups, it is advisable not to use a very large cup. This applies to the cups used by all the participants in the Seder, including women and children (who have reached the age of training in mitzvos) (472:14, 15; *Mishnah Berurah* 33).

After much thought, the Sfas Emes issued a declaration: Anyone who was prepared to bury one of the dead children would be guaranteed a portion in the World to Come. Families heard about the Rebbe's promise, but the streets remained eerily empty, until suddenly, one towering figure emerged. It was Itche Greinemous. With a shovel in his hand, he bent down next to a small child in the middle of the street and wrapped him in a tallis. Then he went to the cemetery and buried the boy. At the end of the day, he showed up at the doorstep of the Sfas Emes.

The Rebbe had heard about his act of selfless dedication and promised him that he would receive a special portion in the World to Come for his mesirus nefesh. But Itche just stood there at the doorstep, exhausted and filthy. "Rebbe, what you promised was based on someone burying one child. I just came from the cemetery. Rebbe, I buried 16 children!"

The Sfas Emes looked incredulously at the broad-shouldered fellow. He could hardly believe what he had just heard. "Sixteen children?" The Rebbe contemplated the immeasurable comfort

Preparing the Table

1. The table should be set with elegant and luxurious articles according to one's means. Although it is usually proper to use moderation in this regard out of mourning for the *Beis HaMikdash*, on Pesach it is encouraged, as this serves as yet another demonstration of our freedom. The table should be set in advance so that the Seder can get underway without delay (so the children should not become too tired) (472:1,2; *Mishnah Berurah* 6).

The Beginning of the Seder

1. Although, as mentioned above, the Seder should begin as promptly as possible, *Kiddush* should not be said before dark (*tzeis hakochavim*) (472:1).
2. It is customary for the leader to wear a *kittel* for the Seder (ibid., *Mishnah Berurah* 12).
3. Only one Seder plate is set, before the leader of the Seder. There are several different opinions as to how the Seder plate should be arranged (see diagrams on page 62).

---

that Itche had provided to those 16 families. Instead of their children being reduced to ash, they now had a final resting place of dignity, where the parents could come visit them and pray.

"So what can I possibly give you as a reward?" the Rebbe asked.

Itche did not hesitate for a moment. He knew exactly what he wanted. It was neither riches nor monetary rewards he was seeking. Nor was he interested in honor or glory. Instead, he asked the Rebbe if he could have the privilege of helping him put on his kittel every year at the Seder. Immediately, the Rebbe agreed. And so it was. Every year, after they came back from davening, the Sfas Emes allowed Itche to help him with his kittel, a privilege that was allowed to no one else.

The obvious connection was never spoken about. While Itche had risked his life to prepare the 16 children he had buried and to dress them in their tachrichim, the Rebbe had given him the privilege of dressing him in his kittel, a special garment reserved for the Seder, and used later for burial.

In the last year of the Sfas Emes's life, as Itche helped him with his kittel, he let out a krechtz, "Oy! There are thousands of Jewish soldiers who have written to me asking that I daven on their

4. The children should be kept awake at least until after reciting עֲבָדִים הָיִינוּ, so that they should hear the basic story of the Exodus. Children who have reached the age of training in mitzvos must participate in all the practices of the entire Seder. (However they must only consume a cheekful of wine, according to the size of their own mouths, for each required cup. Furthermore, there is an opinion that holds that they need not drink the four cups of wine at all.) (472:15; *Mishnah Berurah* 46, 47.)

---

behalf. All they want is that they should be zocheh to receive a kever Yisrael, a proper Jewish burial. How can I begin my Seder with this enormous burden on my shoulders? Who can carry such a burden? I can't do it anymore. I just can't do it."

Anyone who was in the room at that time was greatly moved by the Rebbe's cry, but perhaps no one was more moved than Itche, who had risked his life to bring so many children to Jewish burial.

After the Rebbe's passing that year, Itche continued to perform his yearly practice with the Imrei Emes, the son of the Sfas Emes. Although the Imrei Emes was particular about who touched his clothing, Itche was more angel than man.

Years later, on the first day of Succos, as he stood in the Gerrer beis midrash holding his arba'ah minim, Itche breathed his last breath. With thousands of people in the surrounding area, Itche was taken out of the beis midrash. The following day, he was brought to his final resting place, in one of the largest funeral processions the city of Ger had ever seen. Of course, the Imrei Emes was in attendance, as well.

Itche was buried right near the children he had buried years before.

Four Cups

◄§ To "Halt Cup"

The number four is prevalent throughout the Seder. We ask four questions in the *Mah Nishtanah*, and the Torah speaks of four sons and how to teach each of them. Some commentators say that since one of the three matzos is broken in half, we actually have four of those, as well. According to the *Toras Chaim* on *Maseches*

Reclining

1. One should not recline on his back or stomach, but only on his left side. This applies to left-handed people as well (472:3, *Mishnah Berurah* ad loc.).

2. Someone who is in mourning for a relative should also recline, although he should do so in a less luxurious manner than usual. It is also customary for a mourner not to wear a *kittel* for the Seder, although some opinions permit it (*Mishnah Berurah* 13).

Chullin (brought down in the *sefer Shaarei Leil HaSeder*), we eat four *kezeisim* of matzah (at *Motzi, Matzah, Koreich,* and *Tzafun*). In addition, Hashem used four *leshonos shel geulah,* four expressions of redemption, when telling Moshe about the Exodus. Why the fixation on the number four?

The *Toras Chaim* gives a beautiful answer. At the *bris bein habesarim* (*Bereishis* 15:13), Avraham Avinu was told that the Jewish people were going to be strangers in a land that is not theirs, and they will be enslaved and oppressed for 400 years. However, in *Parashas Bo,* after the fact, the *pasuk* tells us (*Shemos* 12:40) that Bnei Yisrael lived in Egypt for 430 years. In truth, the count of 430 years began at the time of the *bris bein habesarim,* when Hashem told Avraham about the Egyptian exile; hence, the exile was decreed 430 years before the Exodus. The count of 400 began with the birth of Yitzchak, which was 30 years after the *bris bein habesarim.* The *Chida* adds that when Yaakov received gifts from Yosef, included was *yayin yashan,* old wine. The *gematria* of יַיִן יָשָׁן is 430. Yosef was hinting to his father that the exile was beginning now, though it had been decreed that it would last 430 years.

In fact, the actual sojourn in Mitzrayim lasted only 210 years. This is mentioned in the *Haggadah:* "*she'HaKadosh Baruch Hu chishav es haKeitz* — for HaKadosh Baruch Hu calculated the End"; Hashem expedited the redemption from Egypt by 190 years, the *gematria* of the word קֵץ. *Chazal* tell us that the *koshi hashibud,* the harshness of the servitude, was only for 86 years, from the time of Miriam's birth. She was called מִרְיָם, which means *bitter,* because when she was born the Egyptians began to embitter the lives of the Yidden. *Chazal* tell us that Miriam was 86 at the time of the Exodus; thus, we see that the bitter and difficult enslavement lasted 86 years.

3. The custom is that women do not recline (472:4).

4. A student in the presence of his rebbi — or any person in the presence of a great, recognized rabbinical figure — should not recline. This holds true only if they are seated at the same table. (According to some opinions, a student in the presence of his rebbi should ask for permission to recline even if he is sitting at a separate table.) (472:5, *Mishnah Berurah* 18.)

5. A son must recline in the presence of his father, even if his father is also his rebbi (472:5).

The *Toras Chaim* then explains that the Jewish people had to endure only one-fifth of the 430 years, as 86 is one-fifth of 430. The other four-fifths of the 430 years were subtracted. This is why there are four expressions of redemption. We were subjugated for one-fifth of the time designated for enslavement, and were redeemed from the other four parts.

It is also for this reason that we drink four cups of wine, as the word כּוֹס, *cup*, has the numerical value of 86. In His kindness, Hashem had us work for only 86 years, one period of כּוֹס. We thank Hashem for absolving us of the other four-fifths of the enslavement, and we do this by raising the כּוֹס four times: for the four times כּוֹס — 4x86 — that He took off of the calculation.

Though events in our lives may seem coincidental, they are really all part of His Master Plan. In fact, the *gematria* of כּוֹס is equivalent to the numerical value of the Name of Hashem, אֱלֹהִים, which is also equal to the word הַטֶּבַע, the nature. This follows the idea that "nature is a pseudonym for God," since His greatness is revealed in nature and He controls nature.

On the other hand, *Rabbeinu Bachya* writes that טֶבַע is related to the word טְבִיעָה, *drowning*. As nature takes its course, a person can sink or drown as he begins to imagine and let himself believe that everything is happening through him — and not with Hashem's guidance.

This is our *avodah* during the *Leil HaSeder*, to extricate ourselves from the ways of nature and come to the recognition that everything comes from Hashem.

It says in *Tehillim* (116:13): "*Kos yeshuos essa u've'Sheim Hashem ekra* — I will raise the cup of salvations and the Name of Hashem I will invoke."

6. If one forgot to recline for any of the places in the Seder which call for reclining, he has not fulfilled that mitzvah, and it must be performed again. *Raaviah* maintains, however, that since eating in a reclining position is not a sign of freedom and leisure in our culture, the practice need not be followed. Although we do not follow the *Raaviah's* opinion, when redoing one of the mitzvos might lead to a halachic complication, this opinion is adopted and the mitzvah in question is not done over. These exceptions will be noted in appropriate places in the *Haggadah* (472:7, *Mishnah Berurah* 20).

We must constantly be on the lookout for the kindness of Hashem, and raise a cup of salvation to show our gratitude.

Perfect Timing

Yudel Zeigelman and his friends had lost their families in the Holocaust. Thus, when the concentration camp in which they had been interned was abandoned by the Nazis, he and his two friends were left alone in the world. They had only one another.

Since the war was not yet over, they were afraid to be seen on the street, lest a German guard see them and harm them. Luckily, they met a kind non-Jew who allowed them to hide in his stable while he provided for their needs. As rough as the conditions were, they were luxurious compared to the living conditions in the camp. Instead of sleeping on concrete slabs and enduring constant starvation, they had a mattress of straw, drinking water, and daily meals.

Since Pesach was coming, they felt that they could finally celebrate z'man cheiruseinu, the time of our freedom. True freedom was just around the corner, and they could well understand what their forefathers had undergone in Egypt. They, too, had endured what seemed to be endless slavery at the hands of cruel oppressors. Sadly, they could also relate to the many Jews who had lost their family members in the makkah of choshech.

In order to be able to celebrate the Yom Tov, they desperately wanted to get hold of some flour with which to bake matzos. The caring man who hosted them agreed to do what he could to help them.

After a few days, he knocked on the door of the stable, using the special knock they had agreed upon beforehand. When they came out of their hiding place, they were pleasantly surprised to

Drinking the Four Cups

1. Even if one dislikes wine or suffers discomfort when drinking it, he should force himself to drink the four cups (unless it will actually make him ill). The wine may be diluted, as long as it remains fit to be used as *Kiddush* wine.

2. It is preferable to drink the entire cup of wine each time. The minimum amount that must be consumed is a majority of a *revi'is,*

---

see that their host had several bags of flour for them. They thanked him profusely, and the next day they baked matzos.

Although they already had plenty of bitterness in their lives, they got hold of some bitter herbs. At that point, all they were missing to make a complete Seder was wine. They were not even sure how to conduct the Seder properly without it. Thus, the night before the Seder, despite the items they had been able to procure, they were very disappointed.

It was quite windy that evening, and the gusts of wind scattered papers from one end of the farm to the other. Suddenly, the son of the farmer appeared before them with a piece of paper in his hand. He mentioned that he thought that it had Hebrew lettering on it. When Yudel took the piece of paper, he noticed that the boy was right. It was Hebrew lettering. When he looked a bit closer, he was overwhelmed with emotion.

As his two friends looked at the paper, tears formed in their eyes. The paper was a page torn from a Shulchan Aruch. The volume was Orach Chaim. The siman was 483, which discusses how one is to conduct a Seder when he does not have wine!

It was nothing short of miraculous.

It is interesting to think about the path that the page from the Shulchan Aruch may have taken. In all probability, this volume once sat peacefully on someone's sefarim shelf. The owner probably learned it from time to time. And then, this precious sefer was torn from the shelves and destroyed by the German invaders. Yet one page would survive…

And its journey would begin.

The Almighty had sent this very page on a journey to find these lonely young men who had lost nearly everything in their lives. And this paper would somehow console them in a way that nothing else could.

although there is an opinion that one must drink most of the wine in the cup, if the cup is larger than a *revi'is*. The requisite amount of wine should be drunk all at once, or at the very most within a time span of *k'dei achilas pras* (approx. 2-9 minutes) (472:9, *Mishnah Berurah* 30, 33, 34).

3. The four cups must be drunk in their appropriate places in the Seder: one for *Kiddush*, one after *Maggid*, one for *bentching*, and one for *Hallel* (472:8).

That night, they huddled over the torn paper, studying the laws carefully. The next night, they conducted the most memorable Seder they would ever have. They ate their precious little matzos and chewed on the maror. Although they did not have wine, they had something that would carry them through the night and beyond: a torn piece of paper that let them know that Someone was watching over them.

And loved each of them very much.

The war ended three months later, and these young men spent the first few months of the liberation seeking other precious pages of holy books, as if they were looking for members of their families. They lovingly kissed each page and buried them, as their collections grew.

For the rest of their lives, whenever they saw a scrap of paper from a siddur or a sefer, they picked it up and held it close to their lips. And kissed it.

There are moments in our lives in which we are faced with difficult *nisyonos*. At times, we may be tempted to give up, as they sap us of our strength. But although it may be tough to face these challenges, the Almighty gives us the necessary strength to confront them.

For the Almighty will send us a gift. It is impossible to know what that gift may be. But it will be something that will let us know that He loves us and is smiling down upon us.

Always.

The Seder Plate
הקערה

According to the *Arizal*

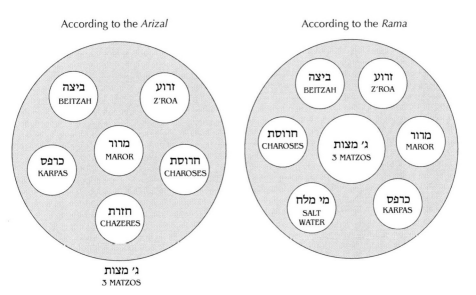

ביצה
BEITZAH

זרוע
Z'ROA

כרפס
KARPAS

מרור
MAROR

חרוסת
CHAROSES

חזרת
CHAZERES

ג' מצות
3 MATZOS

According to the *Rama*

ביצה
BEITZAH

זרוע
Z'ROA

חרוסת
CHAROSES

ג' מצות
3 MATZOS

מרור
MAROR

מי מלח
SALT WATER

כרפס
KARPAS

According to the *Vilna Gaon*

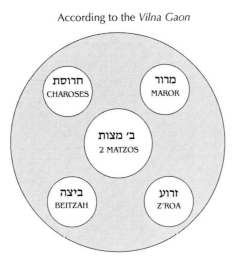

חרוסת
CHAROSES

מרור
MAROR

ב' מצות
2 MATZOS

ביצה
BEITZAH

זרוע
Z'ROA

The Ke'arah / הקערה

בֵּיצָה

Beitzah

⇒§ Inside the Egg

The *Ke'arah* contains six items: *z'roa* (shankbone), *beitzah* (egg), *maror* (bitter herb), *charoses*, *karpas* (vegetable), and *chazeres* (lettuce). Though reasons are given for each of them, there is much mystery hidden within each item, as well. The *Shatzer Rav*, Rav Shalom, illustrated this point with a meaningful parable.

> *In the olden days, in order to grind wheat, the townspeople would harness horses to large millstones and place the wheat between them. When the horses would walk, the stones would grind the wheat into flour.*
>
> *One time, the horse lifted its eyes and asked its owner, "When I walk on a path, I understand my purpose. Before I begin my journey, I am in one place and then, an hour later, I am in a different place; I do not remain in the same spot. However, when I do this work, I am going around and around in circles. I don't understand what purpose there is to my work."*
>
> *The master explained, "You think you are just walking in place, because you don't understand how the millstones work. But I promise you that every step you take accomplishes a tremendous amount. It grinds the wheat into flour, which will eventually be baked into bread that will feed hungry families."*

The same is true with our work this evening. We certainly do not understand the mysterious and secret depths of the Seder. However, through our actions, the exalted "millstones of the Heavens" will accomplish great things and provide spiritual sustenance for hungry souls.

One of the items we place on the Seder plate is the *beitzah*, the egg. Additionally, at the onset of *Shulchan Oreich*, many people have the custom of dipping the egg in salt water and eating it. The *Rema* (*Orach Chaim* 476) provides the following reason. The first day of Pesach always falls on the same day of the week as

Tishah B'Av. Prior to the fast of Tishah B'Av, we eat the *seudah hamafsekes*, which includes an egg dipped in ashes, since egg is a food given to mourners. This reminds us of the destruction of the *Beis HaMikdash*. The *Rema* explains that we eat the egg at the Seder to remember the pain and sense of mourning we have since the *Churban*, which must not be forgotten during our moments of *cheirus*.

And vice versa.

> The Bluzhever Rebbe would sit on the floor as he ate the seudah hamafsekes, a few moments before Tishah B'Av began. At that simple meal, he would include one unique item; he would eat a piece of the afikoman. The Rebbe understood that even at moments of aveilus, we can't forget that we were once free, and that one day soon we will be free again.

The *pasuk* in *Eichah* (3:15) says, "*Hisbi'ani vamerorim hirvani laanah* — He filled me with bitterness, sated me with wormwood." The Midrash (*Eichah Rabbah* 13) notes that "*hisbi'ani vamerorim*" is referring to the *maror* we eat on the first night of Pesach, while "*hirvani laanah*" is the bitterness of Tishah B'Av night.

And yet, do we truly feel the bitterness of Tishah B'Av?

> Two beggars sat on a park bench, lamenting their fate. Neither had any money and both had to beg for their food, but there was one major difference between them. One had always been a pauper, while the other had once been a wealthy man. The bitterness and pain of the formerly wealthy man was exponentially greater than that of the man who was always poor, who had no idea what he was missing.

As the *Yefeh Anaf* explains, there was once a time when we were kings. We tasted the sweetness of freedom and redemption. Now all of that has been replaced by the *laanah*, wormwood. Even so, we do not really know what we are missing.

On Pesach, we, too, taste *cheirus* and we feel so close to the *Ribbono Shel Olam;* more important, He is so happy with us. Yet every year, a few months later on Tishah B'Av, we once more are forced to lament what we no longer have.

If we would truly know and take to heart what we are missing, we would merit the rebuilding of the *Beis HaMikdash* and true *cheirus*, and no longer be in mourning.

Then, Tishah B'Av will be a day of rejoicing.

⤷ Hidden Potential

Rav Meir Shapiro explains why the Jewish people are compared to an egg. The longer an egg remains in hot water, the harder it becomes. So, too, the Jewish people; although they have endured so much suffering and pain, they have become more and more resilient and stronger in their belief and in their Torah.

The *Izhbitzer*, cited in *Mei HaShiloach*, brings another powerful analogy from the egg. Just as the egg itself is not the end result, since one day it will actually become a chicken, the same is true regarding *Yetzias Mitzrayim*. The main point of the Exodus was for the Jews to receive the Torah.

Rav Leibele Eiger adds one more point (*Toras Emes* 5627). When an egg is laid, to the naked eye it appears like an inanimate object. But inside, it is bubbling with potential life. Quoting the *Arizal*, he says that the redemption from Egypt was the first of two births. When we, the Jewish people, first came out of Egypt, we were prepared to receive the Torah, but that was not readily apparent. We first had to go through a 49-day process that could bring us to that point. Therefore, on Seder night, every person reaches very high levels, but that greatness remains locked inside. Only over the next 49 days will we be able to bring that potential to reality.

Just like the egg, which is full of hidden potential.

The Real Reason We Are Here

As the yeshivah of Baranovich struggled to feed its bachurim, Rav Elchanan Wasserman, the Rosh Yeshivah, increased his fund-raising efforts throughout Europe and Russia. But even that did not help much. Rav Elchanan was left with no choice but to travel to America. The ship ride took nearly a month and was physically exhausting for Rav Elchanan. Perhaps most frustrating of all was that once he arrived in America he wasn't making much money. Having spent nearly a year collecting, Reb Elchanan was distraught that he had left the yeshivah for so long and didn't have much to show for it.

Someone who was aware of Rav Elchanan's frustrations suggested that he go to the office of Philip Goodstein, the owner of the most successful coat factory in Manhattan. Formerly Pinchas Goodstein, Philip was an old classmate of Rav Elchanan from his cheder days in Europe. However, 50 years had passed since those days and they had gone in completely opposite directions.

The man who made this suggestion warned Rav Elchanan that there were two problems. First of all, Philip hadn't kept Shabbos in 50 years. And second, despite his vast wealth, Mr. Goodstein had earned a reputation of being tight fisted. Although he could not be sure of the outcome of their meeting, Rav Elchanan was willing to put in the effort. The rest was up to the Almighty.

He came to Philip's office and asked the secretary if he could be seen, and she told him that there were no appointments available for that day. He came back later that afternoon and again was turned away. The third time, he told her to tell her boss that Elchanan Wasserman was waiting to see him. She went back to his office, and a few moments later, Philip emerged. He gave his old friend a warm hello and invited him into his office.

The two of them exchanged pleasantries. Philip told him the story of how he had left Europe and come to America. Before long, he started to make some money and had built up his business, until it had become the most successful coat factory in all of Manhattan.

"So tell me," he turned to the Rosh Yeshivah, "What brings you to Manhattan?"

Rav Elchanan told him that he had just come to say hello. Philip smiled and pushed him further.

"Come on. You traveled for weeks. Tell me the real reason you're here."

Rav Elchanan repeated that he had only come to say hello. They spoke for a few more minutes, and although Philip was not convinced, Rav Elchanan excused himself and went back to the home where he was staying. The next day, he received a phone call. Philip wanted to see him again in his office.

When Rav Elchanan arrived, Philip came out to meet him. "Please, old friend," he entreated. "Tell me the real reason that you're here."

Once again, Rav Elchanan told him that he had only come to say hello. Then finally, after more cajoling, he told Philip that there was another reason he had come to America. "If you look carefully, you can see that I am supposed to have three buttons on my coat. Yet I only have two; one is missing. I came to America so I can have my button sewn on by one of your workers. I figured that if you are the owner of the largest coat factory in Manhattan, then you certainly have someone who can sew on a button for me."

Philip was astounded. What a ludicrous idea. "You mean to tell me that you traveled for four weeks to have one of my workers sew on a button? I've never heard anything so ridiculous in my life."

Rav Elchanan looked at Philip and spoke in a very serious tone. "Our rabbis tell us that it takes 500 years of travel for a soul to make its way through the rakia, firmament. And an additional 500 years to travel between each level of the firmament. That means it takes thousands of years for a soul to make it down to This Earth. Do you think that God sent your soul on a journey that takes thousands of years just so you can sew on buttons and make coats? If you thought it was absurd for me to travel for four weeks from Europe to America to have a button sewn onto my coat, then why is it any less ludicrous for you to do what you're doing and invest your life's efforts into it?"

Philip was rendered speechless, and tears filled his eyes. Finally, he regained his composure. "It has been so long since I have seen the inside of a Gemara. If only I could learn again . . .."

Rav Elchanan reached into his pocket and pulled out a small Gemara. He sat down next to his friend and began to learn with him. As Rav Elchanan read the words, Philip tried to mumble along. Oy, it had been so long. The tears streamed down his cheeks and wet the pages of the Gemara.

Philip begged Rav Elchanan to promise him that he would find him a chavrusa before he went back.

And then he asked his question one last time.

"So tell me, my dear friend. Why did you come to America?"

Rav Elchanan's piercing eyes bore right through him. "I came here to collect money for my yeshivah, which is in a very difficult financial state. The boys have nothing to eat, and I have spent a year trying to raise money for them. Please, help out the yeshivah."

Philip pulled out his checkbook and wrote out a check for an astronomical sum, enough to cover the yeshivah's expenses for a full two years.

But Philip had received much more than he gave. He received the gift of his true identity, the real reason he was here.

He, like every Jew, was full of hidden potential.

Charoses / חרוסת

⋑ The Sweetness of Suffering

The maror, bitter herb, reminds us of the slavery in Egypt. However, when eating the charoses, comprised of wine, apples, almonds, and other sweet-tasting ingredients, it is difficult to understand how that is meant to remind us of the bricks. The taste of the bitter herbs is just that: bitter. How are the sweet ingredients supposed to remind us of the bricks?

It is not sufficient for us to accept the bitterness in our lives, but we must also comprehend that the suffering and bitterness are cushioned with the sweet compassion of the Almighty. The *charoses* contains this duality. On the one hand, it looks like the mortar that was used to create bricks. On the other hand, it tastes sweet and sends us the very clear message that even in times of bitterness, the Almighty is spicing our lives with sweetness.

The word חֲרוֹסֶת contains the word חַס, connoting *compassion*. The remaining letters spell out the name רוּת, who experienced incredible bitterness and suffering in her life. After leaving a life of royalty and becoming a convert, Rus was faced with a life of widowhood, poverty, and derision. No one would have blamed her for being bitter. But she was anything but. In fact, when her mother-in-law, whose name means pleasantness, rejected those who called her נָעֳמִי, insisting that she be called מָרָא, which means bitter, she stood by her side and transformed that bitterness into sweetness (*Rus* 1:20). Her descendant, David, was known as "*ne'im zemiros Yisrael* — the pleasing composer of the songs of Israel" (*II Shmuel* 23:1), because he composed the sweet songs of *Tehillim*, which are recited in the most difficult and bitter times.

Furthermore, the word תּוֹר, which is also formed from the remaining letters, can be referring to a guide, as in the *pasuk* in *Shir HaShirim* (2:12), "*Ve'kol hator nishma be'artzeinu* — And the voice of your guide is heard in the land," signifying the impending *Geulah*.

This is a crucial lesson to convey to our children tonight. There will be times in our life when we experience the bitterness and suffering of the *maror*. But we must dip those bitter herbs into the sweetness of the *charoses*. We must understand that God is "sweet" not only when we experience redemption; rather, even while we are slaves, there is sweetness and love and kindness in those times, as well. In addition, these difficult times are often what signal our impending salvation.

Spiced Up

Reb Aharon, the doctor of Gardiyah, was a disciple of the Mezritcher Maggid. Early on in life, he had not yet discovered the beauty of Torah. Removed from the ways of the Almighty, he pursued a career in medicine and became a doctor of renown, whose services were sought far and wide. Later, he became a baal teshuvah and was quite adept at not only healing human bodies, but human souls, as well. The Maggid respected his opinion and considered him one of his closest disciples.

Reb Aharon walked into shul one Shabbos and noticed a very unhealthy looking fellow; with his keen eye and acute ability to diagnose, he discerned that the man was deathly ill. Immediately, he approached his Rebbe and informed him of his observation.

When the Maggid asked Reb Aharon if anything could be done to save the man's life, Reb Aharon shook his head. "Unfortunately, the only cure for him is a certain type of medicine that burns out the disease. However, this medication is produced with spices that cannot be found anywhere in the vicinity. I'm sorry to tell you that he will not make it till the end of the day."

The Maggid and his disciple were pleasantly surprised when the man walked into the shul to daven Minchah, looking as healthy as can be. The Maggid asked the doctor if it is possible that he was mistaken, but he insisted that his diagnosis had been correct. He, too, was puzzled that the man looked so hale and hearty.

The Maggid called the fellow over and asked him how he was doing and how his Shabbos had gone. The fellow admitted that he was struggling financially, and he and his family had come to the point where their cupboards were bare and there was nothing left to eat in the house.

"Whatever was left in the house had already been given to my children and my wife. I was left with nothing. I was so desperate for food that I grabbed all the spices that we had, made some sort of a concoction, and downed it. It burned through my intestines so deeply that I thought I was going to die. But remarkably, soon thereafter, I began to feel better."

The newly invigorated fellow smiled and walked away.

The Mezritcher turned to his disciple and shared with him a remarkable insight. "You see, there are times when people suffer and endure unimaginable difficulty. Little do they know that it is precisely that suffering that brings about their salvation."

סִימָנֵי הַסֵדֶר

The Order of the Seder

kaddesh	Sanctify the day with the recitation of Kiddush.	קַדֵּשׁ
urechatz	**Wash** the hands before eating Karpas.	וּרְחַץ
karpas	Eat a **vegetable** dipped in salt water.	כַּרְפַּס
yachatz	**Break** the middle matzah. Put away larger half for Afikoman.	יַחַץ
maggid	**Narrate** the story of Yetzias Mitzrayim.	מַגִּיד
rachtzah	**Wash** the hands prior to the meal.	רַחְצָה
motzi	Recite the blessing, **Who brings forth,** over matzah as a food.	מוֹצִיא
matzah	Recite the blessing over **matzah.**	מַצָּה
maror	Recite the blessing for the eating of the **bitter herbs.**	מָרוֹר
korech	Eat the **sandwich** of matzah and bitter herbs.	כּוֹרֵךְ
shulchan orech	The **table prepared** with the festive meal.	שֻׁלְחָן עוֹרֵךְ
tzafun	Eat the Afikoman which had been **hidden** all during the Seder.	צָפוּן
barech	Recite Bircas HaMazon, the **blessings** after the meal.	בָּרֵךְ
hallel	Recite the **Hallel** Psalms of praise.	הַלֵּל
nirtzah	Pray that God **accept** our observance and speedily send the Messiah.	נִרְצָה

[71]   **TOUCHED BY OUR STORY**

קַדֵּשׁ

Kiddush should be recited and the Seder begun as soon after synagogue services as possible; however, not before nightfall. Each participant's cup should be poured by someone else to symbolize the majesty of the evening, as though each participant had a servant.

Some have a custom to say the following declaration of intent:

הִנְנִי מוּכָן וּמְזוּמָּן לְקַדֵּשׁ עַל הַיַּיִן וּלְקַיֵּם מִצְוַת כּוֹס רִאשׁוֹן מֵאַרְבַּע כּוֹסוֹת. לְשֵׁם יִחוּד קֻדְשָׁא בְּרִיךְ הוּא וּשְׁכִינְתֵּיהּ, עַל יְדֵי הַהוּא טָמִיר וְנֶעְלָם, בְּשֵׁם כָּל יִשְׂרָאֵל. וִיהִי נֹעַם אֲדֹנָי אֱלֹהֵינוּ עָלֵינוּ, וּמַעֲשֵׂה יָדֵינוּ כּוֹנְנָה עָלֵינוּ, וּמַעֲשֵׂה יָדֵינוּ כּוֹנְנֵהוּ.

On Friday night begin here:

(וַיְהִי עֶרֶב וַיְהִי בֹקֶר)

יוֹם הַשִּׁשִּׁי וַיְכֻלּוּ הַשָּׁמַיִם וְהָאָרֶץ וְכָל צְבָאָם. וַיְכַל אֱלֹהִים בַּיּוֹם הַשְּׁבִיעִי מְלַאכְתּוֹ אֲשֶׁר עָשָׂה, וַיִּשְׁבֹּת בַּיּוֹם הַשְּׁבִיעִי מִכָּל מְלַאכְתּוֹ אֲשֶׁר עָשָׂה. וַיְבָרֶךְ אֱלֹהִים אֶת יוֹם הַשְּׁבִיעִי וַיְקַדֵּשׁ אֹתוֹ, כִּי בוֹ שָׁבַת מִכָּל מְלַאכְתּוֹ אֲשֶׁר בָּרָא אֱלֹהִים לַעֲשׂוֹת.[1]

On all nights other than Friday, begin here;
on Friday night include all passages in parentheses.

סַבְרִי מָרָנָן וְרַבָּנָן וְרַבּוֹתַי:

בָּרוּךְ אַתָּה יהוה אֱלֹהֵינוּ מֶלֶךְ הָעוֹלָם, בּוֹרֵא פְּרִי הַגָּפֶן.

בָּרוּךְ אַתָּה יהוה אֱלֹהֵינוּ מֶלֶךְ הָעוֹלָם, אֲשֶׁר בָּחַר בָּנוּ מִכָּל עָם, וְרוֹמְמָנוּ מִכָּל לָשׁוֹן, וְקִדְּשָׁנוּ בְּמִצְוֹתָיו. וַתִּתֶּן לָנוּ יהוה אֱלֹהֵינוּ בְּאַהֲבָה (שַׁבָּתוֹת לִמְנוּחָה וּ)מוֹעֲדִים לְשִׂמְחָה חַגִּים וּזְמַנִּים לְשָׂשׂוֹן אֶת יוֹם (הַשַּׁבָּת הַזֶּה וְאֶת יוֹם) חַג הַמַּצּוֹת הַזֶּה, זְמַן חֵרוּתֵנוּ (בְּאַהֲבָה) מִקְרָא קֹדֶשׁ, זֵכֶר לִיצִיאַת מִצְרָיִם. כִּי בָנוּ בָחַרְתָּ וְאוֹתָנוּ

KADDEISH

Kiddush should be recited and the Seder begun as soon after synagogue services as possible; however, not before nightfall. Each participant's cup should be poured by someone else to symbolize the majesty of the evening, as though each participant had a servant.

Some have a custom to say the following declaration of intent:

Behold, I am prepared and ready to recite the *Kiddush* over wine, and to fulfill the mitzvah of the first of the Four Cups. For the sake of the unification of the Holy One, Blessed is He, and His Presence, through Him Who is hidden and inscrutable — [I pray] in the name of all Israel. May the pleasantness of the Lord, our God, be upon us, and may He establish our handiwork for us; our handiwork may He establish.

On Friday night begin here:

(And there was evening and there was morning)

The sixth day. Thus the heaven and the earth were finished, and all their array. On the seventh day God completed His work which He had done, and He abstained on the seventh day from all His work which He had done. God blessed the seventh day and hallowed it, because on it He abstained from all His work which God created to make.[1]

On all nights other than Friday, begin here; on Friday night include all passages in parentheses.

By your leave, my masters and teachers:

Blessed are You, HASHEM, our God, King of the universe, Who creates the fruit of the vine.

Blessed are You, HASHEM, our God, King of the universe, Who has chosen us from all nations, exalted us above all tongues, and sanctified us with His commandments. And You, HASHEM, our God, have lovingly given us (Shabbasos for rest,) appointed times for gladness, feasts and seasons for joy, (this Shabbos and) this Feast of Matzos, the season of our freedom (in love), a holy convocation

---

1. *Bereishis* 1:31-2:3.

קִדַּשְׁתָּ מִכָּל הָעַמִּים, (וְשַׁבָּת) וּמוֹעֲדֵי קָדְשֶׁךָ (בְּאַהֲבָה וּבְרָצוֹן) בְּשִׂמְחָה וּבְשָׂשׂוֹן הִנְחַלְתָּנוּ. בָּרוּךְ אַתָּה יהוה, מְקַדֵּשׁ (הַשַּׁבָּת וְ)יִשְׂרָאֵל וְהַזְּמַנִּים.

On Motza'ei Shabbos, add the following two paragraphs.
Two candles or wicks with flames touching are held and the following blessings are recited. After the first blessing, hold the fingers up to the flame to see the reflected light.

בָּרוּךְ אַתָּה יהוה אֱלֹהֵינוּ מֶלֶךְ הָעוֹלָם, בּוֹרֵא מְאוֹרֵי הָאֵשׁ.

בָּרוּךְ אַתָּה יהוה אֱלֹהֵינוּ מֶלֶךְ הָעוֹלָם, הַמַּבְדִּיל בֵּין קֹדֶשׁ לְחוֹל, בֵּין אוֹר לְחֹשֶׁךְ, בֵּין יִשְׂרָאֵל לָעַמִּים, בֵּין יוֹם הַשְּׁבִיעִי לְשֵׁשֶׁת יְמֵי הַמַּעֲשֶׂה. בֵּין קְדֻשַּׁת שַׁבָּת לִקְדֻשַּׁת יוֹם טוֹב הִבְדַּלְתָּ, וְאֶת יוֹם הַשְּׁבִיעִי מִשֵּׁשֶׁת יְמֵי הַמַּעֲשֶׂה קִדַּשְׁתָּ, הִבְדַּלְתָּ וְקִדַּשְׁתָּ אֶת עַמְּךָ יִשְׂרָאֵל בִּקְדֻשָּׁתֶךָ. בָּרוּךְ אַתָּה יהוה, הַמַּבְדִּיל בֵּין קֹדֶשׁ לְקֹדֶשׁ.

On all nights conclude here:

בָּרוּךְ אַתָּה יהוה אֱלֹהֵינוּ מֶלֶךְ הָעוֹלָם, שֶׁהֶחֱיָנוּ וְקִיְּמָנוּ וְהִגִּיעָנוּ לַזְּמַן הַזֶּה.

The wine should be drunk without delay while reclining on the left side. It is preferable to drink the entire cup, but at the very least, most of the cup should be drained.

וּרְחַץ

The head of the household — according to many opinions, all participants in the Seder — washes his hands as if to eat bread [pouring water from a cup, twice on the right hand and twice on the left], but without reciting a blessing.

in commemoration of the Exodus from Egypt. For You have chosen and sanctified us above all peoples, (and Shabbos) and Your holy festivals (in love and favor), in gladness and joy have You granted us as a heritage. Blessed are You, HASHEM, Who sanctifies (Shabbos,) Israel, and the festive seasons.

On Motza'ei Shabbos, add the following two paragraphs. Two candles or wicks with flames touching are held and the following blessings are recited. After the first blessing, hold the fingers up to the flame to see the reflected light.

B lessed are You, HASHEM, our God, King of the universe, Who creates the illumination of the fire.

B lessed are You, HASHEM, our God, King of the universe, Who distinguishes between sacred and secular, between light and darkness, between Israel and the nations, between the seventh day and the six days of activity. You have distinguished between the holiness of Shabbos and the holiness of a Festival, and have sanctified the seventh day above the six days of activity. You distinguished and sanctified Your nation, Israel, with Your holiness. Blessed are You, HASHEM, Who distinguishes between holiness and holiness.

On all nights conclude here:

B lessed are You, HASHEM, our God, King of the universe, Who has kept us alive, sustained us, and brought us to this season.

The wine should be drunk without delay while reclining on the left side. It is preferable to drink the entire cup, but at the very least, most of the cup should be drained.

URECHATZ

The head of the household — according to many opinions, all participants in the Seder — washes his hands as if to eat bread [pouring water from a cup, twice on the right hand and twice on the left], but without reciting a blessing.

כרפס

All participants take a vegetable other than *maror* and dip it into salt water. A piece smaller in volume than half an egg should be used. The following blessing is recited [with the intention that it also applies to the *maror* which will be eaten during the meal] before the vegetable is eaten.

בָּרוּךְ אַתָּה יהוה אֱלֹהֵינוּ מֶלֶךְ הָעוֹלָם, בּוֹרֵא פְּרִי הָאֲדָמָה.

Karpas / כרפס

⋐ Staying Awake

The Pshevorsker Rebbe shared a story about the Koloshitzer Rebbe. One Rosh Hashanah, when he was 3 years old, he saw his grandfather, the Shinever Rebbe, walk out of his room wearing his kittel and head toward the beis midrash to blow the shofar. He pointed to him and said to his mother, "Look, Mamma, the zeide is going to eat karpas."

On the surface, it seemed to be nothing more than an innocent mistake and a cute story about a 3-year-old. But when his grandfather heard, he said, "Actually, we eat karpas and blow the shofar for the same reason."

In *Haggadah shel Pesach Yeisei VeYifsach*, Rav Moshe Wolfson explains: When we dip the vegetable into the salt water for *karpas*, we are trying to pique the children's interest, and thus prevent them from falling asleep. It is customary to distribute candies to the children throughout the night for that very reason: to keep them awake and get them to ask questions.

This is also why we blow the shofar on Rosh Hashanah: to awaken us from our spiritual slumber. The children to whom we are referring are not merely small children, but all the children of the Almighty. Tonight, on the night of the Seder, we want to be able to awaken our minds and our souls so that we can better understand and strengthen our beliefs.

With this explanation, we can understand the answer that we give to the wicked child. He questions, "*Mah ha'avodah hazos lachem —* Of what purpose is this service to you?" And the *Haggadah* instructs

KARPAS

All participants take a vegetable other than *maror* and dip it into salt water. A piece smaller in volume than half an egg should be used. The following blessing is recited [with the intention that it also applies to the *maror* which will be eaten during the meal] before the vegetable is eaten.

B lessed are You, HASHEM, our God, King of the universe, Who creates the fruits of the earth.

---

us, "*Hakheih es shinav* — Blunt his teeth." What type of response is that?

This son is a *rasha* because he is sleeping from the mitzvos, and that is why he asks the question: "Of what purpose is this service to you?" The *Haggadah* tells us: הַקְהֵה אֶת שִׁנָּיו, meaning that we should knock out his שֵׁינָה, *his sleep*. Rav Wolfson goes on to say that if we remove the letter שׁיִן, alluding to sleepiness (שֵׁנָה), from the word רָשָׁע, and take away the *rasha's* lackadaisical approach to mitzvos, we will be left with the ע and ר, which form the word עֵר, which means to be awake. This is as the *Rambam* says, "*Uru yesheinim mishnaschem* — Awaken, sleepers, from your slumber."

When we dip the vegetable in salt water, we are doing this in order to get the child to ask questions. However, when he does ask, we respond to his question by telling him that we want him to stay awake and keep asking questions. That seems strange. What type of answer is that? He asks why we are dipping. Shouldn't we answer his question?

The answer is that we are telling him that it is all right not to receive an answer to the question. He will always have questions. Whether it is about something he has learned or something he has experienced in life, there will always be a lack of understanding. It is important to be aware that he will not always receive answers to his questions, and we don't become upset because we haven't received the proper answer.

This is how we strengthen our belief tonight.

◄§ It's a Wedding

On the night of the Seder, we recite seven *berachos* before we get up to the matzah (*Borei Pri Hagafen* on the first cup of wine; *Mekadeish*

יחץ

The head of the household breaks the middle matzah in two. He puts the smaller part back between the two whole matzos, and wraps up the larger part for later use as the *afikoman*. Some briefly place the *afikoman* portion on their shoulders, in accordance with the Biblical verse recounting that Israel left Egypt carrying their matzos on their shoulders, and say בְּבֶהָלוּ יָצָאנוּ מִמִּצְרָיִם, "In haste we went out of Egypt."

Yisrael; Shehecheyanu; Borei Pri Ha'adamah; Ga'al Yisrael; Borei Pri Hagafen on the second cup; and Al Netilas Yadayim). According to the Zohar HaKadosh (Raya Mehemna 3:251), these blessings correspond to the Sheva Berachos recited at a wedding, and Chazal tell us that a kallah without a berachah is forbidden to her husband. Therefore, it says in Talmud Yerushalmi, that a person who eats matzah on Erev Pesach is like a man who lives with his betrothed in the home of his father-in-law.

The fourth berachah of the night, Borei Pri Ha'adamah on the karpas, corresponds to the fourth berachah said under the chuppah: "Asher yatzar es ha'adam be'tzalmo be'tzelem demus tavniso ve'hiskin lo mimenu binyan adei ad… — Who fashioned the man in His image, in the image of his likeness and prepared for him, from himself, a building for eternity…"

In Haggadah shel Pesach Yeisei VeYifsach, Rav Moshe Wolfson explains that man is created from the earth. In other words, man is a "pri ha'adamah — fruit of the ground." The word הָאָדָם of the fourth berachah of Sheva Berachos has the same letters as אֲדָמָה, ground, in the fourth berachah of the Seder. We thank Hashem and praise Him that we are the fruit of the land, created from the holy ground of the Beis HaMikdash. And we are confident that the time will yet come when we will return and reunite with our source, and we will form a binyan adei ad, a building for eternity, together with the Beis HaMikdash.

Rav Wolfson expounds further in the name of the Maharal (Sefer HaNetzach 1), that any time there is a set arrangement in the world, even if something causes that order to change, it will eventually revert back to the original arrangement. The arrangement, the seder, of the Jewish people is that they should be residing in Eretz Yisrael because that is where they belong. During their Exile, they

YACHATZ

The head of the household breaks the middle matzah in two. He puts the smaller part back between the two whole matzos, and wraps up the larger part for later use as the *afikoman*. Some briefly place the *afikoman* portion on their shoulders, in accordance with the Biblical verse recounting that Israel left Egypt carrying their matzos on their shoulders, and say בְּבָהְלוּ יָצְאוּ מִמִּצְרַיִם, *"In haste we went out of Egypt."*

---

were uprooted from their land and their *seder*. However, they must return to this arrangement.

It is for this that we are grateful at the Seder, as we say the *berachah* of *Borei Pri Ha'adamah*, which corresponds to the *berachah* of *binyan adei ad*. Indeed, the numerical value of the word כַּלָה is the equivalent of הָאֲדָמָה.

The halachah is that when one makes the *berachah* on the *karpas*, he has in mind also the *maror*, thus exempting himself of the need to make a separate *berachah* of *Borei Pri Ha'adamah* on the bitter herb. In light of our interpretation of the *Borei Pri Ha'adamah*, through this *berachah* we exempt ourselves of the *maror*, the bitterness of the *Galus*, with the faith that we will return to the *Beis HaMikdash*.

In the future, *HaKadosh Baruch Hu* will keep His promise of: *"Ve'lakachti es'chem li le'am ... ve'heiveisi es'chem el ha'aretz —* And I will take you to Me for a people ... and I will bring you to the land" (*Shemos* 6:7,8). The promise of *ve'lakachti* corresponds to the fourth cup, upon which we say *Hallel,* in which we praise Hashem for taking us out of Mitzrayim, and of our present exile. בּוֹרֵא פְּרִי הָאֲדָמָה has the same *gematria* as the word וְלָקַחְתִּי, *And I will take.*

This is how we will endure, and through our faith, we will be redeemed.

Yachatz / יחץ

⁌ Bringing Down the Blessing

Many practices at the Seder are perplexing to children, but one is confusing for adults, too. After breaking the middle matzah, the father hides the larger half behind his pillow for the *afikoman*. It is customary for the children to steal the *afikoman* and hide it so that their father will have to look for it. What an unusual custom this is. Why would we teach our children that they can steal?

Let us think about the only other time where trickery was not only permitted but encouraged: the stealing of the blessings from Eisav (*Bereishis* 27). Yitzchak planned to bless Eisav, and Rivkah instructed Yaakov to steal the *berachos*. *Chazal* (*Pirkei DeRabbi Eliezer* 31) tell us that this incident transpired on the first night of Pesach, and the two goats that Yaakov brought for his father were an allusion to the *korban pesach* and *korban chagigah*.

When Eisav discovered the ruse, Yitzchak said to him, "*Ba achicha be'mirmah va'yikach birchasecha* — Your brother came with cleverness and took your blessing*" (*Bereishis* 27:35). It is interesting to note that the *gematria* of the word בְּמִרְמָה , *with cleverness*, is equivalent to the numerical value of אֲפִיקוֹמָן.

The *Haggadah MiPi Sefarim VeSofrim* explains that since it is the night of Pesach, we try to awaken the power of those *berachos* once more by encouraging the children to steal the *afikoman* from their fathers.

Just as Yaakov was allowed to steal the *berachos* from Eisav, and was even encouraged to do so, we encourage our children to steal the *afikoman*, symbolizing the ability to acquire *berachos* that had been previously unattainable. At times, a person can skip ahead and reach levels of *kedushah* for which he is still unworthy. The *Leil HaSeder* is one such time.

Tonight, when the children steal the *afikoman*, we are encouraging them to shoot for the stars and attempt to reach the highest level possible.

The Best Afikoman Present

For months, Zalman Baharan's mother, Sarah, had begged her husband, Rav Dovid, to bring nine-year-old Zalman to Rav Yehoshua Leib Diskin for a berachah. She desperately wanted him to receive a blessing from the venerated sage, the leader of the Yerushalayim community in the late 1800's. She hoped that when getting the berachah, her son would be able to spend a moment or two in the presence of the great man, for even a short meeting with such a special person would make an everlasting impression on her child. But no matter how many times she suggested it her husband, he would not agree.

He explained his reasoning. "Rav Yehoshua Leib is the gadol hador! Recently, the Beis HaLevi, Rav Yosef Dov HaLevi Soloveitchik, related that when he had written a letter to Rav Yehoshua Leib, his hands had trembled at the thought that he was communicating with such a great man. And if that is the manner in which gedolim react to communicating with this great individual, then how can you expect me to simply bring in our son for a berachah?"

One day, she thought of a plan. With Pesach approaching, she knew her son would have the opportunity to steal the afikoman. Perhaps this year, instead of asking for a present like he usually did, he would ask to be taken to the rav for a special berachah. When she presented her plan to Zalman, he was thrilled with the idea. Then they both waited anxiously for the night of the Seder to arrive.

Seder night began as it always did in the Baharan home, with Rav Dovid discussing in animated fashion the entire story of the Yidden leaving Mitzrayim, just as it was meant to be told: to arouse the hearts and minds of the young ones.

Zalman didn't need much arousing, as he was wide awake. He listened as his father retold the story with all of the Midrashim and explanations. As Rav Dovid's enthusiasm carried him back to the land of Mitzrayim, Zalman's quest took him to the back of his father's chair, where the afikoman had been placed. And under his mother's watchful eye, in the tradition of old, Zalman stole his father's afikoman.

A few hours later, as midnight was fast approaching, Rav Dovid peeked behind his pillow and noticed that his afikoman had been taken. No stranger to this charade, Rav Dovid turned to the obvious culprit and asked, "So Zalman'ke, what is it going to be this year? Should I buy you a Nefesh HaChaim written by Rav Chaim Volozhiner?" Zalman shook his head in a negative manner.

Once again, Rav Dovid offered a nice set of sefarim, this time proposing that he would purchase a set of Pnei Yehoshua. He smiled, as he was certain that this suggestion would certainly do the trick. But again, Zalman refused his father's generous offer. Rav Dovid had not anticipated that young Zalman would drive such a hard bargain.

Finally, he gave up. "All right, Zalman'ke, what is it going to take for me to get my afikoman back?"

Zalman smiled. His response caused his father quite a shock. "All I want is that you take me to Rav Yehoshua Leib for a berachah."

מַגִּיד

Some recite the following declaration of intent before *Maggid*:

הִנְנִי מוּכָן וּמְזוּמָן לְקַיֵּם הַמִּצְוָה לְסַפֵּר בִּיצִיאַת מִצְרַיִם. לְשֵׁם יִחוּד קֻדְשָׁא בְּרִיךְ הוּא וּשְׁכִינְתֵּיהּ, עַל יְדֵי הַהוּא טָמִיר וְנֶעְלָם, בְּשֵׁם כָּל יִשְׂרָאֵל. וִיהִי נְעַם אֲדֹנָי אֱלֹהֵינוּ עָלֵינוּ, וּמַעֲשֵׂה יָדֵינוּ כּוֹנְנָה עָלֵינוּ, וּמַעֲשֵׂה יָדֵינוּ כּוֹנְנֵהוּ:

Although Zalman was bright and confident, Rav Dovid realized that his wife had joined with the boy to propose this "present." Left with no choice, Rav Dovid relented. Because of the trepidation he felt, he could not promise, but he would try his very best to carry out the boy's wish. And so, they decided that the very first day of Chol HaMoed, they would go together to Rav Yehoshua Leib.

After davening, the two of them approached the Rav's small home. Walking toward the house, Rav Dovid's heart was thumping wildly. He had never been so nervous in his life. But he intended to keep his word. Zalman skipped along merrily. Not that he wasn't nervous himself, but his excitement overwhelmed his fear. Before long, they were standing just outside the Rav's home.

Rav Dovid held tightly onto Zalman as he peeked into the Rav's home. The table where the Rav sat was graced with some of the most prominent gedolim of their time. Rav Yosef Chaim Sonnenfeld, Rav Tzvi Hirsch Michel Shapiro, and Rav Eliezer Dan Ralbag all sat quietly in front of their Rebbi. This caused Rav Dovid to almost have a panic attack. How could he possibly barge in on such a gathering? He lost his nerve, knowing he could never interrupt this venerated group ... and introduce himself ... and ask for a berachah. Slowly, he backed away from the door. Zalman stood alone: his dream and his present disappearing. The enormity of it all caused the boy to burst into tears.

Hearing the cries of a child just outside her door, Rav Yehoshua Leib's rebbetzin went outside to check and immediately recognized little Zalman. "What's wrong? Who brought you here? Where's your father?" At that point, Rav Dovid came over, and, having regained his composure, explained what had happened. "My Zalman just wants a berachah from the Rav."

"Well, if he wants a berachah so badly that he's crying over it, then don't you think he deserves one? Come right in. I'll bring him

MAGGID

Some recite the following declaration of intent before *Maggid*:

Behold, I am prepared and ready to fulfill the mitzvah of telling of the Exodus from Egypt. For the sake of the unification of the Holy One, Blessed is He, and His presence, through Him Who is hidden and inscrutable — [I pray] in the name of all Israel. May the pleasantness of the Lord, our God, be upon us, and may He establish our handiwork for us; our handiwork may He establish.

---

over to the Rav myself." And so, the three of them — the rebbetzin, Rav Dovid, and little Zalman — all approached the Rav. The rebbetzin explained what had happened, and all eyes turned to Zalman. As Zalman stood there, the Rav placed his frail hands over the child's head and uttered a simple, one-line berachah, "Yehi ratzon ... du zolst veren an ehrliche Yid — May it be the will of the Almighty that you should become an upstanding Jew."

Then in unison, they all answered, "Amen."

Overjoyed at what had just transpired, Zalman and his father hurried home and were greeted by Sarah, his mother. The child ran into his mother's open arms and she smiled, relieved that obviously the experience had gone as she had hoped.

The Rav's berachah came true. Zalman grew up to become an "ehrliche Yid," and then some. Rav Zalman Baharan's nobility and wisdom inspired all who knew him. He carried on his father's great legacy and became a legend in his own right.

Maggid / מגיד

✒ A Father's Message

The Seder provides a unique opportunity for parents to transmit their *mesorah* to their children. I have an older friend whose Seder extends until the wee hours of the morning, sometimes until 5 or 6 a.m. I once asked him why his Seder takes so long. His answer was sobering. "There is only one time a year that I am able to sit down with my children and grandchildren and really talk to them about *emunah*. Why would I waste the opportunity?"

When put like that, it is hard to fathom why most Sedarim don't last that long. In truth, it is not about how long the Seder lasts, but its quality. However, many fathers feel overwhelmed with the responsibility of talking to and teaching their children about the story of the Exodus. Many children nowadays are more advanced than their fathers in terms of their Torah knowledge. Klal Yisrael enjoys unusual *siyata d'Shmaya* in the proliferation and level of its learning; it is understandable that a parent would feel somewhat inadequate in teaching the story. However, the *sefer Shaarei Leil HaSeder* encourages us by citing an incident that transpired in Chapter 6 of *Sefer Shoftim,* regarding Gideon. From this incident, we will gain insight into the potency and power of the father-and-son relationship, for Pesach and beyond.

While Gideon was still an unknown entity, the people of Midian oppressed the Jewish people, causing them to be afraid to venture out in the open. The Midianites stole from the Yidden and levied heavy taxes; they even scorched the earth to starve them.

Hashem sent an angel to Gideon. When the angel informed Gideon that he would be the savior of the Jewish people because Hashem was with him, Gideon responded, "Is Hashem truly with us? If so, why are we suffering so much? Where are all the wondrous miracles that our forefathers spoke about? Yesterday, on Pesach, my father recited *Hallel* with me, and we read that the Almighty helped the Jewish people at the time of their Exodus. If they were deserving, then Hashem should save us in their merit; and if they were not deserving, then let Hashem save us just as He saved them."

Gideon's father was an idol worshiper. Not only did he worship idols, but he would fatten the cows for seven years before sacrificing them to his idols. It is hard for us to understand, but even though he worshiped idols, he observed the commandments of Pesach. On the night of the Seder, he sat down with his child — not any child but Gideon, the future judge of the Jewish people — and told him the story of the Exodus and how the Jewish people were saved by the Almighty. Despite the fact that he was an ardent idol worshiper, he was able to transmit the story of *Yetzias Mitzrayim* and make it real and alive. So much so, that his son was so impressed that when he met the *malach* the next day, he demanded the same miracles.

It is safe to say that the difference between Gideon and his idol-worshiping father was certainly greater than the difference between us and our children. If Gideon's father was able to inspire him, then we must know that we are given special assistance from the Almighty tonight to inspire our own children.

But a father must prepare, and he must fill himself with exuberance, information, and inspiration to give over to his children. The *Imrei Emes* notes that there is a law (*Chullin* 71a) stating that if there is a space of less than one handbreadth between a dead person and the covering above him, then the impurity of the dead person breaks through the covering and affects everything above it. But if there is a space of a handbreadth, then the impurity is contained beneath the cover.

The same is true with a parent's excitement. If he fills himself with enthusiasm in the story of *Yetzias Mitzrayim*, the excitement will exude from him and bubble over. But if there is some empty space within his efforts and enthusiasm, and the story is not absorbed into his own bones, it will not break out from inside him and enter his children.

This is as the Torah commands us (*Shemos* 10:2), "*U'le'maan tesapeir be'aznei vincha u'ven bincha eis asher hisalalti be'Mitzrayim ve'es ososai asher samti vam vi'datem ki Ani Hashem* — And so that you may relate in the ears of your son and your son's son that I made a mockery of Egypt, and My signs that I placed among them — that you may know that I am Hashem." The *pasuk* does not say: "*ve'yeidu veneichem ki Ani Hashem* — and your children should know that I am Hashem," but: "*vi'datem ki Ani Hashem* — and *you* should know that I am Hashem." This is because once the father is aware of Hashem and he has absorbed and internalized the concepts of *emunah*, only then can he properly fulfill the mitzvah of "*Ve'higadeta le'vincha*," of instilling the lessons of the Exodus in his children.

I Want the Tzaddik to Eat From My Portion

Rav Yosef Goldenthal, the menahel of the yeshivah in Ofakim, arranged to meet Mr. Aharon Lichtenberg, one of the very wealthy benefactors of the yeshivah. He had heard beforehand that Mr. Lichtenberg gave very generously to yeshivos. Although he also gave to other institutions, the vast majority of his donations went to institutions of Torah learning. Eager to discover why, Rav Goldenthal decided that when he came for his meeting, he would ask Mr. Lichtenberg himself.

When he arrived at Mr. Lichtenberg's office, the secretary told him he would see him momentarily, so he made himself comfortable on one of the fancy couches in the waiting room. Indeed, a few moments later, Reb Aharon came out and welcomed him. Rav Goldenthal shared all the pertinent information about his yeshivah, and Mr. Lichtenberg happily wrote out a very generous check to the yeshivah and handed it to Rav Goldenthal. Rav Goldenthal thanked him for the check and then asked him if he could ask a personal question. Reb Aharon, a congenial fellow, readily agreed.

"I know that you are a very generous person, and I know that you give to all types of worthy organizations. But I understand that you give most of your money to yeshivos. May I ask why? Was there any incident that perhaps influenced your decision?"

Rav Goldenthal was afraid that he had overstepped his bounds, but his curiosity had gotten the better of him.

First, Reb Aharon closed his eyes and was quiet for a few moments. Then suddenly, he opened them and a large smile formed on his face.

"I'm happy that you asked me that question. It has been a long time since I thought about the beneficiaries of most of my contributions. I think of it as second nature, but it actually does go back to one particular incident that happened to me when I was a young man. When my mother first brought me to yeshivah, I was scared and very lonely. But besides that, I was very, very hungry. By the time I got settled in my room, it was midafternoon and I had not eaten anything all day. I walked over to the person who was in charge of arranging meals for bachurim, and he told me that it was too late for lunch — that all of the families in town had already eaten — and that perhaps I would be able to get a little bit of supper in someone's home in the evening. I sat down on the bench and began to cry. Here I was, all alone and so hungry.

"The person in charge of meals must have seen that I was crying, and he came back to me. He told me that there was one place in town that he rarely sent anybody to, though the family very much wanted to have guests. However, since the mother was a widow and she had many orphaned children, the yeshivah felt guilty sending them another mouth to feed.

"At that point, I was desperate. The mere thought of a home

filled with sadness broke my heart, but I was really hungry. Thus, after a 10-minute walk, I found myself in front of a small shack of a home on the outskirts of the city, and I knocked on the door. Within seconds, a small boy came to the door, and a wide smile spread across his face as he announced, 'Mommy, a talmid chacham is here.' Although no one else was standing next to me, it did not dawn on me that the boy was referring to me. But then, as I walked into the house, the children all clamored to sit next to me.

"The mother walked into the room and welcomed me. She showed me my seat and she asked the children, 'Who wants to share his portion with the talmid chacham?' I fought to hold back the tears. I had never experienced something like this in my life. The mother placed an empty plate in the middle of the table, and each of the children took a good part of his portion and placed it on that plate. Very quickly, it was more than full.

"Although all eyes in the room were on me, I ignored my discomfort and gobbled down the food. As I ate, each child kept pointing to his piece. 'How come you're not eating mine?' Or: 'Please, why won't you eat from my portion?'

"After the meal, the mother and her children walked me to the door and beyond, and thanked me profusely for coming. It had been so long since they had a guest. It was such a treat for them.

"I left their home and walked back to the yeshivah, and I cried the entire way. I never went back to their home; I just couldn't do it to them. The thought of children not having enough to eat more than took away my hunger.

"World War II broke out soon thereafter. As far as I understand, the entire family was killed. But their memory lives on forever in my heart. And every time I think of their kevod haTorah, I am inspired to give more and more and more. Every penny I've given has always been in their zechus."

Reb Aharon wiped away the tears from his eyes as he finished speaking. Clearly moved from recounting his experience, he doubled the check to the yeshivah and thanked Rav Goldenthal for bringing back this memory.

When I heard this magnificent story, I could not help but think of the story about Yaakov Avinu. In *Parashas Vayeitzei* (*Bereishis* 28:11, *Rashi*), when Yaakov put 12 stones around his head, each one said, "I want the *tzaddik*'s head to rest on me." Echoing that eternal call, each one of these children cried out, "I want the yeshivah boy to eat from my portion."

Sometimes we take it for granted. How privileged we are to have yeshivah boys in our midst, who are learning and aspiring for greatness. It is such a privilege to support their dreams as they continue to perpetuate our *mesorah*. How privileged we are to pass on the torch of *emunah* to our own children, as well.

We must never forget that.

An Awesome Responsibility

It was recently reported that Cardinal John Joseph O'Connor, a widely recognized member of the clergy of the Catholic Church, was really a Jew. His mother, Dorothy, or Devorah as she was named, was the child of a rabbi. Her parents, who lived in Bridgeport, Connecticut, at the turn of the 20th century, were very religious. How different his life would have been had he known his origins, that he was the grandchild of religious Jews.

Yes, ancestry is so important. When we know where we come from it makes all the difference in the world, as it gives us something to which to aspire; we have a clear sense of our responsibility and an understanding of our goals and purpose in life.

In the spring of 2014, I was invited to serve as a scholar-in-residence in Harrisburg, Pennsylvania. Rabbi Akiva Males, who serves as the rabbi of Kesher Israel Congregation, invited our family to his home for Shabbos. Over Shabbos, I noticed an unusual wall hanging. It was a photograph of the Tur Orach Chaim 224. But not just any Tur; it was the Tur that belonged to Rav Yaakov Emden. The page was filled with writing in every space left by the printer. As I took note of a burn in the right-hand corner, I sensed that the page had a deeper meaning and I asked my host what it was.

Rabbi Males shared with me the following story. He had been researching the laws pertaining to a specific berachah: Upon seeing a place where one has earlier experienced a miracle that saved him from imminent danger, he makes a blessing with the following words: "She'asah li neis ba'makom hazeh — Who performed a miracle for me at this place." Rabbi Males was exploring whether one is required to say that blessing with Hashem's Name or not. (See commentaries to Tur and Shulchan Aruch, Orach Chaim 218.)

He discovered that Rabbi Dr. Jacob J. Schacter had written his doctoral dissertation on Rav Yaakov Emden, while studying at Harvard University, and that Rabbi Dr. Schacter had also published a beautiful new edition of Rav Emden's sefer Mor U'Ketziah, on Tur Orach Chaim.

In Mor U'Ketziah, Siman 218, Rav Emden writes that several times, he was up late at night learning by candlelight when he fell asleep from exhaustion, and the papers on his desk, along with some wooden items, caught fire from the candle he had been using. As a result of these fires, he lost many of his papers, notes, and letters. However, he already had copies of those that were lost. He acknowledges that if he hadn't woken up in time from his deep sleep, the desk and his sefarim would have also caught fire, and he would have been in grave danger. As such, when this happened, he bentched HaGomel with a minyan to thank Hashem for saving his life.

He goes on to write that one of the times this occurred, he had been up learning from his Tur, and he fell asleep while it was open to Hilchos Berachos. Embers from that fire burned a hole through several pages of Hilchos Berachos — including Siman 218, which deals with the berachah of "She'asah li neis ba'makom hazeh."

It seems that he saw the burn in his Tur at exactly that spot as a sign from Shamayim that this incident qualified as a neis, and he needed to recite the berachah. He goes on to offer explanations as to why he feels that when this berachah needs to be recited, it should be recited using Hashem's Name — even when the miracle is not supernatural, as in his case.

Framed just below the photograph of the page from Rav Emden's Tur was his accounting of the miracle he had experienced. I looked at the picture of the Tur carefully and stared in wonder. I asked my host how he had gotten hold of that photo. He explained that when he had read the piece about Rav Emden and the fire, he had noticed a footnote in Rabbi Schacter's edition of the Mor U'Ketziah stating that Rav Yaakov Emden's very own set of Tur Shulchan Aruch was located at Columbia University in New York City. Rabbi Males referred back to Rabbi Schacter's PhD dissertation, and was amazed to learn that after a long chain of events, many items from Rav Yaakov Emden's personal library had ended up in Columbia University's Rare Book and Manuscript Library.

The broken matzah is lifted for all to see as the head of the household begins with the following brief explanation of the proceedings.

הָא לַחְמָא עַנְיָא דִי אֲכָלוּ אַבְהָתָנָא בְּאַרְעָא דְמִצְרָיִם. כָּל דִּכְפִין יֵיתֵי וְיֵכוֹל, כָּל דִּצְרִיךְ יֵיתֵי וְיִפְסַח. הָשַׁתָּא הָכָא, לְשָׁנָה הַבָּאָה בְּאַרְעָא דְיִשְׂרָאֵל. הָשַׁתָּא עַבְדֵי, לְשָׁנָה הַבָּאָה בְּנֵי חוֹרִין.

Rabbi Males felt that he had to see Rav Emden's Tur with his own eyes. And so, he contacted the university and arranged a visit, in which a librarian wearing white cloth gloves directed him to a glass-walled room. The librarian removed the precious old volumes and placed them on the table before him. He trembled in disbelief. This volume had so much sanctity, so much history. He turned to the proper page, and there, before his eyes, were the burnt pages of Rav Yaakov Emden's Tur. Sure enough, just as Rav Emden described in his Mor U'Ketziah, the burn passed through Chapter 218. After analyzing the burn, Rabbi Males realized that Rav Emden's Tur Shulchan Aruch had been opened to Chapter 224 when the fire he described had broken out. Though Rabbi Males was excited about his find, he was filled with a tinge of sadness, thinking about how lonely those sacred books must be without anyone to learn from them. However, the staff members at Columbia did allow him to carefully photograph the page upon which the embers had fallen, and that is how the picture ended up on his wall.

As I listened to this incredible tale, I could not believe that I had come to Harrisburg, Pennsylvania, and walked away with such a precious piece of Jewish history.

But the story does not end there.

A few days later, I received an email from a cousin who had an interest in Jewish genealogy. As I read through the email, I was able to trace my father's family from his mother's side 15 generations back — all the way to the Maharal of Prague. As I read through the list of names, I wondered about each person on the list and what kind of life its bearer had led. And then, I read a name and I froze. It was the name of my ancestor from the 1700's — 11 generations back — Rav Yaakov Emden!

I thought again about Harrisburg. I imagined the fire that nearly took Rav Emden's life. And as one of my sons said to me,

This is the bread of affliction that our fathers ate
in the land of Egypt. Whoever is hungry, let
him come and eat! Whoever is needy, let him
come and celebrate Pesach! Now, we are here;
next year may we be in the Land of Israel! Now,
we are slaves; next year may we be free men!

---

*"If he did not catch the fire in time, who knows if we would be
here today?"*

Tonight, we read about our ancestry. It is a storied one, with
much drama and pain. But it is also quite glorious. We come from
greatness and we are destined to be great, as well.

Take a moment to realize all of this. What would our grandparents
think of us? Are we living up to their expectations? Is this what they
sacrificed their lives for?

What an awesome and inspiring responsibility it is.

הָא לַחְמָא עַנְיָא
This is the bread of affliction...

◆§ Open-Door Policy

Ha Lachma Anya includes an invitation: "*Kol dichfin yeisei
ve'yeichol* — Whoever is hungry, let him come and eat." This
is because when we invite those in need and give to others, we
emulate the Almighty and we become providers.

The first halachah in the *Shulchan Aruch* regarding *hilchos
Pesach* (*Orach Chaim* 429:1) is the obligation to review the laws
of Pesach 30 days before the holiday, and the custom to give *maos
chittin*. Immediately thereafter, it states the halachah of: "*Ein noflin
al peneihem be'chol Chodesh Nissan* — They don't fall on their faces
throughout the month of Nissan," which means that we don't say
Tachanun during the entire month.

Rav Baruch'l of Mezhibuzh derives a lesson from the juxtaposition
of these two halachos. One must first provide sustenance to those

in need and make sure they have all they lack, and only after that should he worry about his own needs. This way, he will not have to "fall on his face," and daven out of desperation.

If we take care of others before ourselves, Hashem will take care of us.

Several months before marrying off one of his children, Rav Dovid Schechter (the father of Rav Yaakov Meir Schechter) went to pour out his heart at the Kosel, where he saw someone crying bitterly. Rav Dovid approached the fellow and asked him why he was distraught. The man explained that his child was getting married in a short while, and he had no way of paying for the chasunah. So he had come to the Kosel to cry to Hashem for help.

Rav Dovid told the fellow that he had some extra money and was happy to give it to him. He quickly gathered the full amount of money the man needed for his wedding expenses, and brought it to the man. Rav Dovid was not a man of means by any stretch. However, he had saved up money to pay for his child's wedding, which was coming up in a few months. He gladly gave over the full amount, since he did not need the money just yet, and he trusted in HaKadosh Baruch Hu that He would take care of him when it came time to marry off his own son.

Later that day, Rav Dovid went to daven Minchah in the beis midrash of Rav Shloim'ke of Zhvil. Rav Shoim'ke asked him what mitzvah he had performed that day. At first, Rav Dovid denied that he had done anything special. But Reb Shloim'ke pressed on, until Rav Dovid agreed to tell him on one condition: if the Rebbe would learn with him be'chavrusa. He had asked for this on a number of occasions, and each time he was turned away. But this time, the Rebbe agreed.

Rav Dovid told over the whole story: how he had found a fellow crying bitterly and how he had given him the money he had put away for his own child's wedding. When he finished, Rav Shloim'ke said, "When you walked into the beis midrash, I saw in you a great transformation. Your neshamah has gone through numerous gilgulim," he explained, "and this one act has rectified your soul."

Meanwhile, a man entered the shul to tell the Rebbe that his wife was having trouble giving birth. The Rebbe insisted that Rav Dovid give her a blessing. When Rav Dovid refused, saying that the man had come to Rav Shloim'ke for a berachah and not to him, Rav Shloim'ke countered, "At this time, you are completely clean and pure, and you have the ability to bless Yidden."

From here we see the power of the mitzvah of tzedakah.

We are about to begin the centerpiece of the Seder; a daunting task lies ahead, as we attempt to re-experience the great Exodus of Egypt. At the same time, we hope to instill in our children the faith in the Almighty that our parents instilled in us. For this, we will need great merits. Our open invitation to the poor and needy may serve as that *zechus.*

The Proper Shiur

The Shevus Yaakov, Rav Yaakov Reischer, was delivering his legendary Shabbos HaGadol derashah. This year, he spoke about the minimum shiur of achilas matzah. People came from all over to hear the talmid chacham's intricately woven tapestry of Torah. Even the greatest Torah scholars of the region were in awe of the brilliance and depth of the Shevus Yaakov's speech. After two hours, the Shevus Yaakov concluded his talk. By the time the Rav reached the door of the beis midrash, nearly everyone had said something to him — a comment, a question, an added point, a compliment — about his riveting speech.

But there was one individual who had yet to be heard. A haggard-looking pauper approached the Rav, as he, too, had a kasha on the shiur. "Rebbi, to me it makes no difference what the shiur of achilas matzah is, because I don't have any food or matzah for my family for Pesach!"

The Shevus Yaakov was taken aback. He looked at the down-trodden pauper who stood before him; the man was crying. Immediately, he retreated to the podium where he had delivered the derashah. As he stepped onto the stage in front of the Aron Kodesh, the crowd hushed. They were thrilled that the Rav was going to continue his shiur, and waited with bated breath; then the Rav continued his derashah. "My entire derashah is upgrefrekt [proven wrong].

"The new shiur for achilas matzah is to ensure that every single family has enough food and matzah to eat for Pesach!"

The Seder plate is removed and the second of the four cups of wine is poured. The youngest present asks the reasons for the unusual proceedings of the evening.

מַה נִּשְׁתַּנָּה הַלַּיְלָה הַזֶּה מִכָּל הַלֵּילוֹת?

מַה נִּשְׁתַּנָּה
Why is this night different...

◄§ A Long Bitter Exile

In *Olelos Ephraim*, Rav Shlomo Ephraim Lunshitz, the author of the *Kli Yakar*, explains that the opening question of the *Mah Nishtanah* is a query as to why this night, this *Galus,* is different from all other nights, from all other exiles. Tonight, on a night when we commemorate, relive, and re-experience the Exodus from Egypt, we ask: Why is this Exile so much longer? In addition, why is it different in that we have no idea when it is going to end?

There are four answers to this question, as seen from the four questions and their answers in the *Mah Nishtanah*. The first answer is that while in the other exiles, there were disagreements, hinted to in the word *matzah*, as in *matzah u'merivah* (arguing and dissension), there was also peace, represented by the word *chametz*. But in this Exile, there seems to be only fighting, only *matzah*.

The second reason that this Exile is different is due to our infatuation and obsession with money. In the rest of the exiles, we had "*she'ar yerakos* — many vegetables." This alludes to the fact that we were satisfied with whatever came our way, whatever the potpourri of vegetables may have been. But in this Exile, we are obsessed with amassing wealth, and this causes much bitterness in our lives.

The third source of our lengthy *Galus* is our fixation on *taavah*, desire. We mention that in the other exiles, we did not dip even once. Dipping is symbolic of one who is obsessed with his food and steeped in desire. In this Exile, we are constantly dipping and finding new desires to occupy our hearts and minds.

The fourth reason given for the length of this Exile is our haughtiness. In the other exiles, we ate while we were sitting or while we were reclining. Reclining is a sign of freedom and *gaavah*, pride. The pride factor is quite prevalent in our Exile.

The Seder plate is removed and the second of the four cups of wine is poured. The youngest present asks the reasons for the unusual proceedings of the evening.

Why is this night different from all other nights?

I was once speaking to my host while I was visiting London, and I asked him why the people in London are much more rigid than those in America. He answered me, "We don't mean to insult you, but the people in America are quite comfortable with Galus."

How sad, but how true. We walk down the street as if we own it, as if we belong here. It is not that way all over the world. In other countries, as we know all too well, the Jews are made to feel that they are not wanted and are not welcome.

If we want to end this interminable night, we must work on our unity, our lust for money, our insatiable desires, and our haughtiness. In that way, we will be *zocheh* to see the dawn of Mashiach and the end to all of our questions.

Taking Part

It was Chanukah 1949, and Rav Menachem Mendel Halberstam of Stropkov, who had survived the war, now lived in New York.

His new home was a far cry from the majestic dynasty he had seen in the court of his zeide, Rav Yechezkel Shraga of Shinev. Rav Menachem Mendel remembered what it was like when he was a boy. His zeide had conducted his hadlakas neiros in the same way as his father, the Divrei Chaim of Sanz — with singing and dancing. The Chassidim would gather around, waiting for the Rebbe to light his candles, and then the celebrating would begin. It was a festive occasion with much hoopla, energy, and excitement.

But now, all that seemed like it took place millennia ago. America was not Europe, and New York City was not Sanz or Shinev.

But Rav Menachem Mendel did the best he could. Each night of Chanukah, a small group of his followers came to his apartment, to watch as he lit the candles, and then sing and dance. One day, one of his neighbors — a middle-aged fellow with no family of his own — approached him and asked for a small favor. He was not a religious Jew and did not light the candles himself, yet he tolerated the noise. However, he asked that the following evening, there be no celebration.

Rav Menachem Mendel responded that he would be happy to accommodate him but wondered why; what was happening tomorrow night? The fellow explained that he was hosting a holiday party with some of his non-Jewish buddies and did not want the singing and dancing to compete with his party. Rav Menachem Mendel understood and agreed to the request, but made one small request in return. "Would you please light the menorah at your party? Since I am diminishing my lighting ceremony, would you be able to add a little light to the building?" Somewhat hesitant, the man explained that he had no menorah with which to light. The Rebbe eagerly handed him an extra one, and his neighbor promised to give the matter some thought.

The next night, the Rebbe lit the menorah without much fanfare; the Chassidim came, but there was no singing or dancing. Suddenly, though, they heard a ruckus from down the hall. At first there was yelling and screaming, and then they heard full-blown fighting. Within minutes, there was loud banging on the Rebbe's door. He quickly opened it. There stood his neighbor, with a bruised and beaten face. The Rebbe calmed him down and asked what had happened.

"Rabbi, I thought about what you told me and I figured the guys would be up for it, but soon they began to tease me and tried to prevent me from lighting. The more they tried to prevent me, however, the greater my desire became. A spark ignited inside my soul, which had lain dormant for so long. The innocent teasing soon turned physical, and that's why I look the way I do."

The Rebbe felt terrible about what had happened and asked the fellow what he could do for him. He said that he had only one wish. "I wouldn't mind if you would sing and dance a little. But this time, if you don't mind, let me be a part of it."

◦§ Ask, My Child

Prior to the asking of the four questions in the *Mah Nishtanah*, many *Haggados* offer the instruction, "*Ve'kan haben sho'eil* — And here, the child asks." On the surface, this sentence is simply providing us with basic instructions. But many great *tzaddikim* read something much deeper in these words. This moment is especially ripe for a child to ask. We are not merely referring to young children; rather, we are including the Almighty's children: Jews of all ages. Now is a time that we can ask for anything and everything that our hearts yearn for.

הגדה של פסח [96]

The Satmar Rav used this time to offer special *berachos* for those in need, and many of those *berachos* were fulfilled. The *Yotzer* for *Mussaf* of *Parashas HaChodesh* hints to the potency of the prayers of this month and especially this night: "*Hachodesh asher yeshuos bo makifos* — This month in which salvations follow quickly one upon another." The word *makifos* also shares a root with the word *hakafah*, buying on credit. When one comes to the store and wishes to purchase something but cannot afford it, he will often buy on credit. The same is true tonight. Tonight, the night that we relive the Exodus from Egypt, when the Almighty took us out even though we did not have the necessary merit to be redeemed, He once again offers His children credit. He tells us that even though we may not be deserving of that which we are asking for, tonight He is offering us credit.

> A friend of mine — let's call him Eli — was going through a difficult time. Since he was separated from his wife, he was unable to conduct the Seder with his children. He was bitterly disappointed and distraught beyond measure. He was too embarrassed to go home and spend Yom Tov with his parents, siblings, nieces, and nephews. Instead, he had another idea. He had a friend who was married for over 10 years and had yet to be blessed with children; he and his wife were in desperate need of a yeshuah. They, too, had no interest in spending the Seder night with all of their younger siblings and their children. It would just be too painful to listen to so many children recite the Mah Nishtanah when they had no children, and they were too embarrassed to excuse themselves from the room. Instead, they decided to make their own Seder. Eli asked if he could join them, and they welcomed his company.
>
> When they reached the section of Mah Nishtanah, which was very emotional for the childless couple, Eli told them about the tradition of davening at the time in which the Haggadah instructs us, "Ve'kan ha'ben sho'eil." He shared with them what he had heard about the Satmar Rav on this night, and how his prayers had been answered. Then he suggested that they all daven for a yeshuah.
>
> They did. For the next half-hour, nothing was said. But after buckets of tears were shed, they continued their Seder, with the salt water of their tears still evident on their faces.
>
> The next year, Eli and the young couple no longer needed each other's company. Eli reconciled with his wife and was once more reunited with his children.
>
> And the childless couple was childless no longer.

שֶׁבְּכָל הַלֵּילוֹת אָנוּ אוֹכְלִין חָמֵץ וּמַצָּה,
הַלַּיְלָה הַזֶּה כֻּלּוֹ מַצָּה.

שֶׁבְּכָל הַלֵּילוֹת אָנוּ אוֹכְלִין שְׁאָר יְרָקוֹת,
הַלַּיְלָה הַזֶּה מָרוֹר.

שֶׁבְּכָל הַלֵּילוֹת אֵין אָנוּ מַטְבִּילִין אֲפִילוּ פַּעַם
אֶחָת, הַלַּיְלָה הַזֶּה שְׁתֵּי פְעָמִים.

שֶׁבְּכָל הַלֵּילוֹת אָנוּ אוֹכְלִין בֵּין יוֹשְׁבִין וּבֵין
מְסֻבִּין, הַלַּיְלָה הַזֶּה כֻּלָּנוּ מְסֻבִּין.

In the section that begins with the words: "*Baruch shomer havta-chaso le'Yisrael*," we bless Hashem because He "*chishav es hakeitz* — calculated the end," meaning that He expedited the redemption from Egypt by 190 years, the *gematria* of the word קֵץ. The *Chida* (brought down in *Haggadah Pnei David*) adds that the number 190 is significant for another reason. Avraham waited 100 years to have a child, while Sarah waited 90. This is hinted to in the word קֵץ; the ק signifies the 100 years of Avraham, while the צ represents the 90 years of Sarah. The *Ribbono Shel Olam* took into consideration the pain of one childless couple. Because of their pain, He expedited the *geulah* by 190 years!

We must remember that the Almighty never lets a *Yiddishe trer*, a Jewish tear, go to waste. He counts every one and suffers with us, like a parent who feels the pain of his child.

As we recite the *Haggadah* and listen to our beautiful children ask the *Mah Nishtanah*, let us have in mind all of those who are in need of *refuos* and *yeshuos*. And tonight, the night that we give answers to our children, let the Almighty finally give the answer that His children are waiting for.

כֻּלָּנוּ מְסֻבִּין
We all recline...

⋅ᴇ§ Relying and Reclining

The Seder is divided into two parts: from *Kaddeish* until *Tzafun*; and then the prayer portion, which consists of *Hallel* and *Nirtzah*. Why is this?

1. **On all other nights** we may eat chametz and matzah, but on this night — only matzah.
2. **On all other nights** we eat many vegetables, but on this night [we eat] maror.
3. **On all other nights** we do not dip even once, but on this night, twice.
4. **On all other nights** we eat either sitting or reclining, but on this night we all recline.

The *Shaarei Leil HaSeder* explains the structure of the Seder. The first half of the Seder, in which we read the section of *Maggid*, focuses on the idea of *emunah*. We must repeat to ourselves and our children that everything that happens is orchestrated by *HaKadosh Baruch Hu*. This is most obvious in the paragraph of *Dayeinu*, in which we detail all the specific kindnesses we merited. This teaches us that every detail that happened originated from Hashem. Without Hashem, we have nothing. This is our faith in *Hashgachah Pratis*.

> It is told that Rav Chatzkel Levenstein did not speak during the Seder. However, when he got up to the passage beginning *Mi'techilah*, when he said the pesukim that begin with the words, *"Va'ekach es avichem,"* he said:
> *"Va'ekach es avichem* — I, Hashem, took Avraham.
> *"Va'oleich oso be'chol Eretz Canaan* — I, Hashem, led him throughout the land of Canaan.
> *"Va'arbeh es zaro* — I, Hashem, increased his children.
> *"Va'etein lo es Yitzchak* — I, Hashem, gave him Yitzchak.
> *"Va'etein le'Yitzchak es Yaakov ve'es Eisav* — I, Hashem, gave Yitzchak [sons], Yaakov and Eisav."
> And that is how he continued until the end of the paragraph.

It is every person's obligation to reinforce for himself and his children the message that whatever happens — throughout the generations — is all from Hashem. It is not enough to believe in *"Anochi Hashem Elokecha* — I am Hashem, your God," but we must also believe in *"Asher hotzeisicha mei'Eretz Mitzrayim* — Who took you out of the land of Mitzrayim," which demonstrates belief in *Hashgachah Pratis*.

This is the first half of the Seder.

The Seder plate is returned. The matzos are kept uncovered as the Haggadah is recited in unison. The Haggadah should be translated, if necessary, and the story of the Exodus should be amplified upon.

עֲבָדִים הָיִינוּ לְפַרְעֹה בְּמִצְרָיִם, וַיּוֹצִיאֵנוּ יהוה אֱלֹהֵינוּ מִשָּׁם בְּיָד חֲזָקָה וּבִזְרוֹעַ נְטוּיָה. וְאִלּוּ לֹא הוֹצִיא הַקָּדוֹשׁ בָּרוּךְ הוּא אֶת אֲבוֹתֵינוּ מִמִּצְרַיִם, הֲרֵי אָנוּ וּבָנֵינוּ וּבְנֵי בָנֵינוּ מְשֻׁעְבָּדִים הָיִינוּ לְפַרְעֹה בְּמִצְרָיִם. וַאֲפִילוּ כֻּלָּנוּ חֲכָמִים, כֻּלָּנוּ נְבוֹנִים, כֻּלָּנוּ זְקֵנִים, כֻּלָּנוּ יוֹדְעִים אֶת הַתּוֹרָה, מִצְוָה עָלֵינוּ לְסַפֵּר בִּיצִיאַת מִצְרָיִם. וְכָל הַמַּרְבֶּה לְסַפֵּר בִּיצִיאַת מִצְרַיִם, הֲרֵי זֶה מְשֻׁבָּח.

The second half takes what we have learned in the first half and allows us to implement it. The second half of the Seder focuses on *bitachon,* which follows *emunah. Emunah* means that a person believes with certainty that all is orchestrated by Hashem, while *bitachon* is the application of that *emunah:* how a person lives his life according to his *emunah.* As the *Ramban* points out, "All those who have *bitachon* certainly have *emunah,* but just because one has *emunah* doesn't mean he possesses *bitachon.*" A person must first possess *emunah,* which is the focus of the first part of the *Haggadah,* and that will lead to *bitachon.*

It says in *Parashas Beshalach,* "God led the people roundabout, by way of the wilderness at the Yam Suf" (*Shemos* 13:18). The Midrash (*Shemos Rabbah* 20:18) teaches us a halachah from the word "*Vayaseiv* — And He led roundabout." I.e., even a poor person is required to eat in a reclining position at the Seder. The word *heseibah,* which means reclining, has the same *shoresh* as *vayaseiv:* נ.ס.ב.

What is the connection between these two ideas, other than the obvious similarity of one word? The *Shaarei Leil HaSeder* explains that reclining symbolizes *cheirus,* freedom, since kings sit in a reclining fashion. But there is a deeper meaning in leaning. When someone leans, he is supporting himself on something. When he is being supported, he doesn't worry. When a person

The Seder plate is returned. The matzos are kept uncovered as the *Haggadah* is recited in unison. The *Haggadah* should be translated, if necessary, and the story of the Exodus should be amplified upon.

We were slaves to Pharaoh in Egypt, but HASHEM, our God, took us out from there with a mighty hand and an outstretched arm. Had not the Holy One, Blessed is He, taken our fathers out from Egypt, then we, our children, and our children's children would have remained subservient to Pharaoh in Egypt. Even if we were all men of wisdom, understanding, experience,and knowledge of the Torah, it would still be an obligation upon us to tell about the Exodus from Egypt. The more one tells about the discussion of the Exodus, the more he is praiseworthy.

---

leans on a chair or bed, the object he is leaning on supports him.

The *avodah* of the Seder night is for a person to lean on Hashem, to the point that he can say the words of David in *Tehillim* (71:6), "*Alecha nismachti mi'beten* — I relied on You from my birth."

This is the *inyan* of *heseibah* at the Seder. After we have come to clear *emunah* in *Hashgachah Pratis,* we have no need to worry, because we trust and lean on Hashem.

עֲבָדִים הָיִינוּ
We were slaves...

◆§ The King's Children

"*Ve'chol hamarbeh lesaper bi'tzias Mitzrayim harei zeh meshubach* — And the more one expands upon the discussion of the Exodus, the more he is praiseworthy." The Tiferes Shlomo points out that through the additional retelling of the story, not only will one's children get more out of the story of the Exodus, but the person who is telling the story will become a more praiseworthy person.

Rav Shimon Sofer illustrates this point with a parable:

> *Once upon a time, there was a king whose son was taken captive in a war and forced into slave labor. He worked alongside another*

young captive from his country, a boy who had grown up in a small village. After many years of suffering, the two boys managed to escape. As they approached their homeland, the village boy decided that since they both looked the same — with blackened skin from working in the sun — he would try to pass himself off as the prince. Since it had been such a long time that the king had not seen his son, the villager was certain that he would be able to fool him.

As they came closer to the palace, the villager hurried ahead, in order to enter the palace before the prince. He proclaimed, "I am the captured son of the king!" His declaration caused a tremendous tumult. The servants and other officers in the palace fawned over him, all the while checking the various signs to confirm his identity. Since he had worked with the prince for so many years, he knew all the stories and all the secrets of the kingdom. As they concluded the testing, word began to spread that the prince had finally come home. There was great jubilation in the kingdom.

Then suddenly, the real prince appeared at the doorstep of the palace. His declaration that he was the prince caused another commotion. Nobody knew if he was the real prince or if he was just a fraud.

Although the king was excited to have his son home, he wanted to welcome the son who really belonged to him. One of his advisers claimed that he would be able to determine the truth. The king trusted him and allowed him to interrogate both of the captives.

The man called one of the captives into a room, and he asked him to repeat the entire story of his capture and slave labor. The fellow told how he was beaten and starved and enslaved, forced to work day and night. The officer encouraged him to share more of the story, but the young man said, "Is there anything worse than what I told you?"

Then the adviser called in the second captive and asked him to share his experiences. The boy told him that no words will ever be able to describe the atrocities he endured. He suffered from brutal beatings and infected wounds. But that was not the worst. In a heartbroken voice, he continued:

"I desperately longed to come home. I remembered what it was like living in the palace, while in the labor camp they fed me moldy hard bread without even a table to sit at; I sat on the floor like an animal and I dressed like a peasant. I wasn't able to change my clothing more than once in four weeks, and I couldn't *sleep at night because they refused to give me a decent mattress. It was unbearable not to be able to take a break and have some intellectual stimulation by studying and learning. They forced me to live among wild, barbaric people. Worst of all, I ended up like them." He went on and on and would not stop.*

The king's adviser walked out of the room, convinced that this fellow was the king's son. The fact that he continued to tell the story over and over, and in such detail, was proof that he was the prince. The difficult situation had affected him more than the other fellow, and from his reactions it was obvious that he had grown up as a prince.

The same is true with us. The fact that we want to tell over more and more of the story proves that we are the true princes. When we detail the suffering in Mitzrayim and the subsequent miracles and delve into them at great length, this is proof that we are sons of the King, whose attributes and nature are more refined than those of the average person. We are an *am meshubach,* and the greatest proof of that is that we are *marbeh lesaper.*

The other nations of the world pretend that they are the worthy children of the King. They describe their suffering and tell over their painful stories, but our story — the indignities and suffering that we've endured, which bother us because of our exalted nature — proves that we are His children.

Family Heirloom

Henry Borenstein knocked lightly on Rabbi Nelkin's office door and waited to be admitted into the rabbi's private room. The door opened and Henry was greeted cheerfully by his good friend. "What can I do for you this morning, Henry?"

Henry was a no-nonsense type of guy. Advanced in age, he had been a member of his shul for close to 50 years. Although the rabbi was young enough to be his son, Henry respected him and had come to ask for a favor.

"Rabbi, I'm here to tell you that I'm going to die."

"We're all going to die sooner or later," Rabbi Nelkin joked, in an attempt to lighten up the conversation.

"I mean it, Rabbi Nelkin. I'm not fooling around." Henry's serious tone indicated that this was as serious a discussion as any.

"Have you been to a doctor lately? What makes you think that you're going to die, Henry? You look perfectly fine to me." Rabbi

מַעֲשֶׂה בְּרַבִּי אֱלִיעֶזֶר וְרַבִּי יְהוֹשֻׁעַ וְרַבִּי
אֶלְעָזָר בֶּן עֲזַרְיָה וְרַבִּי עֲקִיבָא
וְרַבִּי טַרְפוֹן שֶׁהָיוּ מְסֻבִּין בִּבְנֵי בְרַק, וְהָיוּ

Nelkin tried his best to calm Henry's nerves, as he seemed to be on edge.

"What can I say? I just know that it won't be long now. And I have a request. I don't want to be buried in tachrichim."

The request surprised Rabbi Nelkin. A proper Jewish burial was something even the non-religious took seriously. What could Henry's reason possibly be?

"Instead, I want you to bury me in the prisoner clothing I wore in the concentration camps. After I pass away, I'll come before the Almighty, and He will ask me how come I didn't keep Shabbos and tefillin and kosher for over three years of my life during the war. I will be able to respond, 'G-d, look at what I'm wearing. I went through the horrors of Auschwitz, and I still raised an observant family.'"

Rabbi Nelkin stared at Henry in disbelief, but then he assured Henry that when the time came he would address the matter, figuring that he had plenty of time before Henry passed on. However, that wasn't the case. Three weeks later, Henry died suddenly. He went to sleep one night and never woke up.

Immediately, Henry's sons began to make the necessary arrangements for the funeral. The chevrah kaddisha was called and preparations for the taharah began. They asked the family for Henry's tachrichim, tallis, and kittel. His children gave them what they asked for, but mentioned to those who would be doing the taharah that they should wait until the family met with Rabbi Nelkin.

"Rabbi, we are aware of our father's unusual request regarding his burial shrouds; however, we ask you not to bury him in his prisoner uniform."

In all of Rabbi Nelkin's years in the rabbinate, this issue was definitely one of his most unusual ones. He thought for a moment and then responded to Henry's sons. "Why should we not bury him in his prisoner's uniform? That was his final request from me. I told him that I would consider it, but I really have not delved into the halachic side of the matter. Still, I can't imagine why you would be opposed to it."

Moshe, Henry's eldest son, stepped forward and spoke on behalf

It happened that Rabbi Eliezer, Rabbi Yehoshua, Rabbi Elazar ben Azaryah, Rabbi Akiva, and Rabbi Tarfon were gathered (at the Seder) in Bnei

of his brothers. "My dear Rabbi, allow me to explain the family's hesitation. Each year, we've been gathering together as a family for the Pesach Seder. Thank G-d, there are already four generations of my father's descendants. You may wonder why we've been going through the trouble of getting together when it would have been more manageable for us to have separate Sedarim.

"The answer is that every year, after all the children would ask the Mah Nishtanah, my father would leave the table. With all his grandchildren watching his every move, he would walk deliberately to the closet, take out a hanger, remove the plastic from it, and then hang it from the chandelier. As the children stared at their grandfather's prisoner uniform, my father would announce in a loud and clear voice, 'Kinderlach, Avadim hayinu leHitler beGermaniah. Children, we were slaves to Hitler in Germany. He tortured and killed millions of our brothers. And some thought that we would never escape the nightmare. But: Vayotzi'einu Hashem Elokeinu misham. Hashem took us out of there, and He allowed us to rebuild our lives. It is to Him that I owe my thanks for all of you.'

"Rabbi, it is that cry of faith that left an indelible impression on each of us, and we don't want to relinquish this family heirloom."

Rabbi Nelkin held onto Moshe as he cried for his father and his children's grandfather.

With a new understanding of the importance of these hallowed garments, the chevrah kaddisha buried Henry in the traditional burial shrouds, but they placed the precious uniform inside the aron, as well. His last request would thus be honored, but the memory of that uniform would remain etched in the minds of his children and grandchildren for years to come.

מַעֲשֶׂה
It happened...

◆§ The Center of Our Circle

Throughout the *Haggadah*, we see the importance of *achdus*, unity. We begin the recitation of *Maggid* with an invitation to all those in need. There may be people who are left out of the loop, and we invite them into our inner circle. The roasting of the *korban pesach* also symbolizes cohesiveness. When a food is cooked, it has a tendency to expand. But when it is roasted, it contracts and becomes more connected. The sheep itself must be roasted whole. In addition, there is an obligation to eat the *korban pesach* as part of a group, also promoting *achdus*.

The *baal Haggadah* tells the story of five Tannaim who met in the city of Bnei Brak and spent the entire night talking about the Jewish people leaving Egypt. The question is: There are thousands of people who have spent the entire night speaking about *Yetzias Mitzrayim;* so why is this particular story noteworthy?

The *Imrei Noam* gives us an answer, which carries with it an important message. Each of these rabbis came with a large entourage, a group of their students. We have a tendency to accord honor and reverence to our own rebbi, rosh yeshivah, Rebbe, rav, or *chacham.* Unfortunately, though, when someone is not our personal leader, we may not accord him the proper respect and honor. But this time it was different.

Notice the usage of the word "*rabboseinu* — our rabbis." The students of each of the five Tannaim all came together, and they accepted each of the others rabbis as their own. This is indeed a noteworthy story: a lesson from which we can all learn.

The Gemara at the end of *Maseches Taanis* (31a) tells us that in the future, the Almighty will make a circle for all the righteous individuals and He will sit among them in Gan Eden. Each one of those *tzaddikim* will point to the Almighty and proclaim the *pasuk* that includes the words: "*Zeh Hashem kivinu lo* — This the Hashem to Whom we hoped" (*Yeshayah* 25:9). Rav Leibele Eiger, in *Toras Emes,* notes that in a circle, every person on the perimeter of the circle is equidistant from the center, although he comes from a different point.

It makes no difference if it will be a Litvishe rosh yeshivah, Chassidishe Rebbe, or Sephardic *chacham.* They will all point to the center of the circle where the Almighty is sitting and declare His Oneness. In this world, it seems as if each person is forging his own path in his service of Hashem, but in the World to Come, in Gan Eden, everyone will realize that it is really all one path.

It is important to point out that Rav Leibele Eiger became a Chassidishe Rebbe, while his grandfather, the renowned Rabbi Akiva Eiger, was a fierce *misnaged,* who was utterly devastated when his grandson chose a different path. Hence, this powerful thought, when quoted from him, holds great value and importance.

There are many ways to serve the Almighty. Each Torah group has its own way of doing so. Perhaps the rabbis who spoke the entire night represent the rabbis who have led us throughout the 2,000 years of our exile. And the *Krias Shema shel Shacharis* that is mentioned in this passage symbolizes our recognition of the Oneness of the Almighty, which will come at the dawn of our Final Redemption. At that time, everyone will gain clarity and point to the center of that circle.

But that day will come only when we are finally able to proclaim one word together:

"*Rabboseinu!*"

The Rizhiner's Ruminations

In the mid-1800's, a terrible plague tore through the city of Yos. Tens of children died, and the people of the town felt devastated and hopeless. They searched for answers but none were forthcoming. Finally, they sent a group to ask the gedolim of the region what brought about the plague. They were told that sinas chinam, in the form of community politics, had caused the tragedy.

The activists of the Yos Jewish community then looked for someone to mediate between the two sides so that they could make peace with each other. One Rebbe originally agreed to be the arbitrator, but then he decided against it when he discovered that his arrival in the city would bring him honor. It was his practice to flee from all personal honor, as he was afraid it would affect him adversely. Instead, he suggested that they approach the Rebbe of Rizhin and solicit his services.

The Rizhiner lived in opulence, but he was completely unaffected by it. His palatial home and his exquisite clothing were a facade, as he viewed himself as an ambassador of the Almighty who needed to look and dress the part. Since he derived no personal benefit from outer trappings, he certainly would not be affected by the honor accorded to him if he came to Yos.

Indeed, they approached him and he agreed to come. But when he arrived, the commotion was much greater than he had anticipated. The police, who were recruited by the local activists to maintain order, had to use force on some individuals who were too pushy in their desire to see and meet the Rebbe. One man was hurt; his injuries were not serious, but he had to be bandaged and sent home.

מְסַפְּרִים בִּיצִיאַת מִצְרַיִם כָּל אוֹתוֹ הַלַּיְלָה. עַד שֶׁבָּאוּ תַלְמִידֵיהֶם וְאָמְרוּ לָהֶם, רַבּוֹתֵינוּ הִגִּיעַ זְמַן קְרִיאַת שְׁמַע שֶׁל שַׁחֲרִית.

אָמַר רַבִּי אֶלְעָזָר בֶּן עֲזַרְיָה, הֲרֵי אֲנִי כְּבֶן שִׁבְעִים שָׁנָה, וְלֹא זָכִיתִי שֶׁתֵּאָמֵר יְצִיאַת מִצְרַיִם בַּלֵּילוֹת, עַד שֶׁדְּרָשָׁהּ בֶּן זוֹמָא, שֶׁנֶּאֱמַר, לְמַעַן תִּזְכֹּר אֶת יוֹם צֵאתְךָ מֵאֶרֶץ מִצְרַיִם כֹּל יְמֵי חַיֶּיךָ.[1] יְמֵי חַיֶּיךָ הַיָּמִים, כֹּל יְמֵי חַיֶּיךָ הַלֵּילוֹת. וַחֲכָמִים אוֹמְרִים, יְמֵי חַיֶּיךָ הָעוֹלָם הַזֶּה, כֹּל יְמֵי חַיֶּיךָ לְהָבִיא לִימוֹת הַמָּשִׁיחַ.

Finally, the Rebbe met with both sides in the dispute, and a short while later they came to an agreement. Peace reigned, and the plague was halted.

Years later, a group of government officials accused the Rebbe of conspiracy against the government. He was thrown into prison, with no visitors allowed. Only after several months was he allowed a visitor. The visitor entered the dark, dank cell, and saw the Rebbe sitting in deep contemplation, tears streaming down his face. After a long and meaningful discussion about why individuals suffer, the Rebbe confided, "As I've been sitting here in solitude, I've been wondering why I had to endure such suffering. What have I done to deserve such a punishment? Finally, I remembered that when I came to the city of Yos, and the townspeople became unruly, the policemen beat some of the people who had gathered. As I understand it, one of them was seriously injured. It was through me that a Jew was hurt. And if one causes another Jew pain, even indirectly, the consequences are severe."

The Rebbe told his visitor to go to his home and retrieve a special key from its hiding place. The man was to use the key to open a safe containing gold coins. "Bring the gold coins to the individual who was beaten by the police. Tell him that it is my gift to him, and that I apologize for any pain he suffered."

The messenger did as he was instructed. However, when he and the other Chassidim arrived at the man's home, his wife informed

Brak. They discussed the Exodus from Egypt all that night until their students came and said to them: "Our teachers, the time has come for the reading of the morning *Shema*."

Rabbi Elazar ben Azaryah said: I am like a seventy-year-old man, but I could not succeed in having the Exodus from Egypt mentioned every night, until Ben Zoma expounded it, as it is stated: "In order that you may remember the day you left Egypt all the days of your life."[1] The phrase "the days of your life" would have indicated only the days; the addition of the word "all" includes the nights as well. But the Sages declare that "the days of your life" would mean only the present world; the addition of "all" includes the era of the Mashiach.

1. *Devarim* 16:3.

---

them that he had passed away a few months earlier. When the messenger explained the purpose of his visit, the woman dismissed the notion that her husband had suffered injuries, other than some cuts and bruises. He had definitely not been seriously injured.

Unwilling to let it go, the small entourage headed straight to the cemetery, to the man's grave, where they davened on the Rebbe's behalf. After they prayed there, they sent a message to the Rebbe that they had fulfilled his wishes. A few days later, he was released and never charged again.

We must be so careful not to hurt others, even indirectly. For the consequences can be devastating.

רַבּוֹתֵינוּ הִגִּיעַ זְמַן

Our teachers, the time has come...

Making the Z'man

The *Ramak*, Rav Moshe Cordovero, says that if one makes a special *kabbalah* regarding *Krias Shema*, he is able to eradicate a

בָּרוּךְ הַמָּקוֹם, בָּרוּךְ הוּא. בָּרוּךְ שֶׁנָּתַן תּוֹרָה
לְעַמּוֹ יִשְׂרָאֵל, בָּרוּךְ הוּא. כְּנֶגֶד אַרְבָּעָה
בָנִים דִּבְּרָה תוֹרָה. אֶחָד חָכָם, וְאֶחָד רָשָׁע, וְאֶחָד
תָּם, וְאֶחָד שֶׁאֵינוֹ יוֹדֵעַ לִשְׁאוֹל.

---

decree, even if that decree was sealed with a *shevuah*, an oath. Rav Biderman shares a story.

> Late one night, a group of avreichim traveled to the kever of R' Shimon bar Yochai to daven on behalf of their chashuve friend, Rav Yaakov Yoel Hirsch, who was very ill. While there, they spoke with one of the gedolei hador, who told them about the Ramak's assurance. Although they were already careful about reciting Krias Shema in a timely manner, they accepted upon themselves with a firm commitment to recite it with the first z'man. They each resolved to do this for a two-week period, and prayed that in that merit, their friend would have a complete recovery. After they finished davening, they got back into the car and headed back toward Yerushalayim.
>
> It was still dark outside when a powerful thunderstorm struck the area. The driver did his best to control the car, but it flipped over, and only through many nissim did all of the avreichim emerge unscathed.
>
> They looked at their watches. The accident — and their miraculous salvation — had occurred at the exact time of mi'sheyakir, the earliest time for reciting Shema. Precisely at the moment that their commitment went into effect, they were all saved.

כְּנֶגֶד אַרְבָּעָה בָנִים
Concerning four sons...

⋖§ The Fifth Son

Each year, my father shares a homiletic insight on the subject of the four sons, who, he says, correspond to four generations of Jews. The wise son is symbolic of the fiercely religious Jew who came to America at the turn of the 20th century, with all of his traditions. Dressed in his strictly Orthodox garb, he hoped to transplant the traditions of old from Europe to America. But when he came here, he realized it would not be so easy.

B lessed is the Omnipresent; blessed is He. Blessed is the One Who has given the Torah to His people Israel; Blessed is He. Concerning four sons does the Torah speak: a **wise** one, a **wicked** one, a **simple** one, and **one who is unable to ask**.

Soon enough, his son rebelled. This wicked son, the *rasha,* was not interested in what his father had to say. He threw away all the age-old customs and commandments he had been taught, and chose a progressive way of life for himself. This *rasha* still comes to the Seder but doesn't relate to his father at all. His father wants him to follow in the footsteps of his ancestors, but he wants to meld into the American way of life.

The third son, the *tam,* the simple son, comes to the Seder and is somewhat confused. He sees his grandfather, who is still dressed as a traditional Jew. Yet, he also sees his father, who appears to be completely different. This simple child, the third generation, grows up with mixed messages, which are especially obvious at the Seder.

Finally, there is the fourth-generation child, the *she'eino yodei'a lishol,* the one who doesn't even know how to ask. His great-grandfather, the *chacham,* is no longer alive. Buried with him are all the traditions of old. The boy's grandfather, the *rasha,* is completely distant from Torah and its lifestyle. His father grew up without Torah, and he is even further removed. This is the fourth generation of American immigrants. Hanging by a thread, they are nearly completely detached from the thousands of years of Torah-rich heritage. At times, they do conduct a Seder, but it is just a meal of matzah balls, and definitely no questions.

Rav Moshe Wolfson has another way of looking at the Jews who no longer keep the Torah. In *Haggadah shel Pesach Yeisei VeYifsach,* he tells us that there is a fifth son, who is not mentioned in the *Haggadah.* This is because, tragically, when we look for the fifth son, we cannot find him at the Seder.

Rav Wolfson then notes that this explanation connects to the interpretation that the four cups of wine, and the four expressions of redemption, correspond to the four sons. The fifth expression of redemption, "*ve'heiveisi* — and I will bring," corresponds to the cup that we pour for Eliyahu, which is not drunk at the Seder. Only with the arrival of the Mashiach will the fifth cup bring with it the advent

חָכָם מָה הוּא אוֹמֵר? מָה הָעֵדֹת וְהַחֻקִּים
וְהַ֫מִּשְׁפָּטִים אֲשֶׁר צִוָּה יהוה אֱלֹהֵינוּ
אֶתְכֶם?[1] וְאַף אַתָּה אֱמָר לוֹ כְּהִלְכוֹת הַפֶּסַח, אֵין
מַפְטִירִין אַחַר הַפֶּסַח אֲפִיקוֹמָן.

רָשָׁע מָה הוּא אוֹמֵר? מָה הָעֲבֹדָה הַזֹּאת
לָכֶם?[2] לָכֶם וְלֹא לוֹ, וּלְפִי שֶׁהוֹצִיא
אֶת עַצְמוֹ מִן הַכְּלָל, כָּפַר בְּעִקָּר — וְאַף אַתָּה
הַקְהֵה אֶת שִׁנָּיו וֶאֱמָר לוֹ, בַּעֲבוּר זֶה עָשָׂה יהוה
לִי בְּצֵאתִי מִמִּצְרָיִם.[3] לִי וְלֹא לוֹ, אִלּוּ הָיָה שָׁם
לֹא הָיָה נִגְאָל.

תָּם מָה הוּא אוֹמֵר? מַה זֹּאת? וְאָמַרְתָּ אֵלָיו,
בְּחֹזֶק יָד הוֹצִיאָנוּ יהוה מִמִּצְרַיִם מִבֵּית
עֲבָדִים.[4]

וְשֶׁאֵינוֹ יוֹדֵעַ לִשְׁאוֹל, אַתְּ פְּתַח לוֹ. שֶׁנֶּאֱמַר,
וְהִגַּדְתָּ לְבִנְךָ בַּיּוֹם הַהוּא לֵאמֹר, בַּעֲבוּר זֶה עָשָׂה
יהוה לִי בְּצֵאתִי מִמִּצְרָיִם.[5]

---

of the Final Redemption. Only then will we be able to rejoice with
the fulfillment of ve'heiveisi.

The same holds true with the fifth son. Only at the time of the
Final Redemption, when Eliyahu comes, will that fifth child find
his way back home, as symbolized by the opening of the door for
Eliyahu HaNavi when we pour the fifth cup of wine.

Indeed, the day will soon come when the fifth son and the fifth
cup will find their calling, with the coming of Eliyahu HaNavi, as the
pasuk says, "Ve'heishiv leiv avos al banim ve'leiv banim al avosam
— And he will turn back to God the hearts of fathers with their sons
and the hearts of sons with their fathers" (Malachi 3:24).

In the meantime, we must try to draw near those who have veered
from the proper path, while keeping the others from straying — with
lots of love, as well as guidance from our gedolim.

The wise son — what does he say? "What are the testimonies, decrees, and ordinances which HASHEM, our God, has commanded you?"[1] Therefore explain to him the laws of the *pesach*-offering: that one may not eat dessert after the final taste of the *pesach*-offering.

The wicked son — what does he say? "Of what purpose is this work to you?"[2] He says, "To you," thereby excluding himself. By excluding himself from the community of believers, he denies the basic principle of Judaism. Therefore, blunt his teeth and tell him: "It is because of this that HASHEM did so for me when I went out of Egypt."[3] "For me," but not for him — had he been there, he would not have been redeemed.

The simple son — what does he say? "What is this?" Tell him: "With a strong hand did HASHEM take us out of Egypt, from the house of bondage."[4]

As for the son who is unable to ask, you must initiate the subject for him, as it is stated: You shall tell your son on that day: "It is because of this that HASHEM did so for me when I went out of Egypt."[5]

---

1. *Devarim* 6:20. 2. *Shemos* 12:26.
3. Ibid 13:8. 4. Ibid V.14.
5. Ibid V.8.

The Right Response

When it comes to educating our children, the Seder is one of the most important nights of the year.

Everyone is searching for the magical formula for raising good, fine, and honest children who follow in the true path of Torah. But with all the challenges and tests we face, it is not an easy task. Every generation has its concerns and issues that threaten our children's souls. In the beginning and middle of the last century, there were the isms: socialism, Zionism, Bundism. Over the past decade, we have fought the battle against social media and Internet. How do we answer our children when they come and ask us if they can partake in these tempting and desirable forbidden activities?

> Perhaps the following story will shed some light on this perplexing matter. Recently, the Lelover Rebbe visited the city of Los Angeles and stayed at the home of the granddaughter of Rav Shloim'ke of Zhvil. After a day or two, she asked him a very unusual question. "How would you react if your granddaughter asked you for permission to attend a movie with some of her friends?"
>
> The Lelover was stunned. He had not expected that type of question. But then the woman answered the question herself by telling him how her own grandfather had reacted and what he had done. "As the Rebbe knows, I grew up in Jerusalem in the early 1940's, and we suffered very much from a lack of food. Looking for diversions, my friends decided to go to the movies. At first, I abstained from these types of activities. But before long, I was swept up and decided to join them. Eager to enjoy my first experience at the theater, I approached my grandfather and asked him for some money for the entrance fee. Though I had been nervous about his reaction, he just pulled out some money from his pocket and handed it to me, without saying a word.
>
> "Then he walked me to the door. As I was about to leave the house, he told me, 'You asked me for money and I gave it to you. But I want you to know that what you're about to do is tearing my heart into pieces.'
>
> "I looked up and I saw that his eyes were filled with tears. He didn't need to say anything more.
>
> "I never thought of going into the theater again."

This story teaches us how we must deal with challenging requests from our children. There are times that they may press us into giving them something that we don't want to give them. There are only so many times we can say no.

We must let them know that we love them unconditionally, but they should also know what makes us proud and what will break our hearts. Hopefully, if we cry and pray hard enough, they will read our minds and our hearts and fulfill the hopes and dreams that we have for them.

Accommodations

In the late 1940's, Shaul and Yosef Hayim, two Sephardic teenagers, went with their father to an interview for Yeshivas Tiferes Tzion in Bnei Brak. The yeshivah, which was under the direction of Rav Shnaidman, had opened its doors a few years earlier, just as the refugees from Europe were arriving in Eretz Yisrael to rebuild their lives. It was there that Shaul and Yosef were hoping to finally begin to learn and become true bnei Torah.

The boys admitted that since they were Sephardim, they did not speak any Yiddish, the language spoken in the yeshivah. At the end of the interview, Rav Shnaidman expressed his regrets but told them that they would not be accepted into the yeshivah. He explained to Mr. Hayim, the boys' father, "We don't speak the same 'nusach.' We teach in Yiddish and your children speak only Ivrit. I'm sorry, but you're going to have to look elsewhere."

The boys and their father were devastated. They begged and pleaded. Shaul and Yosef promised that they would learn the new language and adapt. But their pleas fell on deaf ears. The rosh yeshivah had made his decision and was not going to reverse it. Disappointed and frustrated, the Hayims went to the Chazon Ish, Rav Avraham Yeshayah Karelitz, and poured out their hearts. After listening carefully, he asked them to tell the rosh yeshivah to come see him.

A few hours later, Mr. Hayim appeared at Rav Shnaidman's door, and the rosh yeshivah reiterated his stance. Mr. Hayim explained that he had only come to give the message that the Chazon Ish wanted to speak to Rav Shnaidman. Immediately, the rosh yeshivah dropped what he was doing and ran over to see the gadol hador.

With trepidation, he entered the Chazon Ish's home. The Chazon Ish asked him if the boys had been interviewed and had asked to be accepted into the yeshivah. He acknowledged that they had, but he was unable to accommodate them since they spoke a different nusach. The Chazon Ish asked him to explain, and he responded that the shiurim in yeshivah were given in Yiddish, and these boys only spoke Ivrit.

The Chazon Ish spoke directly and firmly. "Then teach in Ivrit."

Rav Shnaidman listened and did not question. The Chazon Ish had spoken.

The following Sunday, the Chazon Ish arrived in the yeshivah and gave his weekly bechinah. In Ivrit.

יָכוֹל מֵרֹאשׁ חֹדֶשׁ, תַּלְמוּד לוֹמַר בַּיּוֹם
הַהוּא, אִי בַּיּוֹם
הַהוּא, יָכוֹל מִבְּעוֹד יוֹם, תַּלְמוּד לוֹמַר בַּעֲבוּר זֶה.

Shaul and Yosef grew by leaps and bounds. Before long, they were well on their way to becoming leaders of the Sephardic community.

We must always remember: Our children don't have to fit into our "nusach." We must fit into theirs.

Building a Connection

Eli had only recently lost his father and was having a very difficult time; he was struggling in so many areas. With his spotty attendance in school, he was not able to follow the classes when he did show up. In addition, though his friends wanted to help, they had no idea how to reach him. As he continued his downward spiral, Eli seemed more and more hopeless.

The school administrators recommended a child psychologist, and Eli began therapy. The therapist suggested that Eli stay home from school, except for an hour each day. The hours of therapy drained the family's already strained resources, and a group of individuals approached Rav Avrohom Ganochofsky, Rosh Yeshivah of Tchebin, to see if he would able to assist with the fund-raising efforts.

Rav Avrohom listened carefully to the entire story. After hearing the details, he asked that the boy be brought to him the next day. When Eli arrived and sat across from him, Rav Avrohom asked Eli what he likes to do. At first, Eli was shy and did not know how to respond. After some prodding, he admitted that he likes to play kugelach. Already prepared, Rav Avrohom reached into his desk drawer and pulled out a set of five square gold-colored rocks. He sat down on the floor next to Eli, and the two of them began to play the well-known Jewish variation of jacks. After a half-hour, the boy was smiling and happy.

Rav Avrohom thanked his new friend and told him that he would love to play longer, but he has to go to school and teach. He added, "Just like you, Eli, I have to get back to school. But before you leave, I have an idea. Once a week, I am going to write a riddle for you. Take it with you to school and show it to the boys in your class. When you come back to me with the answer, I will give you prizes to distribute to the boys who figured out the riddle. Then, I

One might think [that the obligation to discuss the Exodus commences] from the first day of the month of Nissan, but the Torah says: "You shall tell your son on that day." But the expression "on that day" could be understood to mean only during the daytime; therefore the Torah adds: "It is because of this [that HASHEM did so for me when I went out of Egypt]."

---

will give you another riddle for the next week. What do you think?" With that, he presented Eli with his first riddle.

Eli was overjoyed; he could not control his smile. Beaming, he ran outside, where his brother was waiting for him. His brother hardly recognized Eli. It had been so long since his little brother had smiled.

The next day, Eli went to school and presented the riddle. All the children surrounded him, and they were superimpressed with the riddle and the story behind it. They could not believe that Eli had such a great person as a close friend. Before long, everyone wanted to be involved with Eli. He distributed the prizes and conveyed the riddle week after week. Before long, he was, once more, a growing and happy child, like all of his friends.

With time, Eli developed into a true ben Torah and a budding talmid chacham. Eventually, he was blessed with a warm and loving family of his own.

At times, we have to bring ourselves down to a child's level in order to reach him. But once we connect, there is no telling how high he will soar.

יָכוֹל מֵרֹאשׁ חֹדֶשׁ
One might think...

◄§ The *Havah Amina* of Life

The *baal Haggadah* states: One may think that the obligation to discuss the Exodus commences with the first day of the month of Nissan, but the Torah says, *"Ve'higadeta le'vincha ba'yom hahu* — You shall tell your son on that day" (*Shemos* 13:8). The *baal Haggadah* then suggests that we may think that one may begin while it is still day, on Erev Pesach. Therefore, the *pasuk* reveals that the mitzvah to discuss the Exodus must be fulfilled at a time when the matzah and *maror* lie before you, which is at the Seder.

Why did the author choose to use this particular paragraph, and with this terminology? Why all the back-and-forth? Additionally, why is this the paragraph that concludes the first part of the narrative, which speaks about the questions and answers, and serves as a prelude to the second part of the narrative, which speaks about our forefathers serving idols?

Rav Simchah Bunim of Pshis'cha would say, "One needs to exert much effort on the *havah amina* [thought process] of the Gemara, for the *chiyus* of *Olam Hazeh* comes from the *havah amina*. And the *maskana* [conclusion] is *Olam Haba.*" As an answer to our question, the *Lev Simchah* would quote his father, the *Imrei Emes*, who would take Rav Simchah Bunim's statement one step further. Not only do the energy and *chiyus* of *Galus* come through the *havah amina* of the Gemara, but specifically through the *havah amina* of this passage in the *Haggadah.*

The *Haggadah Likkutei Av* explains that this world is the thought process. It is here that we struggle to understand all the twists and turns of Creation. We have so many questions and so few answers. However, there will come a time when all of our questions will be answered, when we will understand everything and gain the clarity we so desperately seek.

The main topic of study in our Exile is the Talmud Bavli, which is filled with one *havah amina* after another. There are times when there is no answer at all, when the Gemara concludes with the word תֵּיקוּ, which means "let it stand [unresolved]," but which has homiletically been said to stand for: "תִּשְׁבִּי יְתָרֵץ קוּשְׁיוֹת וְאַבָּעְיוֹת — Eliyahu [HaTishbi] will answer our questions and our problems."

On a deeper level, this does not refer only to the questions on the Gemara, but it refers to the many questions we have in trying to understand our pain and suffering. Some of those questions will remain unanswered while we are in Exile. When Eliyahu HaNavi comes, he will answer all of those questions. Indeed, *teiku.*

Rav Nachman of Breslov writes that תֵּיקוּ is a shortened version of תִּיקוּן, which means complete and total rectification. Perhaps we can take this further and say that תִּיקוּן contains the same letters as קִינוֹת, the Lamentations we cry for the painful events that have transpired over the last 2,000 years. When Eliyahu HaNavi arrives, there will be a *tikkun* for our *Kinnos,* as well.

The Talmud Yerushalmi, on the other hand, is comprised mostly of the final *maskana* of the Gemara. The *Sifsei Tzaddik* once said that when Mashiach comes, our main *limud* will be Talmud Yerushalmi; at that time, all of our questions will be answered. The thought process will be complete. But until then, we must struggle to understand. The harder we work at it, the more energy and *chiyus* we will gain.

Perhaps it is for this reason that we conclude the first portion of the narrative with this paragraph. We must know that there will be questions. We will try to answer as many of them as possible. We will tell our children as much as we know. But they must realize that at times, we will have no answers. There will be tragedies that leave us speechless, but that is part of the process.

This paragraph — and the above explanation — serve as the perfect prelude to the next portion of the narrative. As we ready ourselves to enter the exile of Egypt, we must be aware that there will be many questions. Children will be drowned in the river, while others will be used as mortar for bricks. There will be senseless bloodshed. Indeed, there will be many a *havah amina*.

But in the end, there will be a *maskana*, one that we will truly understand.

Tatte Leben

It was a few short days before Pesach, and a prominent rav from the southern part of Eretz Yisrael was scheduled to go on a trip, along with his wife and several of his children. Another one of his daughters also wanted to come along, but she was not feeling well. She begged her father over and over, but he was firm in his stance. If she was sick, she could not join them.

Frustrated that she was being left behind, she blurted out, "Abba, you don't love me!"

That night, the rav, Rav Shimshon Pincus, lost his life in a horrific car accident, along with his wife and daughter; several of his children were injured, one critically.

The daughter who was left behind is alive and well.

Perhaps that was Rav Shimshon's dying message to his daughter. There are times when, despite all of our efforts, we don't get what we want in life. Inevitably, we think that it is because our Father, the Almighty, does not love us.

But He knows what is best for us. He knows the truth.

בַּעֲבוּר זֶה לֹא אָמַרְתִּי אֶלָּא בְּשָׁעָה שֶׁיֵּשׁ מַצָּה וּמָרוֹר מֻנָּחִים לְפָנֶיךָ.

And the truth is that our Abba loves us.
It is all part of the *havah amina*.

A second-grade rebbi told me that in his first year of teaching, one of the children in his class lost his father. He was uncertain, as a teacher, how to handle the situation. At the time, he had been teaching the boys the Mah Nishtanah. As many teach it, he began with the Yiddish words, "Tatte leben — dear Father..." The rebbi knew that when the boy was going to recite the Mah Nishtanah, it would, no doubt, be a heartrending scene.

His colleagues suggested that he teach him, "Mama leben — dear Mother," as the boy was going to be saying it to his mother. Finally, the rebbi asked one of the leading roshei yeshivah what to do. He told him that the boy should say, "Tatte leben," because the child still had his Tatte in Himmel — his loving Father in Heaven.

Although we cannot comprehend all the suffering we see, and we have not yet arrived at the *maskana*, we must remember that we always have a loving Father in Heaven.

בְּשָׁעָה שֶׁיֵּשׁ מַצָּה וּמָרוֹר
At the time when matzah and maror...

The Mechutanim

The *Beis Avraham/ Beis Aharon Haggadah*, written by Rav Avraham Aharon Friedman during World War II, is a remarkable *Haggadah*. It brings nine distinctive ways to understand the *Haggadah*. Included is the following story.

*Great Chassidic leaders would occasionally glean inspiration from simple Jews. For this reason, one Seder night, the Sar Shalom, Rav Shalom of Belz, went for a walk accompanied by his Chassidim. As they passed the home of an ignorant Jew, they heard him reading from the paragraph of Yachol MeiRosh Chodesh. Instead of reading "be'sha'ah she'yeish matzah u'maror **munachim** lefanecha — at the*

The pronoun "this" implies something tangible, thus, "You shall tell your son" applies only at the time when matzah and maror lie before you — at the Seder.

---

time when matzah and maror **lie** before you," the simpleton read, "be'sha'ah she'yeish matzah u'maror **mechutanim** lefanecha — at the time when matzah and maror **are related by marriage** before you." The Rebbe read deeply into the innocent mistake, and he explained his feelings with a story:

A wealthy and prominent individual had a daughter whom he cherished, and he wouldn't marry her off to just anyone. Eventually, he came across a young man who, he believed, was the perfect match. However, the boy came from a very poor home, where there was very little to eat. In fact, when the match was suggested, the boy's father requested that they wait a few months until he could pay for his end of the wedding. But the rich man was so anxious and eager that he was willing to forgo a fancy wedding; he was even prepared to make do with black bread.

Once they were married, the magnate planned to put his son-in-law into business. He knew that with his talents, the young man would become successful immediately. Still, he always wanted to be able to remind his son-in-law how much he had given him. Therefore, he took one of the torn garments that the young man wore prior to the wedding and put it aside, to use whenever a reminder was necessary.

The son-in-law was also prepared to remind his father-in-law how badly he had wanted him to marry his daughter. So he took some of the black bread that was served at the wedding, and put it aside to remind his father-in-law how he had wanted to make the wedding without delay, so that no one else would snatch him away.

Sure enough, after a number of years, the father-in-law was ready to remind his son-in-law of his humble beginnings. He pulled out a torn jacket and showed it to his son-in-law. His son-in-law would not be outdone. He took out a bag that contained a moldy piece of black bread from the wedding, to show his father-in-law just how badly he had wanted him as a son-in-law.

As the Sar Shalom concluded his story, the explanation was clear to all. The Almighty, the rich Man, had a beautiful daughter, the Torah, and searched for the proper mate. Finally, He found us,

מִתְּחִלָּה עוֹבְדֵי עֲבוֹדָה זָרָה הָיוּ אֲבוֹתֵינוּ,
וְעַכְשָׁו קֵרְבָנוּ הַמָּקוֹם לַעֲבוֹדָתוֹ.
שֶׁנֶּאֱמַר, וַיֹּאמֶר יְהוֹשֻׁעַ אֶל כָּל הָעָם, כֹּה אָמַר
יְהוה אֱלֹהֵי יִשְׂרָאֵל, בְּעֵבֶר הַנָּהָר יָשְׁבוּ אֲבוֹתֵיכֶם
מֵעוֹלָם, תֶּרַח אֲבִי אַבְרָהָם וַאֲבִי נָחוֹר, וַיַּעַבְדוּ
אֱלֹהִים אֲחֵרִים. וָאֶקַּח אֶת אֲבִיכֶם אֶת אַבְרָהָם
מֵעֵבֶר הַנָּהָר, וָאוֹלֵךְ אוֹתוֹ בְּכָל אֶרֶץ כְּנָעַן,
וָאַרְבֶּה אֶת זַרְעוֹ, וָאֶתֵּן לוֹ אֶת יִצְחָק. וָאֶתֵּן
לְיִצְחָק אֶת יַעֲקֹב וְאֶת עֵשָׂו, וָאֶתֵּן לְעֵשָׂו אֶת
הַר שֵׂעִיר לָרֶשֶׁת אוֹתוֹ, וְיַעֲקֹב וּבָנָיו יָרְדוּ
מִצְרָיִם.[1]

---

the perfect groom, the Jewish people, and He wanted to make the
wedding immediately. But He always wanted to remind us of our
origins. This is symbolic of the bitter herb, the maror, that we eat.
It signifies where we come from — Egypt — with all of its suffering
and persecution. But we, as the son-in-law, also want to remind
our Father-in-law how quickly He wanted to make the wedding.
He did not wait to make a large affair. Instead, we celebrated over
some black bread — the matzah — that we carried on our backs
out of Egypt. Even when we are lowly, Hashem still wants us.

Tonight, at the Seder, to remind us of all that Hashem, our Father-
in-law, did for us, and to remind Him of how badly He wanted us,
the son-in-law, we eat the bitter herbs and we eat the matzah.

Indeed, *"be'sha'ah she'yeish matzah u'maror* **mechutanim**
lefanecha."

מִתְּחִלָּה
Originally...

◄§ Feeling the Closeness

The *baal Haggadah* writes that our ancestors served idols, and
now the Almighty has brought us close to His service. The *Chasan
Sofer* gives a magnificent insight into the length that Hashem goes to

Originally our ancestors were idol worshipers, but now the Omnipresent has brought us near to His service, as it is written: Yehoshua said to all the people, "So says HASHEM, God of Israel: Your fathers always lived beyond the Euphrates River, Terach the father of Avraham and Nachor, and they served other gods. Then I took your father Avraham from beyond the river and I led him through all the land of Canaan. I multiplied his offspring and gave him Yitzchak. To Yitzchak I gave Yaakov and Eisav; to Eisav I gave Mount Seir to inherit, but Yaakov and his children went down to Egypt."[1]

---

1. *Yehoshua* 24:2-4.

---

show us His love. We would think that since the Jewish people had served idols, we had, in essence, felt that we were alienated from our Father in Heaven. Yet, He did just the opposite and brought us closer to His service.

When the *Haggadah* uses the word "*ve'achshav* — and now," this one word says it all. Hashem, in His kindness and benevolence, does not look at our past; He looks only at the way we are now. This means that even though the Jewish people worshiped idols in the past, that is all but erased. Hashem chooses to focus on the here and now. This word — *ve'achshav* — brings with it so much hope, so much encouragement. We need not be bogged down with guilt and insecurity about our inadequacies and shortcomings. We don't have to wallow in the mistakes we have made. It is all about the present: what we want to do now; what we hope to become now.

The Gemara in *Berachos* (7a) tells the story of Rabbi Yishmael ben Elisha, the Kohen Gadol. One Yom Kippur, he went into the innermost chambers of the *Beis HaMikdash* — the Holy of Holies. There, in a vision, he saw the angel Kasriel sitting in front of Hashem. Hashem then asked Rabbi Yishmael for a blessing. The blessing he gave Him was that Hashem should be able to control His anger with compassion and be merciful toward His children, the Jewish people.

On the day of Yom Kippur, we would have expected that Hashem wants us to focus on serving Him. Nevertheless, He showed His love

בָּרוּךְ שׁוֹמֵר הַבְטָחָתוֹ לְיִשְׂרָאֵל, בָּרוּךְ הוּא.
שֶׁהַקָּדוֹשׁ בָּרוּךְ הוּא חִשַּׁב אֶת הַקֵּץ,
לַעֲשׂוֹת כְּמָה שֶׁאָמַר לְאַבְרָהָם אָבִינוּ בִּבְרִית
בֵּין הַבְּתָרִים, שֶׁנֶּאֱמַר, וַיֹּאמֶר לְאַבְרָם, יָדֹעַ תֵּדַע
כִּי גֵר יִהְיֶה זַרְעֲךָ בְּאֶרֶץ לֹא לָהֶם, וַעֲבָדוּם וְעִנּוּ

for us by asking for a *berachah*, in which Rabbi Yishmael blessed
Him that He should have mercy on Klal Yisrael.

For Hashem just wants to be close to us.

Never Give Up

*The pasuk in Devarim (20:14) states: "Ve'achalta es shelal oivecha
— You shall eat the booty of your enemies." Rav Yaakov Galinsky
quoted a well-known statement from Rav Nachman of Breslov.
The word אֹיְבֶיךָ, your enemies, can stand for: אֵין יֵאוּשׁ בָּעוֹלָם כְּלָל —
There is no [reason for] despair in the world at all.*

Yei'ush, despair, is really our worst enemy. It keeps us from
getting closer to the *Ribbono Shel Olam*, and closer to our goals.

To prove his point, Rav Galinsky told the following story.

*The Novaradok Yeshivah in Mezritch was struggling mightily to
provide food for its students. The rosh yeshivah, Rav Dovid Bliacher,
asked the Jews of the neighboring villages if they could host the
boys and provide them with food. This is the way he sustained
the nearly 200 boys in his yeshivah, as well as the others who were
under his authority.*

*Before Pesach, he had the additional responsibility of raising
money to provide flour for matzos. Somehow, he managed to
procure the flour, which he placed in the attic of the beis midrash,
to make sure that it did not come into contact with water. Knowing
how difficult the yeshivah's financial situation was, when the boys
learned that they would have enough matzos for all of them, they
were ecstatic. But their joy was short lived.*

*Right before Pesach, a torrential downpour soaked the city. The
fierce storm broke through the roof of the beis midrash and ruined
the flour that was stored there. Though they were devastated,
the boys set out once more to try to get hold of matzos. But it
seemed almost impossible, and they began to grow despondent.*

B lessed is He Who keeps His pledge to Israel; Blessed is He! For the Holy One, Blessed is He, calculated the end of the bondage in order to do as He said to our father Avraham at the Covenant between the Parts, as it is stated: He said to Avram, "Know with certainty that your offspring will be aliens in a land not their own, they will serve them, and they will oppress

---

Rav Dovid called the boys together to give them hope and encouragement. "Rabbosai, I have four questions to ask you. First of all, Who commanded us to eat matzah?" They looked at each other quizzically. Obviously it was the Almighty.

Rav Dovid continued. "The second question is: Who helped me collect the flour the first time when most thought I would never be able to do it?" Again, they answered that this was the work of the Almighty.

"The third question I have is: Who is the one Who brought this ferocious and fierce storm, which broke our roof and ruined the flour?" Once more, they nodded toward each other in agreement. Of course, it was the Almighty.

"Finally, my fourth question is: Who will be the One to enable us to procure the flour one more time so we can have beautiful matzos?" One last time, they called out, "The Ribbono Shel Olam will."

With newfound vigor, energy, and hope, they waited to see how the matter would be resolved. Sure enough, that evening, a letter arrived in the mail. It contained a large sum of money from a donor — enough to purchase the very best matzos for the entire yeshivah. Ein yei'ush ba'olam klal!

בָּרוּךְ שׁוֹמֵר

Blessed is He Who keeps...

∽§ Unimaginable Sacrifices

As mentioned earlier (To "Halt Cup") the 430 years of the *Galus* of Mitzrayim began with the *bris bein habesarim*. At the time of the treaty (*Bereishis* 15), the Almighty commanded Avraham to take

אֹתָם, אַרְבַּע מֵאוֹת שָׁנָה. וְגַם אֶת הַגּוֹי אֲשֶׁר
יַעֲבֹדוּ דָן אָנֹכִי, וְאַחֲרֵי כֵן יֵצְאוּ בִּרְכֻשׁ גָּדוֹל.[1]

---

three goats, three heifers, three rams, a turtledove, and a young dove. Avraham cut up all the animals, but not the birds. Birds of prey then descended upon the carcasses and Avraham drove them away. Later, Avraham fell into a deep sleep, and Hashem told him about the *Galus* of Mitzrayim and the subsequent Exodus. Then a smoky furnace appeared, from which a torch of fire passed through the pieces. What does all this represent?

The *Sefer HaIkrim* explains that the Jewish people are connected to the Almighty, as one unit. At the *bris bein habesarim*, when Hashem passed through the cut-up pieces with a torch of fire, He demonstrated the strong connection between Hashem and Bnei Yisrael — that we are really one; we are connected more closely than two parts of one animal.

When the Yidden were ready to leave Mitzrayim, they were saved on account of two commandments, which have the trait of *mesirus nefesh* at their core: *bris milah* and *korban Pesach*. *Chazal* (*Gittin* 57b) say that the *pasuk* in *Tehillim* (44:23): "*Ki alecha horagnu chol hayom* — Because for Your sake we are killed all the time*,*" is referring to *bris milah*. When a man takes his precious 8-day-old infant and spills his blood, it is considered just like a *korban* before Hashem. When the Jewish people sacrificed the *korban pesach* in Mitzrayim, they displayed great self-sacrifice, as the lamb was the deity of Egypt, and the Egyptians could have stoned them for using their god as an offering. By performing the mitzvos of *bris milah* and *korban pesach*, the Yidden demonstrated that they were willing to sacrifice for the Almighty, and they became one with Him.

The *Chassid Yaavetz* notes that during the period of the Spanish Inquisition, the first ones who gave up their lives without any questions were the women and the simple individuals. This is because there were many brilliant philosophers in Spain, who reached exalted levels of belief through their deep philosophical discussions. When it came to practice, however, they had all the reasons in the world to explain why they should save themselves. But when one receives his *emunah* as a transmission from father to son, going all the way back to *Maamad Har Sinai* and *Yetzias*

them four hundred years; but also upon the nation which they shall serve will I execute judgment, and afterward they shall leave with great possessions."[1]

---

1. *Bereishis* 15:13-14.

Mitzrayim, then there are no questions. Hence, there is no need for answers, as an act of *mesirus nefesh* is performed simply because this is what we learned from our parents.

We say in *Hallel* (*Tehillim* 114:2), "*Hayesah Yehudah le'kadsho* — Yehudah became His sanctuary." In his *Haggadah Maaseh Nissim*, *Rav Yaakov of Lisa* asks: Shouldn't the *pasuk* have said "*hayah* — he was," in the male form, rather than "*hayesah* — she was"? He answers that the *pasuk* is referring to Tamar, who was prepared to jump into the fire to save Yehudah from embarrassment (*Bereishis* 38). As the great-great-great-grandmother of Nachshon ben Aminadav, she instilled in him the courage and ability to sacrifice himself for the Almighty. That is where he received the power to jump into the Yam Suf with *mesirus nefesh* (*Sotah* 37a). This is because women have the ability to imbue future generations with *emunah* and *mesirus nefesh*.

The *Zera Kodesh of Ropshitz* explains that the reason the *Haggadah* tells us the story of the five great *tzaddikim* who spent the night in Bnei Brak is to show that we culminate the night with the declaration of *Krias Shema*, the ultimate declaration of belief in Hashem and our willingness to sacrifice our lives for His Name. That is the purpose of the entire Seder: to understand that our lives are to be lived with *mesirus nefesh* for the *Ribbono Shel Olam*. And it was specifically the *Krias Shema* of *Shacharis*, not the one from *Maariv*. Why?

Rav Dessler explains that the *Krias Shema* of *Shacharis,* which is said in the morning when we can see clearly, symbolizes free choice. The *Krias Shema* of *Maariv* represents our declaration in the dark period of night. During those times, we really have no choice but to serve the Almighty. But in the morning, we have a choice, and we still choose to serve the Almighty by declaring *Shema Yisrael*.

A Meaningful Life

Lieutenant Emanuel Yehudah Moreno was referred to as one of the most prestigious soldiers in the Israeli Army, and was revered by his fellow officers. This was not only because he spearheaded

The matzos are covered and the cups lifted as the following paragraph is proclaimed joyously. Upon its conclusion, the cups are put down and the matzos are uncovered.

וְהִיא שֶׁעָמְדָה לַאֲבוֹתֵינוּ וְלָנוּ, שֶׁלֹּא אֶחָד בִּלְבַד עָמַד עָלֵינוּ לְכַלּוֹתֵנוּ. אֶלָּא שֶׁבְּכָל דּוֹר וָדוֹר עוֹמְדִים עָלֵינוּ לְכַלּוֹתֵנוּ, וְהַקָּדוֹשׁ בָּרוּךְ הוּא מַצִּילֵנוּ מִיָּדָם.

---

highly dangerous rescue missions. Rather, he also imbued in his fellow soldiers respect for one's fellow man, and a deep love for a fellow Jew. He even found time to learn Daf Yomi and hilchos lashon hara, along with Sefer HaTanya.

Perhaps his greatest legacy was a conversation he had with a fellow soldier, which took place a few hours before a fateful mission. The following letter, which describes this conversation, was written by that comrade to Emanuel's family after Emanuel was killed in battle.

I would like to share with you a conversation I had with Emanuel on Friday, just a few hours before we boarded the helicopter. I don't remember the exact words, but this is the gist of it. We sat and talked about different things that could happen to us, and what we would do in each case. This was just two weeks after the sad incident in which a helicopter was hit by a rocket and five soldiers were killed, and so there was a general vague apprehension regarding flying helicopters over Lebanon.

Emanuel asked me, "So what would you do if, God forbid, our chopper is hit by a missile and you have five seconds left until it crashes?" I answered, "I don't know. I guess I would be very sad and scared, and I would close my eyes and wait for my life to end as quickly and as painlessly as possible." Emanuel thought for a moment and then said, "What I would do — and this is what you should do, too — is say Shema Yisrael."

I looked at him and said, "O.K., you'll say Shema Yisrael. But what will it give you? Either way, a second later, the helicopter will crash and we will all die." Then he told me something that I'm convinced will remain with me all my life:

"If a person has five seconds left to live, and those seconds still have significance for him, that means that his whole life had meaning. But if the person has five seconds left, and he does not realize their

I t is this that has stood by our fathers and us. For not only one has risen against us to annihilate us, but in every generation they rise against us to annihilate us. But the Holy One, Blessed is He, rescues us from their hand.

---

importance, then apparently his whole life had no meaning. For we don't live just to satisfy our desires, or just for momentary pleasures; our lives are a stop on the way to the next stage."

This thought has been with me from the moment of the terrible tragedy, and it helps me, in that I know that as far as Emanuel is concerned, his life did not end with that terrible wound that killed him. Rather, one stage ended and he proceeded to the next stage, one that is even more important than this one: a stage that can be reached only by living this life.

It is crucial to convey this lesson to our children. We are deeply connected to the Almighty and willing to die for Him. We live our lives with the knowledge that if we would ever have to, we will be prepared to give our souls back to Him and proclaim, "*Shema Yisrael Hashem Elokeinu Hashem Echad.*"

וְהִיא שֶׁעָמְדָה
It is this that has stood...

אֶלָּא שֶׁבְּכָל דּוֹר וָדוֹר
but in every generation...

In Every Generation

It was customary for the Chortkover Rebbe, Rav Yisrael Friedman, to conduct his tisch on Friday evenings during the winter months, and on Shabbos mornings in the summer. One week during the winter months, he notified his attendants that the coming Shabbos he would be eating privately with his family.

That Shabbos, Rav Yosef of Sanik planned to visit the Rebbe and attend the tisch. When he arrived, however, he was disappointed

צֵא וּלְמַד מַה בִּקֵּשׁ לָבָן הָאֲרַמִּי לַעֲשׂוֹת לְיַעֲקֹב אָבִינוּ, שֶׁפַּרְעֹה לֹא גָזַר אֶלָּא עַל הַזְּכָרִים, וְלָבָן בִּקֵּשׁ לַעֲקוֹר אֶת הַכֹּל. שֶׁנֶּאֱמַר:

to hear that the Rebbe was planning on conducting a private meal that Friday night. He had traveled specifically to join the Rebbe's tisch, and now he would not have the opportunity. He decided that he was going to hide in the Rebbe's dining room and watch the goings-on at the Rebbe's Shabbos table from his hiding place.

On Friday night, Rav Yosef somehow managed to hide in the room. First, he watched the Rebbe sing Shalom Aleichem. Rav Yisrael then raised the cup of wine to make Kiddush, and lingered for a short while. For some reason, he put the cup down and made an announcement. "It is accepted among our family that when one finds himself in the midst of a frightening situation, he should articulate, 'Gut fun Levi Yitzchak ben Sarah Sasha, helf mir — G-d of Levi Yitzchak son of Sarah Sasha, help me.' [This invokes the merit of the great defender of Israel, Rav Levi Yitzchak of Berditchev.]" And then, once more, he picked up the cup and made Kiddush.

Rav Yosef presumed that the Rebbe must have known somehow that he was hiding in the room and was directing his words toward him. He knew that there would come a time in which he would need to invoke the merit of Rav Levi Yitzchak of Berditchev, and this would bring about a salvation. After the meal, he waited until everyone left before sneaking out of his hiding place. Later, he told his family about what had transpired, and instructed them to remember the phrase, to recite in their moment of desperation.

Many years passed. Although Rav Yosef left this world, his children and grandchildren continued to hold onto this treasured segulah. They still did not know when it would be needed, but they sensed that one day it would.

The year was 1940, and the Nazis came rolling through Europe, destroying everyone and anything in their path. They came into one village, Krasnau, and rounded up 30 Jews from the city, including one of Rav Yosef's grandchildren. The men were taken outside of the city and instructed to dig graves for themselves. At the last

$$\bigodot \text{o and learn what Lavan the Aramean attempt-}$$
ed to do to our father Yaakov! For Pharaoh
decreed only against the males, and Lavan attempted to uproot everything, as it is said:

---

moment, as the Nazis were about to shoot, Rav Yosef's grandchild
cried out, "Gut fun Levi Yitzchak ben Sarah Sasha, helf mir!"

The Nazi guards grabbed him and demanded that he reveal
what he had just said. He replied, "I was crying to go back to my
house." The sadistic commanding officer decided to grant his
wish. He commanded him to stop digging and to run toward
the nearby river. As soon as he jumped into the shallow river and
began making his way across, the Nazis began to shoot. Although
they sprayed bullets all around him, miraculously, none of them
hit him. When he reached the other side, he climbed out of the
river and ran into the forest, where he hid for the next three days.
Eventually, he returned home.

When he entered his house, he found his family members
sitting shivah for him. Upon seeing him, they began to cry, but this
time the tears were tears of joy.

The man survived the war, and raised a family of bnei Torah.

We say in *Ve'hi She'amdah,* "For not only one has risen against
us to annihilate us, but in every generation they rise against us to
annihilate us. But *HaKadosh Baruch Hu* rescues us from their hand."

צֵא וּלְמַד
Go and learn...

בְּדָמַיִךְ חֲיִי
Through your blood shall you live!

◆§ Through the Blood and the Silence

The *baal Haggadah* quotes the *pasuk* from *Yechezkel* (16: 6) that
says that the Almighty sees that we are wallowing in our blood, and He
declares, "*Be'damayich cha'yi … be'damayich cha'yi* — Through your
blood you shall live … through your blood you shall live." To what does
this double expression refer? And how are we wallowing in our blood?

אֲרַמִּי אֹבֵד אָבִי, וַיֵּרֶד מִצְרַיְמָה וַיָּגָר שָׁם בִּמְתֵי מְעָט, וַיְהִי שָׁם לְגוֹי, גָּדוֹל עָצוּם וָרָב.[1]

וַיֵּרֶד מִצְרַיְמָה. אָנוּס עַל פִּי הַדִּבּוּר.

וַיָּגָר שָׁם. מְלַמֵּד שֶׁלֹּא יָרַד יַעֲקֹב אָבִינוּ לְהִשְׁתַּקֵּעַ בְּמִצְרַיִם, אֶלָּא לָגוּר שָׁם. שֶׁנֶּאֱמַר, וַיֹּאמְרוּ אֶל פַּרְעֹה, לָגוּר בָּאָרֶץ בָּאנוּ, כִּי אֵין מִרְעֶה לַצֹּאן אֲשֶׁר לַעֲבָדֶיךָ, כִּי כָבֵד הָרָעָב בְּאֶרֶץ כְּנָעַן, וְעַתָּה יֵשְׁבוּ נָא עֲבָדֶיךָ בְּאֶרֶץ גֹּשֶׁן.[2]

בִּמְתֵי מְעָט. כְּמָה שֶׁנֶּאֱמַר, בְּשִׁבְעִים נֶפֶשׁ יָרְדוּ אֲבֹתֶיךָ מִצְרַיְמָה, וְעַתָּה שָׂמְךָ יהוה אֱלֹהֶיךָ כְּכוֹכְבֵי הַשָּׁמַיִם לָרֹב.[3]

וַיְהִי שָׁם לְגוֹי. מְלַמֵּד שֶׁהָיוּ יִשְׂרָאֵל מְצֻיָּנִים שָׁם.

גָּדוֹל עָצוּם. כְּמָה שֶׁנֶּאֱמַר, וּבְנֵי יִשְׂרָאֵל פָּרוּ וַיִּשְׁרְצוּ וַיִּרְבּוּ וַיַּעַצְמוּ בִּמְאֹד מְאֹד, וַתִּמָּלֵא הָאָרֶץ אֹתָם.[4]

Simply understood, the *Haggadah* is referring to the two mitzvos involving blood: the *korban pesach* and *bris milah*. These two mitzvos, which the Jews performed right before the Exodus, provided them with the merit they needed in order to be able to leave Egypt.

But the Klausenberger Rebbe, Rav Yekusiel Yehudah Halberstam, gave another explanation.

The Rebbe lost his entire family — his wife and 11 children — in the war. His entire universe was no longer. With incredible fortitude, he rebuilt his life and rebuilt the lives of thousands of others. People turned to him for advice and hung onto his every word. His upbeat perspective infused the hopeless and lifeless souls with the belief that they had what to live for.

He constructed new Sanz-Klausenberg communities in the city of Netanya in Israel, and in Union City, New Jersey, and was behind many important Torah and chesed institutions and initiatives.

An Aramean attempted to destroy my father. Then he descended to Egypt and sojourned there, with few people; and there he became a nation — great, mighty, and numerous.[1]

Then he descended to Egypt — compelled by Divine decree.

He sojourned there — this teaches that our father Yaakov did not descend to Egypt to settle, but only to sojourn temporarily, as it says: They (the sons of Yaakov) said to Pharaoh: "We have come to sojourn in this land because there is no pasture for the flocks of your servants, because the famine is severe in the Land of Canaan. And now, please let your servants dwell in the land of Goshen."[2]

With few people — as it says: With seventy persons, your forefathers descended to Egypt, and now HASHEM, your God, has made you as numerous as the stars of heaven.[3]

There he became a nation — this teaches that the Israelites were distinctive there.

Great, mighty — as it says: And the Children of Israel were fruitful, increased greatly, multiplied, and became very, very mighty; and the land was filled with them.[4]

---

1. *Devarim* 26:5. 2. *Bereishis* 47:4.
3. *Devarim* 10:22. 4. *Shemos* 1:7.

One year at the Pesach Seder, when he was already living in the United States, as he came to the words "Be'damayich cha'yi," the Rebbe launched into a powerful and meaningful derashah. He explained that the word "be'damayich" can have two meanings: blood, which is the basic explanation, and silence, as in "Vayidom Aharon — And Aharon was silent" (Vayikra 10:3).

The Rebbe then raised his voice and said, "On this holy night, we sit together and we speak about the greatness of the Jewish people, how they accept upon themselves the yoke of our exile with total trust in the Almighty. The Almighty says, 'I know that you have endured some of the most horrific atrocities man has ever seen; I saw you wallowing in your blood — *misboseses be'damayich*. But, *va'omar lach* — I can tell you: Be'damayich cha'yi ... *be'damayich cha'yi*. Your whole life is filled with spilled blood and sacrifices in the Name of Hashem, but even so, you accept it all in silence and love, without complaint.'"

The Rebbe confirmed that he witnessed this uncompromising faith in the darkest moments of the death camps, and he said, "Hashem also witnessed all this."

With that he concluded, "And we hope that soon a Bas Kol will comfort us with the coming of Mashiach."

In a similar vein . . .

At the Leil HaSeder Rav Yehudah Leib Nekritz, the rosh yeshivah of Novaradok, said that when his yeshivah was sent to Siberia during the war, they were all sentenced to 20 years of imprisonment. He explained that despite the intense cold and suffering, the yeshivah bachurim and rebbeim had only one goal: to live their lives as Jews. At the end of the summer, they already began to worry about how they were going to obtain matzah.

At great risk, they began to squirrel away stalks of grain each day as they worked, and they brought them to their quarters. After several months, they separated the wheat from the chaff, and ground the kernels in a coffee grinder that they found. Step by step, they used makeshift contraptions to prepare the dough for a few matzos, and they worked tirelessly to make the oven in their quarters kosher for Pesach. They stayed up many nights, finally managing to bake a few tiny and very hard matzos.

Their landlords, a non-Jewish farmer and his wife, kept a watchful eye on them on the night of the Seder, waiting for the moment when they would mix the blood into the matzos, as they had heard so many times during their youth.

In truth, Rav Nekritz concluded, the matzos were mixed with blood, which oozed from their bleeding hearts: "Be'damayich cha'yi."

By Your Blood You Shall Live

The following story was related by Reb Dani Halperin. About a decade ago, Reb Dani's wife gave birth to a healthy baby boy. When *he asked his grandfather, Reb Yisroel Menachem (Joe) Plawes, to serve as sandak, his grandfather adamantly refused. It seemed that his grandfather never accepted the honor, and his reason seemed to be connected to his experiences during World War II and his queasiness upon seeing blood.*

After Reb Dani pressed his grandfather for an explanation, he told him the following story:

"During the war, the Nazis lined us up in front of a firing squad, and began shooting; they hit most of us, but not me. Next to me stood a dear friend. As he died, he fell on me and his blood poured onto me. One sadistic Nazi, not satisfied with merely shooting at us all, actually began poking us to ensure that he had successfully murdered all his prey. I lay there, feigning death. The ruse worked. Since I was so still and I was covered in the blood of my friend, he presumed I was dead.

"Dani, do you know which pasuk flashed through my mind at those harrowing moments? 'Va'e'evor alayich va'ereich misboseses be'damayich, va'omar lach be'damayich cha'yi — And I passed over you and saw you wallowing in [your] blood and I said to you: Through [your] blood you shall live.' Hashem determined that through this blood — the blood of my friend — would come my yeshuah.

"So now, Dani, do you fully understand why I get queasy when seeing blood? That's why I cannot accept sandeka'us."

Instead of saying that he understood and then excusing his grandfather, Reb Dani replied, "Zeidy, that's exactly why you should accept sandeka'us."

His grandfather was incredulous and asked for an explanation. Reb Dani said, "Zeidy, you stopped after the first time it says 'be'damayich cha'yi.' Yet, the pasuk repeats these words. And from here, Chazal learn that there were two bloods: the blood of korban pesach and the blood of bris milah.

"You clearly experienced the blood of the korban, so please honor us by being sandak and fulfilling the second 'be'damayich cha'yi' at our son's bris milah."

Hearing these words, his grandfather accepted the honor of the second blood.

✑ Giving Our Lives

For many years, blood libels have stalked the Jewish people. We have suffered immeasurable pain and countless deaths because of these false charges. How can it be that something that has no kernel of truth to it can continue to endure? In *Kovetz Maamarim,* Rav Elchanan Wasserman explains that the blood libels are a punishment, which is measure for measure, for the original sin of "*Va'yitbelu es hakutones ba'dam* — And they dipped the tunic in the blood" (*Bereishis* 37:31), which the *shevatim* did to trick Yaakov after selling Yosef. This is a sin for which we are still paying through the generations.

Rav Chaim Palagi cites a *Pirkei DeRabbi Eliezer.* It says "*be'damayich cha'yi*" twice in the *pasuk* to teach us that just as the blood of *milah* and the blood of the *korban pesach* provided us with the merit to be redeemed from Egypt, they will also serve as our *zechus* when we are redeemed from this Exile.

But the question is: How will the blood of the *korban pesach* serve as a merit if we cannot bring that offering while in this Exile?

Tragically, because of the blood libels, which come about because of our observance of the festival of Pesach, all the sins of the Jewish people will be forgiven. That is what is meant by the blood of the *korban pesach.*

> Though not technically a blood libel, a harrowing incident of suspected wrongdoing occurred in the city of Lvov in 1728. A Jew who had become an apostate regretted his horrible actions and repented. When the priests of the town discovered that he had returned to the Jewish fold, they captured him and put him in prison. During their investigation, they told him that if he puts the blame for his return to Judaism on one of the Jews, then nothing would happen to him. In his moment of weakness, he claimed that the rabbis of the city had convinced him to return to his native religion. But he also said that he did not know their names. However, if he would see them, he would recognize them. The judges of the city ordered that the rabbis of the city be arrested and imprisoned on the Seder night; among them were the two great brothers, Rav Chaim and Rav Yehoshua Reitzes.

> The two brothers were tortured so that they would "admit" to the sin of convincing a Jew to return to his roots. However, they maintained that they were completely innocent and that they had been framed. At one point, the head priest decided to make a procession in front of the apostate, so that he could identify who had caused him to return to his religion. As he passed the priest and the apostate, Rav Chaim declared in Latin, "I am totally free of all wrongdoing. You have suspected me for no reason. Why did you torture my brother and me for 40 days?"

When the apostate heard these words, he became infuriated, like a stark, raving mad dog, and he screamed, "You are guilty and so is your brother! And for your terrible sins, you will be put to death publicly."

Rav Chaim was 41 years old, and his brother was only 32 years old. The authorities agreed to commute the sentence if these two brothers would be willing to convert to Christianity. But there was nothing to discuss. They embraced the privilege and opportunity to sanctify God's Name and die for the sake of their religion, al kiddush Hashem.

Throughout their seven-week ordeal, the brothers shared many deep conversations. Since they had been imprisoned on Pesach, Rav Yehoshua asked his brother, "Why has so much innocent Jewish blood been spilled on Pesach, the holiday when the Almighty performed so many miracles on behalf of the Jewish people?"

Rav Chaim answered his younger brother with fire in his eyes. "This is the reason we were taken out of Mitzrayim: to sanctify the Name of Hashem in this world. The pasuk says [Vayikra 22:32], 'Ve'nikdashti be'soch Bnei Yisrael Ani Hashem mekadishchem. Hamotzi eschem meiEretz Mitzrayim lihyos lachem Lei'lokim Ani Hashem — I should be sanctified among the Children of Israel; I am Hashem Who sanctifies you, Who took you out of the land of Egypt to be a God unto you; I am Hashem.' Rashi explains, 'Al menas kein.' Hashem took us out of Mitzrayim on this condition: that we sanctify Him.

"Now let us go and sanctify the Name of Hashem Yisbarach in joy!"

As the two brothers were taken out to be killed in front of the townspeople, their mother hired 10 Jews to disguise themselves as non-Jews and be present when her sons were killed, so that they could fulfill the mitzvah of dying al kiddush Hashem in front of 10 Yidden.

After publicly refusing to convert, these two kedoshim were burned alive and their bodies reduced to ash. The kehillah bribed one of the guards to collect their ashes and give them over for burial. On their tombstone it is written that these ashes will stand alongside the ashes of Yitzchak from the Akeidah (which, although they never materialized, are considered a zechus), and the ashes of the Asarah Harugei Malchus.

Be'damayich cha'yi. . .

רְבָב. כְּמָה שֶׁנֶּאֱמַר, רְבָבָה כְּצֶמַח הַשָּׂדֶה נְתַתִּיךְ, וַתִּרְבִּי וַתִּגְדְּלִי וַתָּבֹאִי בַּעֲדִי עֲדָיִים, שָׁדַיִם נָכֹנוּ וּשְׂעָרֵךְ צִמֵּחַ, וְאַתְּ עֵרֹם וְעֶרְיָה; וָאֶעֱבֹר עָלַיִךְ וָאֶרְאֵךְ מִתְבּוֹסֶסֶת בְּדָמָיִךְ, וָאֹמַר לָךְ, בְּדָמַיִךְ חֲיִי, וָאֹמַר לָךְ, בְּדָמַיִךְ חֲיִי.[1]

וַיָּרֵעוּ אֹתָנוּ הַמִּצְרִים, וַיְעַנּוּנוּ, וַיִּתְּנוּ עָלֵינוּ עֲבֹדָה קָשָׁה.[2]

וַיָּרֵעוּ אֹתָנוּ הַמִּצְרִים. כְּמָה שֶׁנֶּאֱמַר, הָבָה נִתְחַכְּמָה לוֹ, פֶּן יִרְבֶּה, וְהָיָה כִּי תִקְרֶאנָה מִלְחָמָה, וְנוֹסַף גַּם הוּא עַל שֹׂנְאֵינוּ, וְנִלְחַם בָּנוּ, וְעָלָה מִן הָאָרֶץ.[3]

וַיְעַנּוּנוּ. כְּמָה שֶׁנֶּאֱמַר, וַיָּשִׂימוּ עָלָיו שָׂרֵי מִסִּים, לְמַעַן עַנֹּתוֹ בְּסִבְלֹתָם, וַיִּבֶן עָרֵי מִסְכְּנוֹת לְפַרְעֹה, אֶת פִּתֹם וְאֶת רַעַמְסֵס.[4]

וַיִּתְּנוּ עָלֵינוּ עֲבֹדָה קָשָׁה. כְּמָה שֶׁנֶּאֱמַר, וַיַּעֲבִדוּ מִצְרַיִם אֶת בְּנֵי יִשְׂרָאֵל בְּפָרֶךְ.[5]

וַיִּתְּנוּ עָלֵינוּ עֲבֹדָה קָשָׁה

They imposed hard labor upon us...

Just Tears

Moshe Rabbeinu's care and concern for the Jewish people are what made him the perfect leader. He was *nosei be'ol im chaveiro* — sharing in the burden of his friend. Though he was a member of Shevet Levi and not required to work in Mitzrayim, the *pasuk* (Shemos 2:11) tells us, "*Va'yeitzei el echav vay'ar be'sivlosam* — And he went out to his brethren and saw their burdens." Rashi tells us: "*Nassan einav ve'libo li'h'yos meitzar aleihem* — He focused his eyes and heart to be distressed over them." Moshe allowed their suffering to penetrate his heart and he truly felt the pain of the Jewish people; he helped them through his actions, as well.

Numerous — as it says: I made you as numerous as the plants of the field; you grew and developed, and became charming, beautiful of figure; your hair grown long; but you were naked and bare. And I passed over you and saw you downtrodden in your blood and I said to you: "Through your blood shall you live!" And I said to you: "Through your blood shall you live!"[1]

The Egyptians did evil to us and afflicted us; and imposed hard labor upon us.[2]

The Egyptians did evil to us — as it says: Let us deal with them wisely lest they multiply and, if we happen to be at war, they may join our enemies and fight against us and then leave the country.[3]

And they afflicted us — as it says: They set taskmasters over them in order to oppress them with their burdens; and they built Pithom and Raamses as treasure cities for Pharaoh.[4]

They imposed hard labor upon us — as it says: The Egyptians subjugated the Children of Israel with hard labor.[5]

---

1. *Yechezkel* 16:7,6. 2. *Devarim* 26:6.
3. *Shemos* 1:10. 4. Ibid. 1:11.
5. Ibid. 1:13.

Rav Moshe Soloveitchik of Switzerland, the grandson of Rav Chaim Brisker, was known for his exceptional sensitivity toward his fellow Jews. The following story was told by his son, who was present at the time. Late one night, when Rav Moshe was learning with his son, the telephone rang. After his rebbetzin answered the phone, she told her husband that someone was calling from the hospital. The man had explained to her that he and his wife had been childless for eight years, and finally, his wife was about to give birth. But the doctors had notified him that there were serious complications. He called to ask Rav Moshe to pray on behalf of his wife and unborn child.

וַנִּצְעַק אֶל יהוה אֱלֹהֵי אֲבֹתֵינוּ, וַיִּשְׁמַע יהוה אֶת קֹלֵנוּ, וַיַּרְא אֶת עָנְיֵנוּ, וְאֶת עֲמָלֵנוּ, וְאֶת לַחֲצֵנוּ.[1]

וַנִּצְעַק אֶל יהוה אֱלֹהֵי אֲבֹתֵינוּ. כְּמָה שֶׁנֶּאֱמַר, וַיְהִי בַיָּמִים הָרַבִּים הָהֵם, וַיָּמָת מֶלֶךְ מִצְרַיִם, וַיֵּאָנְחוּ בְנֵי יִשְׂרָאֵל מִן הָעֲבֹדָה, וַיִּזְעָקוּ, וַתַּעַל שַׁוְעָתָם אֶל הָאֱלֹהִים מִן הָעֲבֹדָה.[2]

וַיִּשְׁמַע יהוה אֶת קֹלֵנוּ. כְּמָה שֶׁנֶּאֱמַר, וַיִּשְׁמַע אֱלֹהִים אֶת נַאֲקָתָם, וַיִּזְכֹּר אֱלֹהִים אֶת בְּרִיתוֹ אֶת אַבְרָהָם, אֶת יִצְחָק, וְאֶת יַעֲקֹב.[3]

וַיַּרְא אֶת עָנְיֵנוּ. זוֹ פְּרִישׁוּת דֶּרֶךְ אֶרֶץ, כְּמָה שֶׁנֶּאֱמַר וַיַּרְא אֱלֹהִים אֶת בְּנֵי יִשְׂרָאֵל, וַיֵּדַע אֱלֹהִים.[4]

Rav Moshe closed his Gemara, and he and his son each opened up a Tehillim to pray. After a few minutes, the phone rang again. The rebbetzin picked it up, listened for a moment, and then entered his room once again. In a soft voice, she told her husband that there was no need for him to pray any further. The child was born. A stillborn. The child's mother was fine.

Rav Moshe decided to go to the hospital to visit the bereft father. But there was one problem. He had no idea which hospital they were in. Zurich is a very large city, with thousands of people. But Rav Moshe was not deterred. He sat at the telephone and began calling every delivery room in the city. He asked them if there had been a stillbirth there in the last hour. After two hours of inquiries, the rebbetzin suggested that he wait until tomorrow to visit the man.

Rav Moshe admitted that he did not really have any words of comfort to offer, but he felt that the man needed a shoulder to cry on. "I just want him to know that I am thinking of him," he explained. "He is most probably waiting to receive official documentation of his child's death. Who can imagine his pain?"

The hour was extremely late — 4 a.m. — by the time Rav Moshe

We cried out to HASHEM, the God of our fathers; and HASHEM heard our cry and saw our affliction, our burden, and our oppression.[1]

We cried out to HASHEM, the God of our fathers — as it says: It happened in the course of those many days that the king of Egypt died; and the Children of Israel groaned because of the servitude and cried; their cry because of the servitude rose up to God.[2]

HASHEM heard our cry — as it says: God heard their groaning, and God recalled His covenant with Avraham, with Yitzchak, and with Yaakov.[3]

And He saw our affliction — that is the disruption of family life, as it says: God saw the Children of Israel and God knew.[4]

---

1. *Devarim* 26:7. 2. *Shemos* 2:23.
3. Ibid. 2:24. 4. Ibid. 2:25.

---

found the right hospital. He and his son made their way there, and together they walked through the spic-and-span corridors. They soon spotted the bereft young man, utterly broken. When the man heard the footsteps, he lifted his head. He recognized Rav Moshe and burst out crying. It was a scene that was hard to forget.

The fellow ran up to Rav Moshe and buried his head on Rav Moshe's shoulder, yet he did not say a word. His wife was resting and he did not want to make too much noise outside her room, but he could no longer hold in his tears. He cried and cried and cried. For 20 minutes, he did not lift up his head. Finally, Rav Moshe spoke.

"For eight years, you waited for this child. How can I possibly imagine your pain? I bless you that you should merit the Almighty's help to have a healthy child, from whom you will see much nachas."

Rav Moshe stayed for a few minutes longer and then he left. Six months later, the fellow approached Rav Moshe's son and he said, "Your father saved me. I was so devastated that I had considered ending my life that night. For two hours, my parents and my wife's parents kept calling us to find out what happened. They knew that we were going to the hospital but had not heard any news. I did not have the courage or the strength to tell them that my child had died.

וְאֶת עֲמָלֵנוּ. אֵלּוּ הַבָּנִים, כְּמָה שֶׁנֶּאֱמַר,כָּל הַבֵּן הַיִּלּוֹד הַיְאֹרָה תַּשְׁלִיכֻהוּ, וְכָל הַבַּת תְּחַיּוּן.[1]

וְאֶת לַחֲצֵנוּ. זוֹ הַדְּחַק, כְּמָה שֶׁנֶּאֱמַר,וְגַם רָאִיתִי אֶת הַלַּחַץ אֲשֶׁר מִצְרַיִם לֹחֲצִים אֹתָם.[2]

וַיּוֹצִאֵנוּ יהוה מִמִּצְרַיִם בְּיָד חֲזָקָה, וּבִזְרֹעַ נְטוּיָה, וּבְמֹרָא גָּדֹל, וּבְאֹתוֹת וּבְמֹפְתִים.[3]

"When your father came, he was like an angel from Heaven. He did not push off his visit until the next day, but came at 4 in the morning and supported me at my darkest hour. I had never been so alone in my life, but he was there for me."

We must think of the pain and suffering of another Jew. We must help shoulder our friend's burden.

Sometimes there are no words. Sometimes there are only tears.

This is what earned Moshe the right to be the redeemer of the Jewish people.

וְאֶת עֲמָלֵנוּ. אֵלּוּ הַבָּנִים
Our burden — refers to the children ...

What Won't a Mother Do?

Rav Yisrael Baal Shem Tov usually conducted his Pesach Seder in the company of many of his closest disciples. Among them were the Toldos Yaakov Yosef of Polonnoye, Rav Dov Ber of Mezritch, Rav Zev Wolf Kitzes, Rav Yechiel Michel of Zlotchov, and the Shpolya Zeide and his brother-in-law, Rav Boruch Gershon of Kitov. Celebrating the Exodus from Egypt brought the Baal Shem Tov great joy, as he found within its story the yearly salvations of the Jewish people.

But this year, something was different; something was troubling the Rebbe. Beginning less than 36 hours before the Seder, as he attended to the necessary preparations, the Baal Shem wore a worried expression. He set out the 10 pieces of bread and conducted the search for them. However, even after finding

Our burden — refers to the children, as it says: Every son that is born you shall cast into the river, but every daughter you shall let live.[1]

Our oppression — refers to the pressure expressed in the words: I have also seen how the Egyptians are oppressing them.[2]

HASHEM took us out of Egypt with a mighty hand and with an outstretched arm, with great awe, with signs and with wonders.[3]

---

1. *Shemos* 1:22. 2. Ibid. 3:9. 3. *Devarim* 26:8.

---

the pieces and thereby finding the representation of the se'or she'be'issah hidden inside us all, he was still troubled. He then told his disciples that he planned on conducting a special service of Tikkun Chatzos that night, hoping to bring about some sort of redemption.

The disciples sat with their master as they prayed fervently and cried bitterly. But even after their long prayer session, nothing seemed to have changed. As the holiday drew closer, the pained expression on their Rebbe's face remained. A heavy cloud hung over their master and the entire city, whose inhabitants sensed something was wrong.

The Baal Shem Tov and his students went to shul and exalted in the recital of Maariv and Hallel, but the heaviness remained. The Rebbe arrived home, donned his kittel, and set up the Seder plate, yet his deep, mystical thoughts could not break the sadness. During the Seder, the Baal Shem would generally discuss mystical topics and sing joyously. But now, he seemed to be going through the motions without the usual celebration.

When they came to the section of the Haggadah that speaks of the decree that every male be cast into the sea, the master suddenly smiled. Then he began to sing and share deep thoughts. The dark cloud was lifted and the ebullient joy of the holiday was restored.

One of his closest disciples mustered up the courage to ask his teacher what had happened. The Baal Shem closed his eyes and tears began to stream forth, as he recounted the following.

"Hashem had decreed that anti-Semites would stage a pogrom against the people of a nearby village, and all of its Jews would be

וַיּוֹצִאֵנוּ יהוה מִמִּצְרַיִם. לֹא עַל יְדֵי מַלְאָךְ, וְלֹא עַל יְדֵי שָׂרָף, וְלֹא עַל יְדֵי שָׁלִיחַ, אֶלָּא הַקָּדוֹשׁ בָּרוּךְ הוּא בִּכְבוֹדוֹ וּבְעַצְמוֹ. שֶׁנֶּאֱמַר, וְעָבַרְתִּי בְאֶרֶץ מִצְרַיִם בַּלַּיְלָה הַזֶּה, וְהִכֵּיתִי כָל בְּכוֹר בְּאֶרֶץ מִצְרַיִם מֵאָדָם וְעַד בְּהֵמָה, וּבְכָל אֱלֹהֵי מִצְרַיִם אֶעֱשֶׂה שְׁפָטִים, אֲנִי יהוה.[1]

וְעָבַרְתִּי בְאֶרֶץ מִצְרַיִם בַּלַּיְלָה הַזֶּה — אֲנִי וְלֹא מַלְאָךְ. וְהִכֵּיתִי כָל בְּכוֹר בְּאֶרֶץ מִצְרַיִם — אֲנִי וְלֹא שָׂרָף. וּבְכָל אֱלֹהֵי מִצְרַיִם אֶעֱשֶׂה שְׁפָטִים — אֲנִי וְלֹא הַשָּׁלִיחַ. אֲנִי יהוה — אֲנִי הוּא, וְלֹא אַחֵר.

בְּיָד חֲזָקָה. זוֹ הַדֶּבֶר, כְּמָה שֶׁנֶּאֱמַר, הִנֵּה יַד יהוה הוֹיָה בְּמִקְנְךָ אֲשֶׁר בַּשָּׂדֶה, בַּסּוּסִים בַּחֲמֹרִים בַּגְּמַלִּים בַּבָּקָר וּבַצֹּאן, דֶּבֶר כָּבֵד מְאֹד.[2]

וּבִזְרֹעַ נְטוּיָה. זוֹ הַחֶרֶב, כְּמָה שֶׁנֶּאֱמַר, וְחַרְבּוֹ שְׁלוּפָה בְּיָדוֹ, נְטוּיָה עַל יְרוּשָׁלָיִם.[3]

וּבְמֹרָא גָדֹל. זוֹ גִּלּוּי שְׁכִינָה, כְּמָה שֶׁנֶּאֱמַר, אוֹ הֲנִסָּה אֱלֹהִים לָבוֹא לָקַחַת לוֹ גוֹי מִקֶּרֶב גּוֹי, בְּמַסֹּת, בְּאֹתֹת, וּבְמוֹפְתִים, וּבְמִלְחָמָה, וּבְיָד חֲזָקָה, וּבִזְרֹעַ נְטוּיָה, וּבְמוֹרָאִים גְּדֹלִים, כְּכֹל אֲשֶׁר עָשָׂה לָכֶם יהוה אֱלֹהֵיכֶם בְּמִצְרַיִם לְעֵינֶיךָ.[4]

וּבְאֹתוֹת. זֶה הַמַּטֶּה, כְּמָה שֶׁנֶּאֱמַר, וְאֶת הַמַּטֶּה הַזֶּה תִּקַּח בְּיָדֶךָ, אֲשֶׁר תַּעֲשֶׂה בּוֹ אֶת הָאֹתֹת.[5]

וּבְמֹפְתִים. זֶה הַדָּם, כְּמָה שֶׁנֶּאֱמַר, וְנָתַתִּי מוֹפְתִים בַּשָּׁמַיִם וּבָאָרֶץ:[6]

HASHEM took us out of Egypt — not through an angel, not through a seraph, not through a messenger, but the Holy One, Blessed is He, in His glory, Himself, as it says: I will pass through the land of Egypt on that night; I will slay all the firstborn in the land of Egypt from man to beast; and upon all the gods of Egypt will I execute judgments; I, HASHEM.[1]

"I will pass through the land of Egypt on that night" — I and no angel; "I will slay all the firstborn in the land of Egypt" — I and no seraph; "And upon all the gods of Egypt will I execute judgments" — I and no messenger; "I, HASHEM" — it is I and no other.

With a mighty hand — refers to the pestilence, as it says: Behold, the hand of HASHEM shall strike your cattle which are in the field, the horses, the donkeys, the camels, the herds, and the flocks — a very severe pestilence.[2]

With an outstretched arm — refers to the sword, as it says: His drawn sword in His hand, outstretched over Jerusalem.[3]

With great awe — alludes to the revelation of the Shechinah, as it says: Has God ever attempted to take unto Himself a nation from the midst of another nation by trials, miraculous signs, and wonders, by war and with a mighty hand, and outstretched arm, and by awesome revelations, as all that HASHEM your God did for you in Egypt, before your eyes?[4]

With signs — refers to the miracles performed with the staff as it says: Take this staff in your hand, that you may perform the miraculous signs with it.[5]

With wonders — alludes to the blood, as it says: I will show wonders in the heavens and on the earth:[6]

---

1. *Shemos* 12:12.
2. Ibid. 9:3.
3. *I Divrei HaYamim* 21:16.
4. *Devarim* 4:34. 5. *Shemos* 4:17. 6. *Yoel* 3:3.

As each of the words דָּם, *blood*, אֵשׁ, *fire*, and עָשָׁן, *smoke,* is said, a bit of wine is removed from the cup, with the finger or by pouring.

דָּם וָאֵשׁ וְתִמְרוֹת עָשָׁן.

דָּבָר אַחֵר בְּיָד חֲזָקָה, שְׁתַּיִם. וּבִזְרֹעַ נְטוּיָה, שְׁתַּיִם. וּבְמֹרָא גָּדֹל, שְׁתַּיִם. וּבְאֹתוֹת, שְׁתַּיִם. וּבְמֹפְתִים, שְׁתַּיִם: אֵלּוּ עֶשֶׂר מַכּוֹת שֶׁהֵבִיא הַקָּדוֹשׁ בָּרוּךְ הוּא עַל הַמִּצְרִים בְּמִצְרַיִם, וְאֵלּוּ הֵן:

---

murdered in cold blood. I tried desperately to alter the decree, but to no avail. Then tonight, something happened, and it was able to accomplish what all of our prayers could not.

"A couple in that small village has not been blessed with children. Although they have prayed for many years, they are still childless. As they conduct their Seder, it is difficult to overcome their feelings of loneliness. There are no children to ask the Four Questions and no children with whom to share the story of the Exodus. Yet, they have accepted their fate with faith; they don't question the Almighty's actions.

"Tonight, the woman listened as her husband read about the decree that every male baby be thrown into the river, and she cried out, 'How could He do it? How could the Almighty allow His children to be drowned in the river? Why didn't He protect them? The Almighty is their Mother, and a Jewish mother doesn't allow her children to be tortured and killed in that manner. Why didn't He stop it? Why? Why? If I will ever be blessed with children, I will make sure to protect them. I will never let anyone touch my children; they would have to kill me first. I don't understand how He let it happen.'

"The childless woman cried bitterly as the pain and suffering of so many years came rushing out. Her husband tried to calm her and reassure her that the Jewish people were saved and the Almighty took them out of Egypt. Still, she continued to protest and continued to cry.

"In Heaven, a great debate ensued. The decree had been issued that the Jews of the village were to be wiped out in a terrible pogrom. However, this woman insisted that a Yiddishe mamma must protect her children. And if that was the case, the decree

As each of the words דָּם, *blood*, אֵשׁ, *fire*, and עָשָׁן, *smoke*, is said, a bit of wine is removed from the cup, with the finger or by pouring.

Blood, fire, and columns of smoke.

Another explanation of the preceding verse: [Each phrase represents two plagues,] hence: **mighty hand** — two; **outstretched arm** — two; **great awe** — two; **signs** — two; **wonders** — two. These are the Ten Plagues which the Holy One, Blessed is He, brought upon the Egyptians in Egypt, namely:

---

should be abolished; the greatest Mother of all, the Ima Ila'a, must protect Her children from the pogrom.

"Finally, the decree was abolished. The childless woman saved her village. With her heartfelt tears, she accomplished what we were not able to, with our deep and mystical prayers."

That night, the Seder continued in the manner in which the Baal Shem had always conducted it: with great joy, deep insights, and beautiful song.

The following year, the couple in the nearby town once again sat down to their Seder. But this time, after 20 years as a childless couple, they were joined by their newborn baby.

אֵלוּ עֶשֶׂר מַכּוֹת
These are the Ten Plagues...

דָּם
Blood

A Brother's Pain

When the Bluzhever Rebbe, Rav Yisrael Spira, arrived in America from Europe after World War II, it was arranged that he would speak at the Bialystoker Shul on the Lower East Side of Manhattan. A large crowd assembled to hear the harrowing details of what had transpired in Europe over the course of the war. The Rebbe shared the heartrending details, and the crowd was moved by all they heard about the diabolical Nazis who had exterminated so many people and destroyed so many communities. By the time

As each of the plagues is mentioned, a bit of wine is removed from the cup. The same is done by each word of Rabbi Yehudah's mnemonic.

דָּם. צְפַרְדֵּעַ. כִּנִּים. עָרוֹב. דֶּבֶר. שְׁחִין.

בָּרָד. אַרְבֶּה. חֹשֶׁךְ. מַכַּת בְּכוֹרוֹת.

רַבִּי יְהוּדָה הָיָה נוֹתֵן בָּהֶם סִמָּנִים:

דְּצַ"ךְ. עֲדַ"שׁ. בְּאַחַ"ב.

The cups are refilled. The wine that was removed is not used.

---

the Rebbe was finished, there was not a dry eye in the crowd.

When the speech was over, Moreinu Yaakov Rosenheim, the president of Agudas Yisrael, handed him an envelope with a large sum of money. The Rebbe looked at him in bewilderment. "What is this for?"

Moreinu Rosenheim explained that it is customary in America to pay a speaker for the trouble he goes through in preparing his speech. At the time, the Rebbe had no money whatsoever. Nevertheless, he adamantly refused to take any of the money and returned the envelope to Rav Yaakov, along with an explanation.

"You are correct. It is a very proper and admirable custom to give a speaker remuneration for his efforts. But in this speech, I spoke about the suffering of our brethren. For that, I cannot take any money.

"Chazal tell us [Midrash Shocher Tov] that during the plague of blood, in order for an Egyptian to be able to drink water, he had to pay for the water. Rabbi Avin says that through this money, the Jewish people became wealthy. However, Rabbi Yosi disagrees. He suggests that they became wealthy when their Egyptian neighbors gave them their riches as they left Egypt. The question is: Why didn't Rabbi Yosi agree with the first explanation? What is wrong with the Jews becoming wealthy during the plague of blood? According to Rabbi Yosi, it is not proper for a Jew to become wealthy from someone else's suffering, even if it is the suffering of a non-Jew. This is not a Jewish trait."

The Bluzhever concluded, "The disagreement concerns only whether a Jew can make money off a non-Jew's suffering, but there is no disagreement when it comes to the suffering of a Jew. That is not a time for a person to become rich. One does not make money off of his brother's pain.

As each of the plagues is mentioned, a bit of wine is removed from the cup. The same is done by each word of Rabbi Yehudah's mnemonic.

1. Blood 2. Frogs 3. Lice 4. Wild Beasts
5. Pestilence 6. Boils 7. Hail 8. Locusts
9. Darkness 10. Plague of the Firstborn.

Rabbi Yehudah abbreviated them by their Hebrew initials:

D'TZACH, ADASH, B'ACHAV.

The cups are refilled. The wine that was removed is not used.

"So how can I possibly take money for speaking about the suffering and pain of our brothers and sisters?"

צְפַרְדֵּעַ

Frogs

◆§ Frogs Here, Frogs There, Frogs Singing (?!) Everywhere

People who lack the ability to carry a tune are sometimes told that they "sing like a frog." At first glance, it would appear that this is an insult. After all, frogs are not viewed as gracious animals, and they have, well, froggy voices.

And yet, the *Yalkut Shimoni* on *Tehillim* (889) tells us that after David HaMelech completed *Sefer Tehillim,* he asked the Almighty if any other creature's praise could measure up to the praise he offered the Almighty. The answer was shocking. A frog stepped forward and showed David three ways in which his *shirah* outperformed the praise of David.

First, the frog said that he praises Hashem more than David. Second, he mentioned that he adds 3,000 *meshalim* for each praise he sings. Third, he explained that there is a creature that lives on the edge of the sea, which can be fed only from the water. The frog offers himself to be eaten by this animal.

The *Mabit* on *Perek Shirah* adds that the frogs were one of four living creatures used during the *makkos*. The others were *kinim* (lice), *arov* (wild animals), and *arbeh* (locust). Regarding the frogs, the *pasuk* says (*Shemos* 8:2), "*Va'taal hatzefardei'a* — And the frog-infestation ascended." The frogs left their natural habitat — water — and rose to carry out the Almighty's will. Furthermore, they were ready to sacrifice their lives, and they entered the ovens and were burned alive during the plague, in order to punish the Egyptians (*Pesachim* 53b).

We see that the rise of the *tzefardei'a* may be understood not only in the physical sense but in the spiritual sense as well. They rose to fulfill the will of the Al-mighty. Their commitment to sacrifice themselves is precisely what makes their *shirah* so exalted. For the *shirah* of an individual is not measured by the tone and timbre of his voice, but by the generosity of his soul.

And nothing gives more than the *tzefarde'a*.

When we look at the *shirah* designated for the *tzefardei'a* in *Perek Shirah*, we discover that it is the words of *Chazal* (*Pesachim* 56a) that we are allowed to articulate audibly only once a year: "*Baruch Sheim kevod malchuso le'olam va'ed* — Blessed is the Name of His glorious kingdom for all eternity."

Let's examine the words "*le'olam va'ed* — for all eternity."

Rabbi Klonimus, a contemporary of the *Rashba*, wrote a *sefer* titled *Iggeres Baalei Chaim*. In this *sefer* (*Shaar Sheni*, *Perek Beis*), he mentions two outstanding incidents in which the *tzefardei'a* earns his title as the *rav hatishbachos* — the greatest of those who give praise. The first incident is when Avraham was thrown into the fiery furnace by Nimrod. At that time, a frog jumped into the furnace and extinguished the flames in order to save Avraham. The second incident transpired when the frog volunteered for the *makkah* of *tzefardei'a*. *Rabbi Klonimus* adds that the *tzefardei'a* is one who is consistently "davening." Day and night, he croaks his *shirah*, *le'olam va'ed*.

His continuous, steady song teaches us much about how we are to approach the song that is our lives, the learning of Torah. It is the unbroken, ceaseless learning of Torah that upholds the world; one moment without it and the world would be destroyed. The *tzefardei'a* knows that its sacrifice must be unremitting and persistent. So it is with our learning of Torah. We cannot be deterred or discouraged. We must always be willing to sacrifice for Torah: in comfort, and even more so in pain.

The *Gra* (*Eitz Yosef*, *Bava Basra* 73b) says that the Egyptians were smitten with *tzefardei'a* because they caused the Jewish people to be *mevatel Torah*. The frogs teach us that we must not be *mevatel Torah*, not for one second!

When Chananiah, Mishael, and Azariah were threatened by Nevuchadnetzar to be thrown into a furnace unless they bowed down to his *avodah zarah*, they said, "If a frog can throw himself into a furnace for the sake of God, shouldn't we?"

The Midrash says that during *arov*, all the animals attacked the Egyptians. The *Malbim* asks: Then why send the *tzefardei'a* separately?

The answer is: To teach us these very lessons. The Egyptians had to be punished, but at the same time, the Yidden had to learn these incredible lessons of the *tzefardei'a*: Torah, *tefillah*, and *mesirus nefesh*.

Our *tefillah* must be constant; our Torah must be consistent.

We cannot ever stop. And we must be willing to sacrifice everything for it.

Even our lives.

Serving Him With Every Cell

The *Yefei Einayim* (*Pesachim* 53b) tells us that the only frogs that did not die at the end of the plague of *tzefardei'a* were the ones that had jumped into the ovens.

When our focus is the *Ribbono Shel Olam*, and we do our best to fulfill His will constantly and consistently, He will protect us.

> On the 23rd day of Elul, 5770, Moshe and Shira Moreno were traveling back to their home in Maale Ephraim. It was a quiet night and the road was dark. After a while, Moshe noticed a car in his rearview mirror flashing his high beams at him. Moshe tried to ignore it, but it seemed that the man was trying to pass him. Finally, he decided to pull over at the side of the road and let the driver in the other car go past him.
>
> It was a decision that nearly cost him his life.
>
> Immediately after he pulled over, the car behind him also came to a stop. Then suddenly, he and his wife were under attack. A ruthless terrorist unleashed a barrage of gunfire on Moshe's car. He shattered the windows and punctured the tires. Miraculously, only one bullet hit Moshe, in his leg. Shira was slightly injured by some shattered glass that cut her head. They were very grateful that the terrorist finished off his bullets on the car, but they knew it was only a matter of time before he would reload his gun and finish the job.
>
> In the meantime, the two of them jumped from the side of the road, and somehow, after tumbling about 75 feet below the road,

landed in a wadi. Although it was pitch dark, they realized they had only a few minutes before they would be discovered by the terrorist.

As they had fled their car, Shira had the presence of mind to take her cellphone with her. Now, she placed a call to the nearby police station. The police found them before their attacker did, and subdued the perpetrator.

As they were pulled to safety, the commanding officer asked them how they had managed to make the phone call. Not understanding the question, Shira readily displayed her phone. But the officer shook his head. "You don't understand. There's no cellphone service here."

Realizing that their rescue was nothing short of miraculous, they thanked the Ribbono Shel Olam for their salvation. Additionally, six months later, after they were both completely healed, the grateful couple made a special seudas hoda'ah, in which they thanked Hashem in public. At the festive meal, one of Moshe's friends spoke about the kindness of the Almighty, and how we must thank Him for His constant Providence. Then he added a stunning postscript.

"As many of you are aware, our friends managed to make the phone call that saved their lives in a place where there was no cellphone service. I believe I know how that phone call was made.

"Ten years ago, our dear friend Reb Moshe created a movement to stop all cellphone use in our shuls. His initiative caught on, and before long, cellphone use during davening decreased dramatically in our area. Perhaps it is in that merit that when he needed it most, inexplicably, his cellphone worked.

"Because he was so committed to shutting off his phone when speaking to the Almighty, when he needed to speak to the police, the Almighty ensured that his phone would be on."

בָּרָד
Hail

◆§ The Power of Our Cries

The power of a Jewish teardrop is immeasurable.

Chazal (Shemos Rabbah, Va'eira 12) tell us that the Almighty suspended the large hailstones of the plague of barad in midair.

When Yehoshua battled the Amorites (*Yehoshua* 10:11), the Almighty allowed those hailstones to continue to fall. The rest of them are destined to fall during the war of *Gog U'Magog*. Rabbeinu Bachya adds that the loud noises that accompanied the *barad*, as it says (*Shemos* 9:23), "*VaHashem nassan kolos u'varad* — And Hashem sent loud noises and hail," were also suspended at that time. They, too, continued at a later date, during the days of Elisha, where it says (*II Melachim* 7:6), "*VaHashem hishmia es machaneh Aram kol rechev kol sus kol chayil gadol* — Hashem had caused the camp of Aram to hear the sound of chariot, the sound of horse, the sound of a great army."

There is an obvious question. Did the Almighty lack additional hail that He had to suspend these hailstones in midair? It is understandable that a human being would take some of his ammunition and save it for a later date. But the Almighty lacks nothing. Why did He choose to save this hail for a future battle?

The *Darash Mordechai* explains that the hail of Egypt was extremely dear to Hashem, since it was created from the groans of the Jewish people: "*Va'yei'anchu ... Va'yitzaku ...* — And they groaned ... And they cried out ..." (*Shemos* 2:23). Each ball of hail was suffused with the tears of the men, women, and children of the Jewish people. Each and every sigh went up to the Heavens and pierced the firmaments. From these hot tears were created the fire within the hail. Such creations are dear to Hashem and possess great merit; they also have the ability to take revenge against the Jews' enemies and the nations that torment us and want to destroy us.

The hail of Egypt was miraculous in that the fire and water, two natural enemies, made peace with each other to protect the Jews and punish their enemies. The tears that flowed like water combined with the groans, which were mixed with Jewish blood, to form special creations that were saved for later: to destroy the fire that fueled the hatred of the *reshaim*. The fact that the Jews were capable of enduring all they did was in itself miraculous. This was symbolized by these hailstones, which to Hashem are very dear. Therefore, He stored them and hid them until the days of Yehoshua and Mashiach.

The same was true with the sounds of the cries, which helped create the loud noises of *barad*. The cries that ascended to Heaven, as it says (ibid.), "*Va'taal shavasam el haElokim* — Their outcry went up to God," were what formed the sounds that accompanied the *barad*.

These were sounded on the camp of Aram. One pure and sincere cry from the heart of a Jew forms the necessary ammunition for battle.

This idea is found in another Midrash (*Otzar HaMidrashim, Midrash Asarah Harugei Malchus*). When the Romans seized Rabbi Shimon ben Gamliel and Rabbi Yishmael Kohen Gadol, they offered them a choice of who should be killed first. Rabbi Shimon came from a distinctive line of princes, and Rabbi Yishmael descended from a line of Kohanim; hence, each one of them felt he should be the first to be killed. Ultimately, a lot was cast and Rabbi Shimon "won" the lottery. The caesar commanded that his head be cut off. After the Romans beheaded Rabbi Shimon, Rabbi Yishmael took hold of Rabbi Shimon's head and lamented with bitter tears, "How could the tongue that translated the Torah into 70 languages now lick the dust?" The caesar asked him why he was crying for his friend and not crying for himself. He responded, "My friend was greater than I in wisdom, and he was fortunate to ascend to the Heavenly Yeshivah first. For that I cry."

The *Zohar* tells us that Rabbi Nehorai heard the sounds of rams crying for a lion that was engraved on the Heavenly Throne. Rabbi Nechemiah informed him that the cries were those of Rabbi Yishmael, whose cries will never cease from the Heavenly Throne — until Hashem takes His final revenge against the nations of the world.

The cries of Rabbi Yishmael, and the others who cried, continue to reverberate. These cries will tear open the heart of Heaven, and eventually bring the Jews to their Final Redemption.

The Three Times Rav Mottel Cried

Recently, the Torah world commemorated 50 years since the passing of the great Telshe rosh yeshivah, Rav Chaim Mordechai Katz, known to the world as Rav Mottel. He was renowned for his pikchus (cleverness) and warmth, and people from all over the world turned to him for advice. Although his life was filled with tzaros, he managed to rebuild his family and his yeshivah in Cleveland. With tremendous fortitude, unfathomable strength, and unshakable faith, Rav Mottel steered the ship of Telshe in its most vulnerable times, not only during the war years, but later on, as well.

After a fire broke out in the yeshivah on New Year's Day in 1963, in which the lives of two talmidim were lost, Rav Mottel announced that the yeshivah would rebuild. Many people thought that this was one tragedy too many, and that Rav Mottel was being completely unrealistic. But history would prove otherwise. Indeed, he spearheaded a campaign in which the yeshivah reached even greater heights than before.

My grandmother once shared a powerful story. When my grandfather, Herbert I. Spero, a very dear friend of Rav Mottel, was sick in a hospital in Boston with the illness that would eventually take his life, Rav Mottel came to visit. Though my grandmother was a devoted wife who never left her husband's side, when Rav Katz asked to speak with my grandfather privately for a few moments, my grandmother couldn't say no. Later, my grandmother remarked, "I don't know what the two of them spoke about, but when I looked at Rav Katz as he left the room, I couldn't help but think that I had never seen a grown man cry so hard."

When I shared this with Rav Mottel's son, Rav Yankel Velvel, he told me that he was somewhat surprised by the story because his father was not a crier. Then he told me about another time that he heard that his father had cried, as was retold by Rav Mordechai Kamenetsky. Rav Mordechai's father, Rav Binyamin, had learned be'chavrusa with one of Rav Mottel's sons in yeshivah in Lithuania. Tragically, Rav Mottel lost 10 children, including Rav Binyamin's chavrusa, in the war. Later, Rav Binyamin recalled that after he was married, he once received a call from Rav Mottel in the middle of the night, and Rav Mottel was crying. "Binyaminka," he said through his tears. "Ich ken nit shloffen — I cannot sleep. I forgot the name of my son who was your chavrusa. What was it?"

The third story is one that was told by Rav Moshe Mendel Glustein, at the 50th yahrtzeit gathering in the yeshivah. Many years ago, Rav Glustein and his wife suffered the loss of their infant son. Though Rav Glustein was living in Cleveland at the time, Rav Mottel did not come to be menachem avel. Only afterward did he call up Rav Moshe Mendel and ask him to come out to the yeshivah.

When Rav Glustein walked into Rav Mottel's office, Rav Mottel looked at his broken talmid and spoke. "You lost a child and I lost my children. Lomer veinen tzuzamen — Let us cry together…"

Then they cried and cried and cried.

And that was Rav Glustein's greatest nechamah.

These tears, too, will eventually break through the gates of Shamayim.

רַבִּי יוֹסִי הַגְּלִילִי אוֹמֵר: מִנַּיִן אַתָּה אוֹמֵר
שֶׁלָּקוּ הַמִּצְרִים בְּמִצְרַיִם עֶשֶׂר
מַכּוֹת, וְעַל הַיָּם לָקוּ חֲמִשִּׁים מַכּוֹת? בְּמִצְרַיִם
מָה הוּא אוֹמֵר, וַיֹּאמְרוּ הַחַרְטֻמִּם אֶל פַּרְעֹה,
אֶצְבַּע אֱלֹהִים הִוא.[1] וְעַל הַיָּם מָה הוּא אוֹמֵר,
וַיַּרְא יִשְׂרָאֵל אֶת הַיָּד הַגְּדֹלָה אֲשֶׁר עָשָׂה יהוה
בְּמִצְרַיִם, וַיִּירְאוּ הָעָם אֶת יהוה, וַיַּאֲמִינוּ בַּיהוה
וּבְמֹשֶׁה עַבְדּוֹ.[2] כַּמָּה לָקוּ בְאֶצְבַּע? עֶשֶׂר מַכּוֹת.
אֱמוֹר מֵעַתָּה, בְּמִצְרַיִם לָקוּ עֶשֶׂר מַכּוֹת, וְעַל הַיָּם
לָקוּ חֲמִשִּׁים מַכּוֹת.

רַבִּי אֱלִיעֶזֶר אוֹמֵר. מִנַּיִן שֶׁכָּל מַכָּה וּמַכָּה
שֶׁהֵבִיא הַקָּדוֹשׁ בָּרוּךְ הוּא
עַל הַמִּצְרִים בְּמִצְרַיִם הָיְתָה שֶׁל אַרְבַּע מַכּוֹת?
שֶׁנֶּאֱמַר, יְשַׁלַּח בָּם חֲרוֹן אַפּוֹ — עֶבְרָה, וָזַעַם,
וְצָרָה, מִשְׁלַחַת מַלְאֲכֵי רָעִים.[3] עֶבְרָה, אַחַת.
וָזַעַם, שְׁתַּיִם. וְצָרָה, שָׁלֹשׁ. מִשְׁלַחַת מַלְאֲכֵי
רָעִים, אַרְבַּע. אֱמוֹר מֵעַתָּה, בְּמִצְרַיִם לָקוּ אַרְבָּעִים
מַכּוֹת, וְעַל הַיָּם לָקוּ מָאתַיִם מַכּוֹת.

רַבִּי אֱלִיעֶזֶר אוֹמֵר
Rabbi Eliezer said…

◆§ How We Have Suffered

Rav Shlomo Wolbe, the mashgiach in the yeshivah in Be'er
Yaakov, once suggested to his *bachurim* a meaningful approach
to the structure of *Kinnos*. Rav Wolbe noticed that on the day of
Tishah B'Av, we recite 40 *Kinnos*. He posits that the number 40 is
significant.

He quoted the *Maharal* in *Gevuros Hashem* on the *Haggadah shel
Pesach,* which discusses the opinion of Rabbi Eliezer that Hashem

Rabbi Yose the Galilean said: How does one derive that the Egyptians were struck with 10 plagues in Egypt, but with 50 plagues at the sea? — Concerning the plagues in Egypt the Torah states: The magicians said to Pharaoh, "It is the finger of God."[1] However, of those at the sea, the Torah relates: Israel saw the great "hand" which HASHEM laid upon the Egyptians, the people feared HASHEM, and they believed in HASHEM and in His servant Moshe.[2] How many plagues did they receive with the finger? Ten! Then conclude that if they suffered 10 plagues in Egypt [where they were struck with a finger], they must have been made to suffer 50 plagues at the sea [where they were struck with a whole hand].

Rabbi Eliezer said: How does one derive that every plague that the Holy One, Blessed is He, inflicted upon the Egyptians in Egypt was equal to four plagues? — for it is written: He sent upon them His fierce anger: wrath, fury, and trouble, a band of emissaries of evil.[3] [Since each plague in Egypt consisted of] 1) wrath, 2) fury, 3) trouble, and 4) a band of emissaries of evil, therefore conclude that in Egypt they were struck by 40 plagues and at the sea by 200!

1. *Shemos* 8:15. 2. Ibid. 14:31. 3. *Tehillim* 78:49.

did not inflict only 10 *makkos* on the Egyptians; He actually inflicted four times that amount. This is based on the *pasuk* (*Tehillim* 78:49), "*Yeshalach bam ... evrah va'zaam ve'tzarah, mishlachas malachei ra'im* — He sent upon them ... fury and wrath and trouble, a band of emissaries of evil." He divides this *pasuk* into four categories: *evrah, tzarah, zaam,* and *mishlachas malachei ra'im.*

Each category contains a different form of pain.

Evrah, fury, says the *Maharal,* represents the extensiveness of the *makkah.* It does not affect only one area; rather, it punishes an entire region. *Zaam,* wrath, focuses on the intensity of the *makkah. Tzarah,* trouble, highlights the fear of the impending *makkah*; imagine the suffering of one who awaits his death, knowing that at any moment he is going to die. Finally, *mishlachas malachei ra'im,* a band of emissaries of evil, signifies the continuity and relentlessness of the *makkah*; it never lets up.

In Mitzrayim, there were 10 *makkos* that multiplied into 40, due to the four aspects of each *makkah.* Throughout history, the Jewish people have endured their own 40 *makkos.* In each *Kinnah,* we read of another element of these "*makkos*" that the Jewish people have suffered through.

How we have suffered!

Destruction. Murders. Deaths of *tzaddikim.* Deaths of children. Brutality. Torture. Inquisitions. Crusades. Holocausts. Suicide bombings.

Evrah. Zaam. Tzarah. Mishlachas malachei ra'im.

The Bookbinder's Tricks:

Rav Yitzchak of Rudvil once instructed his attendant to draw water for him to wash his hands at the Seder. The attendant went to carry out his wishes, but did not return for a long time. Curious about the delay, Rav Yitzchak sent his wife to see why his attendant had not returned. However, she, too, did not return. Left with no choice, he went outside himself. As he approached the well, he was surprised to see a large crowd. Along with his wife and his attendant were a number of other individuals, perhaps 20 in all, and everyone was listening to a simple Jew recite the Haggadah.

He would read a page from the Haggadah, and then a page from Megillas Eichah. He began with Mah Nishtanah (toward the beginning of Maggid) and continued with the words: "Eichah yashvah badad" (the first pasuk of Eichah). The group watched with smiles on their faces, unable to control their laughter. It was obvious that the simple man had no clue what he was saying.

It seems that in the middle of the year, the man had given two books to the bookbinder. The first was his Haggadah, and the second was his Kinnos with Eichah. The bookbinder pulled a prank on the unsuspecting man, and he bound the two of them together, mixing up the pages. In the meantime, the fellow had no idea that the bookbinder had tricked him.

But one person was not smiling at all. Instead, tears began to stream down Rav Yitzchak's face. When the crowd realized that the Rebbe was crying, they asked him why. He responded, "Do you realize that we are not the only ones standing here right now? The entire Heavenly entourage has come to listen to the exalted prayers of this well-meaning Jew. There is a reason that you cannot move from here; it is not just to observe the silliness, but because your souls are being pulled by the holiness that surrounds this man."

This simple individual somehow revealed a truth that most of us do not know. The two days are indeed intertwined. Providentially, the bookbinder put together the two of them to allow him to read what they already know in Heaven.

Right now, Tishah B'Av is the saddest day of the year. As we mourn the destruction of our Temple, we wait for the Almighty to rebuild it. There is no better time to pray for our Final Redemption than Seder night, when we relive the Exodus from Egypt.

Then, we will have no reason to dwell on the never-ending *makkos* with which we are plagued.

The Torn Kesubah

There is a reason that we are still in *Galus*, as we have forsaken the Torah and we are not yet ready to be redeemed.

One Tishah B'Av night, the great Chozeh of Lublin came to shul and sat down on the floor for Kinnos. As Eichah was set to begin, his personal badchan, Rav Mordechai Rakover, approached him with a shailah.

"Rebbe, someone just came over to me and asked me to present a shailah to you. He and his wife have been suffering from marital discord of late. During the course of one of their arguments, his wife grabbed her kesubah and tore it into hundreds of pieces. Soon after, though, she calmed down and realized that she could not live with her husband without a proper kesubah.

"She managed to glue it back together, but now she has a shailah. The glue she used is chametz; will she be permitted to her husband over Pesach?"

The small crowd that had gathered began to chuckle, as they

רַבִּי עֲקִיבָא אוֹמֵר. מִנַּיִן שֶׁכָּל מַכָּה וּמַכָּה שֶׁהֵבִיא הַקָּדוֹשׁ בָּרוּךְ הוּא עַל הַמִּצְרִים בְּמִצְרַיִם הָיְתָה שֶׁל חָמֵשׁ מַכּוֹת? שֶׁנֶּאֱמַר, יְשַׁלַּח בָּם חֲרוֹן אַפּוֹ, עֶבְרָה, וָזַעַם, וְצָרָה, מִשְׁלַחַת מַלְאֲכֵי רָעִים. חֲרוֹן אַפּוֹ, אַחַת. עֶבְרָה, שְׁתַּיִם. וָזַעַם, שָׁלֹשׁ. וְצָרָה, אַרְבַּע. מִשְׁלַחַת מַלְאֲכֵי רָעִים, חָמֵשׁ. אֱמוֹר מֵעַתָּה, בְּמִצְרַיִם לָקוּ חֲמִשִּׁים מַכּוֹת, וְעַל הַיָּם לָקוּ חֲמִשִּׁים וּמָאתַיִם מַכּוֹת.

כַּמָּה מַעֲלוֹת טוֹבוֹת לַמָּקוֹם עָלֵינוּ.

אִלּוּ הוֹצִיאָנוּ מִמִּצְרַיִם וְלֹא עָשָׂה בָהֶם שְׁפָטִים דַּיֵּנוּ.

---

saw the humor in the question. But they noticed that the Chozeh had taken the opposite approach. He was sobbing bitterly, unable to control his emotions.

After he calmed down, he explained, "This is not just a silly question. The Husband is Hashem, and we are the wife. In our rebelliousness, we began to bicker and fight with our dear Husband. Finally, we took that which is most precious — our kesubah, our holy Torah — and we tore it up into hundreds of pieces, by abandoning its teachings and forsaking its message. Then, however, like the wife, we realized that we cannot be together with our Husband without it. And so, we have tried to glue together the many loose ends.

"Throughout this Exile," continued the Chozeh, "we've struggled to hold onto bits and pieces. Perhaps that may be good enough for us to survive in Galus, but the question is: Will it be good enough for Pesach, for the time when we will have our Final Redemption?"

Their smiles were no longer evident. The Chozeh lowered his head. Eichah began.

Let us hope that soon, we will be zocheh to patch up the kesubah properly, so that we may be worthy of the real Exodus, the Final Redemption.

Rabbi Akiva said: How does one derive that each plague that the Holy One, Blessed is He, inflicted upon the Egyptians in Egypt was equal to five plagues? — for it says: He sent upon them His fierce anger, wrath, fury, trouble, and a band of emissaries of evil. [Since each plague in Egypt consisted of] 1) fierce anger, 2) wrath, 3) fury, 4) trouble, and 5) a band of emissaries of evil, therefore conclude that in Egypt they were struck by 50 plagues and at the sea by 250!

**The Omnipresent has bestowed
so many favors upon us!**

Had He brought us out of Egypt,
but not executed judgments against the Egyptians,
it would have sufficed us.

כַּמָּה מַעֲלוֹת טוֹבוֹת
So many favors...

◆§ A Pesach Confessional

In *Haggadah shel Pesach HaLekach VeHaLibuv* (5774), Rav Avrohom Schorr suggests that the recitation of *Dayeinu* is a form of *viduy,* confession. We admit that it would have been enough if Hashem had taken us out of Mitzrayim, but since He did so much more for us, we have so much more to thank Him for. Because of all the favors He has bestowed upon us, we are indeed obligated to increase our level of *avodas Hashem,* yet we have not served Him as we should have.

Rav Schorr further explains that when we say the opening paragraph of *Maggid, Ha Lachma Anya,* some have the custom to stand. Why? He cites the *Chida,* who reveals that the second word of the paragraph, לַחְמָא, when read backward, stands for the first words of the prayer of *Avinu Malkeinu:* אָבִינוּ מַלְכֵּנוּ חָטָאנוּ לְפָנֶיךָ, which mean: "Our Father, our King, we have sinned before You." This declaration is a confession of sorts. Now, as we are about to begin the primary component of the Seder, the retelling of the Exodus, we

אִלּוּ עָשָׂה בָהֶם שְׁפָטִים
וְלֹא עָשָׂה בֵאלֹהֵיהֶם — דַּיֵּנוּ.
אִלּוּ עָשָׂה בֵאלֹהֵיהֶם
וְלֹא הָרַג אֶת בְּכוֹרֵיהֶם — דַּיֵּנוּ.
אִלּוּ הָרַג אֶת בְּכוֹרֵיהֶם
וְלֹא נָתַן לָנוּ אֶת מָמוֹנָם — דַּיֵּנוּ.
אִלּוּ נָתַן לָנוּ אֶת מָמוֹנָם
וְלֹא קָרַע לָנוּ אֶת הַיָּם — דַּיֵּנוּ.
אִלּוּ קָרַע לָנוּ אֶת הַיָּם
וְלֹא הֶעֱבִירָנוּ בְתוֹכוֹ בֶּחָרָבָה — דַּיֵּנוּ.
אִלּוּ הֶעֱבִירָנוּ בְתוֹכוֹ בֶּחָרָבָה
וְלֹא שִׁקַּע צָרֵינוּ בְּתוֹכוֹ — דַּיֵּנוּ.
אִלּוּ שִׁקַּע צָרֵינוּ בְּתוֹכוֹ
וְלֹא סִפֵּק צָרְכֵּנוּ בַּמִּדְבָּר אַרְבָּעִים שָׁנָה — דַּיֵּנוּ.
אִלּוּ סִפֵּק צָרְכֵּנוּ בַּמִּדְבָּר אַרְבָּעִים שָׁנָה
וְלֹא הֶאֱכִילָנוּ אֶת הַמָּן — דַּיֵּנוּ.
אִלּוּ הֶאֱכִילָנוּ אֶת הַמָּן
וְלֹא נָתַן לָנוּ אֶת הַשַּׁבָּת — דַּיֵּנוּ.

---

must first confess our sins, for we have come up short in our *avodas Hashem*. It is for this reason that we stand, as one is required to stand during *viduy*.

By admitting his deficiencies, a person receives the power to leave his מְצָרִים — his own narrow straits of physicality that hold him back from reaching his spiritual goals — and merits a personal exodus.

Rav Hutner notes the similarity between the word הוֹדָאָה, *thanks*, and וִידּוּי, *confession*. When one gives thanks, he is admitting that a kindness has been done on his behalf. Thus, it is befitting that tonight, a night of *hakaras hatov*, we begin our recitation of *Maggid* with a declaration of *viduy*.

As we think of all the goodness we received as a nation, it is

Had He executed judgments against them,
but not upon their gods,   it would have sufficed us.
Had He executed [judgments] against their gods,
but not slain their firstborn,
it would have sufficed us.
Had He slain their firstborn,
but not given us their wealth,
it would have sufficed us.
Had He given us their wealth,
but not split the sea for us,
it would have sufficed us.
Had He split the sea for us,
but not led us through it on dry land,
it would have sufficed us.
Had He led us through it on dry land,
but not drowned our oppressors in it,
it would have sufficed us.
Had He drowned our oppressors in it,
but not provided for our needs in the desert
for 40 years,   it would have sufficed us.
Had He provided for our needs in the desert
for 40 years, but not fed us the manna,
it would have sufficed us.
Had He fed us the manna,
but not given us the Shabbos,
it would have sufficed us.

---

also important for us to contemplate as well as articulate all the personal good that has been bestowed upon us. If every person would stop for a moment and think about all the good in his life, he would feel a stronger obligation to serve Hashem to the best of his ability.

What About Hakaras Hatov?

Hakaras hatov is a crucial part of our *avodas Hashem*. We are constantly finding ways to thank the Almighty for His kindness. We

אִלּוּ נָתַן לָנוּ אֶת הַשַּׁבָּת

וְלֹא קֵרְבָנוּ לִפְנֵי הַר סִינַי דַּיֵּנוּ.

אִלּוּ קֵרְבָנוּ לִפְנֵי הַר סִינַי

וְלֹא נָתַן לָנוּ אֶת הַתּוֹרָה דַּיֵּנוּ.

אִלּוּ נָתַן לָנוּ אֶת הַתּוֹרָה

וְלֹא הִכְנִיסָנוּ לְאֶרֶץ יִשְׂרָאֵל דַּיֵּנוּ.

אִלּוּ הִכְנִיסָנוּ לְאֶרֶץ יִשְׂרָאֵל

וְלֹא בָנָה לָנוּ אֶת בֵּית הַבְּחִירָה דַּיֵּנוּ.

עַל אַחַת כַּמָּה וְכַמָּה טוֹבָה כְפוּלָה וּמְכֻפֶּלֶת לַמָּקוֹם עָלֵינוּ. שֶׁהוֹצִיאָנוּ מִמִּצְרַיִם, וְעָשָׂה בָּהֶם שְׁפָטִים, וְעָשָׂה בֵאלֹהֵיהֶם, וְהָרַג אֶת בְּכוֹרֵיהֶם, וְנָתַן לָנוּ אֶת מָמוֹנָם, וְקָרַע לָנוּ אֶת הַיָּם, וְהֶעֱבִירָנוּ בְּתוֹכוֹ בֶּחָרָבָה, וְשִׁקַּע צָרֵינוּ בְּתוֹכוֹ, וְסִפֵּק צָרְכֵּנוּ בַּמִּדְבָּר אַרְבָּעִים שָׁנָה, וְהֶאֱכִילָנוּ אֶת הַמָּן, וְנָתַן לָנוּ אֶת הַשַּׁבָּת, וְקֵרְבָנוּ לִפְנֵי הַר סִינַי, וְנָתַן לָנוּ אֶת הַתּוֹרָה, וְהִכְנִיסָנוּ לְאֶרֶץ יִשְׂרָאֵל, וּבָנָה לָנוּ אֶת בֵּית הַבְּחִירָה, לְכַפֵּר עַל כָּל עֲווֹנוֹתֵינוּ.

are instructed to make 100 blessings a day in order to constantly have Him in our thoughts. Our initial persecution in Mitzrayim began when Pharaoh exhibited a lack of *hakaras hatov*, when he very conveniently forgot all that Yosef had done for him. It is thus incumbent upon us to emphasize the importance of *hakaras hatov*, and perhaps even more important, to exhibit such behavior: to Hashem, and to other human beings.

When Rav Aryeh Levin was yet a young man, he had already earned a reputation as an outstanding scholar in his mastery of Seder Nashim. He was also known for his unusual sensitivity and warmth. He was an outstanding lamdan and ba'al middos, an ideal talmid for any yeshivah.

Had He given us the Shabbos,
but not brought us close to Mount Sinai,
                    it would have sufficed us.
Had He brought us close to Mount Sinai,
but not given us the Torah,
                    it would have sufficed us.
Had He given us the Torah,
but not brought us into the Land of Israel,
                    it would have sufficed us.
Had He brought us into the Land of Israel,
but not built the Temple for us,
                    it would have sufficed us.

Thus, how much more so should we be grateful to the Omnipresent for all the numerous favors He showered upon us: He brought us out of Egypt; executed judgments against the Egyptians; executed [judgments] against their gods; slew their firstborn; gave us their wealth; split the sea for us; led us through it on dry land; drowned our oppressors in it; provided for our needs in the desert for 40 years; fed us the manna; gave us the Shabbos; brought us close to Mount Sinai; gave us the Torah; brought us to the Land of Israel; and built us the Temple, to atone for all our sins.

When Aryeh was 16, Rav Baruch Ber Leibowitz opened a yeshivah in Halusk, and Aryeh wanted to join. When Rav Baruch Ber met him, he was impressed with what he saw, and was excited to have such a bachur in his yeshivah. In fact, he asked Aryeh to learn with him two full sedarim: one in which they would learn Gemara, Maseches Eruvin, and one in which they would learn halachah from the Even HaEzer.

What a dream chavrusashaft it was for the young bachur. He cherished every day and grew immensely. Perhaps that is why it was so shocking when he approached Rav Baruch Ber a year later and told him he was leaving.

Rav Baruch Ber was very upset. He tried to convince him to stay,

רַבָּן גַּמְלִיאֵל הָיָה אוֹמֵר. כָּל שֶׁלֹא אָמַר שְׁלֹשָׁה דְּבָרִים אֵלּוּ בַּפֶּסַח, לֹא יָצָא יְדֵי חוֹבָתוֹ, וְאֵלּוּ הֵן,

פֶּסַח. מַצָּה. וּמָרוֹר.

פֶּסַח שֶׁהָיוּ אֲבוֹתֵינוּ אוֹכְלִים בִּזְמַן שֶׁבֵּית הַמִּקְדָּשׁ הָיָה קַיָּם, עַל שׁוּם מָה? עַל שׁוּם שֶׁפָּסַח הַקָּדוֹשׁ בָּרוּךְ הוּא עַל בָּתֵּי אֲבוֹתֵינוּ בְּמִצְרָיִם. שֶׁנֶּאֱמַר, וַאֲמַרְתֶּם, זֶבַח פֶּסַח הוּא לַיהוה, אֲשֶׁר פָּסַח עַל בָּתֵּי בְנֵי יִשְׂרָאֵל בְּמִצְרַיִם בְּנָגְפּוֹ אֶת מִצְרַיִם, וְאֶת בָּתֵּינוּ הִצִּיל, וַיִּקֹּד הָעָם וַיִּשְׁתַּחֲווּ.[1]

---

but there was nothing to talk about. Aryeh had made up his mind; he was going to learn in Volozhin. In truth, Rav Baruch Ber was so upset that years later, Rav Aryeh commented that he felt that he had certain difficulties in life because of the pain he had caused his rebbi.

Many years later, he revealed the reason for his departure. As in many yeshivos in those days, there was no dormitory in Halusk. Hence, Aryeh stayed at the home of a family that lived near the yeshivah. His hosts saw that he was diligent and bright, and they encouraged him to learn other languages. They tried to influence him to broaden his horizons, and tried to expose him to secular culture. Sensing the spiritual danger, he decided that he must leave.

When he gave this explanation years later, Rav Aryeh was asked why he did not share his reasoning with his rebbi. He would have certainly understood. Rav Aryeh asked in wonderment, "What about hakaras hatov? How could I have told Rav Baruch Ber? He would have approached the family and castigated them for driving me away. And this was a family that fed me and gave me room and board for a year. It would have shown a glaring lack of hakaras hatov."

Thus, he was willing to endure the consequences of causing pain to Rav Baruch Ber, rather than display a lack of hakaras hatov.

R abban Gamliel used to say: Whoever has not explained the following three things on Passover has not fulfilled his duty; namely,

Pesach — the pesach-offering;
Matzah — the unleavened bread;
Maror — the bitter herbs.

P esach — Why did our fathers eat a pesach-offering during the period when the Temple still stood? Because the Holy One, Blessed is He, passed over the houses of our fathers in Egypt, as it is written: You shall say: "It is a pesach-offering for HASHEM, Who passed over the houses of the Children of Israel in Egypt when He struck the Egyptians and spared our houses"; and the people bowed down and prostrated themselves.[1]

---

1. *Shemos* 12:27.

רַבָּן גַּמְלִיאֵל הָיָה אוֹמֵר
Rabban Gamliel used to say...

מַצָּה
Matzah

Cherishing a Mitzvah

Rabban Gamliel taught: "Whoever has not explained the following three things on Pesach has not fulfilled his duty; namely, *pesach, matzah,* and *maror.*"

Even in the darkest hours of Jewish history, our fellow Jews showed their love for the mitzvos connected to Pesach. Though their lives were at stake and they were not obligated to bake matzos, there were some individuals who cherished the mitzvah and would not give it up, no matter what.

Rav Yitzchak Shlomo Unger, the rosh yeshivah of Machaneh Avraham in Bnei Brak, told the following story. Hungarian Jewry

The middle matzah is lifted and displayed while the following
paragraph is recited.

מַצָּה זוּ שֶׁאָנוּ אוֹכְלִים, עַל שׁוּם מָה? עַל שׁוּם
שֶׁלֹּא הִסְפִּיק בְּצֵקָם שֶׁל אֲבוֹתֵינוּ
לְהַחֲמִיץ, עַד שֶׁנִּגְלָה עֲלֵיהֶם מֶלֶךְ מַלְכֵי הַמְּלָכִים
הַקָּדוֹשׁ בָּרוּךְ הוּא וּגְאָלָם. שֶׁנֶּאֱמַר, וַיֹּאפוּ אֶת
הַבָּצֵק אֲשֶׁר הוֹצִיאוּ מִמִּצְרַיִם עֻגֹת מַצּוֹת כִּי לֹא
חָמֵץ, כִּי גֹרְשׁוּ מִמִּצְרַיִם, וְלֹא יָכְלוּ לְהִתְמַהְמֵהַּ,
וְגַם צֵדָה לֹא עָשׂוּ לָהֶם.[1]

was spared the horrors of the Nazi regime until 1944. At that point,
with the Nazis sensing defeat, they decided that their last efforts
would be invested in annihilating Hungarian Jewry. Within two
months, they wiped out over 800,000 Jews.

Moshe's wife and children were sent to the gas chambers. Left
alone in Auschwitz, he continued to survive on the measly piece
of bread and murky bowl of soup he received every day. Sleeping
next to him in the barracks was Naftali, a scion of one of the most
prestigious and meyuchas'dike families in all of Europe. Naftali
gave Moshe the encouragement he needed, and attempted to
inject him with small doses of faith, which he had gleaned from
his father and grandfather.

With Pesach fast approaching, Naftali asked his friend, "In
Auschwitz, we have maror, bitternesss, in abundance. But where
are we going to get a kezayis of matzah?"

Moshe was aware of a large sack of wheat in the camp. But
anybody who tried to smuggle it into the barracks was liable to
be beaten to death. Nevertheless, he told his friend that he was
willing to bake some matzos, even if it meant putting his life at
risk. On Erev Pesach, Moshe and Naftali built a makeshift grinding
stone and oven. They managed to thresh out a little bit of flour, with
which they baked one thick matzah, enough for two ke'zeisim.

It was Moshe who was faced with the difficult task of smuggling
the matzah into the camp. He placed the thick piece of matzah under
his shirt. As he made his way toward the barracks, one of the German
guards asked him what he was hiding there. At first, he denied that
he was hiding anything, but then the matzah fell to the ground.

The middle matzah is lifted and displayed while the following
paragraph is recited.

M atzah — Why do we eat this unleavened
bread? Because the dough of our fathers
did not have time to become leavened before the
King of kings, the Holy One, Blessed is He, revealed Himself to them and redeemed them, as it
is written: They baked the dough which they had
brought out of Egypt into unleavened bread, for
it had not fermented, because they were driven
out of Egypt and could not delay, nor had they
prepared any provisions for the way.[1]

1. *Shemos* 12:39.

---

*Infuriated, the Nazi guard dug his boots into the matzah,
smashing it to smithereens. Then he began to pummel Moshe
with ferocious blows to the head and the body, until Moshe bled
profusely, and he felt he was losing consciousness. Even so, once
the Nazi stomped away, Moshe managed to gather some of the
crumbs. With his last bit of strength, he limped to the barracks,
collapsed onto the slab of concrete that was the Nazi excuse for a
bed, and closed his eyes.*

*A short while later, Naftali discovered what had happened to
his friend. He brought him some water and gave him a drink. As
he revived him, he noticed that Moshe had a smile on his face.
Looking at his bruised and bloody face, he could not understand
what he was smiling about. Then Moshe pulled out his hand, with
his fist closed. He opened it up, and there was a treasure inside:
one fistful of matzah — a kezayis.*

*Naftali could not believe his eyes. Tears streamed down his
cheeks. It was as if he were staring at a hand filled with diamonds. He
called out, "Ah heilige matzah! A holy matzah!" He was overjoyed
that he had matzah here in the valley of death. It was a beacon of
light! A sight that provided a medium of comfort. But what a shame
that only one of them would be able to fulfill his obligation.*

*Naftali immediately asked Moshe to give him the matzah. "I
have never missed eating matzah in my life. Please, I beg of you.
Let me have it."*

[169] **TOUCHED BY OUR STORY**

The *maror* is lifted and displayed
while the following paragraph is recited.

מָרוֹר זֶה שֶׁאָנוּ אוֹכְלִים, עַל שׁוּם מָה? עַל
שׁוּם שֶׁמֵּרְרוּ הַמִּצְרִים אֶת חַיֵּי אֲבוֹתֵינוּ
בְּמִצְרַיִם. שֶׁנֶּאֱמַר, וַיְמָרְרוּ אֶת חַיֵּיהֶם, בַּעֲבֹדָה
קָשָׁה, בְּחֹמֶר וּבִלְבֵנִים, וּבְכָל עֲבֹדָה בַּשָּׂדֶה, אֶת
כָּל עֲבֹדָתָם אֲשֶׁר עָבְדוּ בָהֶם בְּפָרֶךְ.[1]

Moshe could not believe what he was hearing. As he lay there more dead than alive, he wondered how his friend could ask him for the matzah. After all, he had sacrificed everything and almost lost his life doing so. The matzah was rightfully his.

But Naftali was not ready to give up so fast. He proposed that since he knows the Haggadah by heart, he would recite it aloud, and thus, he would get to eat the matzah. But Moshe was not ready to give in. Naftali cried out, "I lost my wife and children. Please let me have the matzah. It is all I have left in this world." But Moshe quickly retorted that he was in the same position. He had also lost his wife and children.

After much negotiating, Moshe agreed to the following proposition: Naftali would eat the matzah and recite the Haggadah, while Moshe would receive the reward for the mitzvah. That night, the two of them celebrated the Seder in this very manner.

The next day, truly inspired by the previous evening's events, Naftali prayed quietly in the middle of his work. But when he came to the words of Hallel, he could no longer control his exuberance and began to sing the words aloud. When the Nazi guard saw that he was praying, he shot Naftali on the spot. Moshe was brokenhearted.

He managed to survive the war and rebuild his life in Bnei Brak, and became a member of Rav Unger's congregation, Chug Chasam Sofer. One day in the 1970's, he told this story to Rav Unger. Then he told the rav that the previous night, Naftali had come to him in a dream. "He looked like an angel," explained Moshe to his rav, "yet he had a despondent look on his face. He asked if I would relinquish the reward for the mitzvah of eating the matzah that night. I reminded him that we had made a deal that he would get to eat the matzah, while I would receive the reward. But he begged me over and over.

Maror — Why do we eat this bitter herb? Because the Egyptians embittered the lives of our fathers in Egypt, as it says: They embittered their lives with hard labor, with mortar and bricks, and with all manner of labor in the field: Whatever service they made them perform was with hard labor.[1]

---

1. *Shemos* 1:14.

"That is why I came here today, to ask you if I am supposed to relinquish the reward of the mitzvah to my friend."

Awed by the story, the rav told Moshe that this is not a question for a rav, but for a Chassidic Rebbe. He directed him to the tzaddik, the Machnovka Rebbe. The Machnovka Rebbe listened carefully to the story and the question, and gave a very surprising response. "If you want to do what's yashar, you should be mevater on the reward of the mitzvah."

Yashrus?! Moshe could not believe what he had just heard. His only question was if he should go beyond the call of duty. But he certainly felt that he was entitled to keep the reward if he wanted to.

The Machnovka Rebbe explained, "Look at what he has and look at what you have. Your friend was killed. What does he have? He has only the mitzvos and the rewards he acquired through them. This is one mitzvah he did not receive the reward for. However, you are alive. You have the opportunity to don tallis and tefillin, make berachos, learn Torah, and do countless other good deeds. Additionally, you have children whom you have educated to follow in your footsteps. Don't you think that it is only yashrus to allow him to have the reward for this one mitzvah?"

Hearing it put that way, Moshe immediately agreed to give over the reward for this mitzvah. "Fine, I will be mevater."

But the Rebbe was not satisfied. He told him that it was not enough. He pulled out a ring of keys and instructed him to go into the empty beis midrash nearby. "Open the door and light the candles inside. Open the Aron with this key, put your head inside, and pour out your heart to Hashem. Tell Him how you knew your friend; speak about the close friendship you shared, and the strength and the encouragement you gained from him.

בְּכָל דּוֹר וָדוֹר חַיָּב אָדָם לִרְאוֹת אֶת עַצְמוֹ
כְּאִלּוּ הוּא יָצָא מִמִּצְרָיִם. שֶׁנֶּאֱמַר, וְהִגַּדְתָּ
לְבִנְךָ בַּיּוֹם הַהוּא לֵאמֹר, בַּעֲבוּר זֶה עָשָׂה יהוה
לִי, בְּצֵאתִי מִמִּצְרָיִם.[1] לֹא אֶת אֲבוֹתֵינוּ בִּלְבָד גָּאַל
הַקָּדוֹשׁ בָּרוּךְ הוּא, אֶלָּא אַף אֹתָנוּ גָּאַל עִמָּהֶם.
שֶׁנֶּאֱמַר, וְאוֹתָנוּ הוֹצִיא מִשָּׁם, לְמַעַן הָבִיא אֹתָנוּ
לָתֶת לָנוּ אֶת הָאָרֶץ אֲשֶׁר נִשְׁבַּע לַאֲבוֹתֵינוּ.[2]

The matzos are covered and the cup is lifted and held until it is to be drunk. According to some customs, however, the cup is put down after the following paragraph, in which case the matzos should once more be uncovered. If this custom is followed, the matzos are to be covered and the cup raised again upon reaching the blessing אֲשֶׁר גְּאָלָנוּ, *Who has redeemed us* (p. 182).

Tell Hashem about what happened that night, the last night of his life. Tell how Naftali was even willing to give up the reward for the mitzvah just for the opportunity to perform the mitzvah. Then cry that you are willing to give up the reward for your friend, to give nachas ruach to his neshamah."

Moshe followed the instructions to a T. Afterward, he was completely exhausted. He closed the Aron, kissed the Paroches, and returned the keys to the gabbai. He did not have the strength to go to the Rebbe, but promised himself that he would visit him the next day. That night, his friend appeared to him once more. But this time, his face was glowing as he came to thank Moshe for his selfless act.

The next morning, Moshe went to the Rebbe and informed him of the previous night's dream. The Rebbe responded, "Your friend was the progeny of a special family. No doubt, he performed countless mitzvos throughout his lifetime. He was even privileged to die by sanctifying God's Name. If he had committed any sins in his lifetime, they were certainly erased. Our Sages tell us that if a person is murdered as he sanctifies God's Name, no one can stand in his proximity in Gan Eden. Nevertheless, it was worth it for him to leave the comfort of basking in the glow of the Almighty to come down to ask you for the reward for one more mitzvah. One mitzvah!"

And we? How many mitzvos are just sitting there at our feet waiting for us to perform them? How many minutes a day do we

In every generation it is one's duty to regard himself as though he personally had gone out of Egypt, as it says: You shall tell your son on that day: "It was because of this that HASHEM did for 'me' when I went out of Egypt."[1] It was not only our fathers whom the Holy One, Blessed is He, redeemed from slavery; we, too, were redeemed with them, as it says: He brought "us" out from there so that He might take us to the land which He had promised to our fathers.[2]

The matzos are covered and the cup is lifted and held until it is to be drunk. According to some customs, however, the cup is put down after the following paragraph, in which case the matzos should once more be uncovered. If this custom is followed, the matzos are to be covered and the cup raised again upon reaching the blessing אֲשֶׁר גְּאָלָנוּ, *Who has redeemed us* (p. 182).

_____

1. *Shemos.* 13:8. 2. *Devarim* 6:23.

---

squander when we could be accumulating countless rewards? How much learning? Davening? *Chesed?*

Indeed, Moshe gave up the reward for that one mitzvah, but this story gave him much greater understanding about how we must continue to live our lives: cherishing every mitzvah.

בְּכָל דּוֹר וָדוֹר
In every generation...

וְהִגַּדְתָּ לְבִנְךָ
You shall tell your son...

Saved by a Father

The Pesach Seder revolves around one primary mitzvah: "*Ve'higadeta le'vincha* — You shall tell your son" (*Shemos* 13:8). It is very important for a father to prepare properly and share all that he knows about the Exodus with his child. It is crucial that he instill faith in his children by sharing with them the miracles that the Jewish people experienced so many years ago.

It is also worth noting the people whose lives were saved because of this mitzvah.

This story takes place in 1944, the year the Germans set their eyes on Hungary, and annihilated so many Jews in a very short period of time. Though he was only in his late 20's, the Yeshuos Moshe, Rav Moshe Yehoshua Hager of Vizhnitz, led a congregation in the community of Vilkhovitz, in the Ukraine. Upon hearing the devastating news of the German atrocities, he strengthened and encouraged his people.

As Pesach drew near, however, he had an overwhelming desire to travel to his father, the Imrei Chaim, in Grosswardein, which was in Hungary, so that his father could fulfill the commandment of "Ve'higadeta le'vincha." Although he was much safer in his village, and his community pleaded with him not to endanger himself, he felt an urgency to see his father and spend Pesach with him. He was already a leader of many families, yet he still felt that he was a child in need of guidance, and that he would benefit from being close to his father.

Though traveling in general was extremely risky, it was impossible to travel by train. If a Jew would be seen on a train, he was at risk of being shot. The Hungarian non-Jews hated the Jews as much as the Germans did, and they were more than happy to help out the Nazis. The Rebbe thought of an ingenious plan. He had his assistants rent an ambulance, pretending he was ill and in urgent need of medical attention. They informed the authorities that he was going to a hospital in Klausenberg, which was not far from Grosswardein. His wife and daughter escorted him on the journey.

There were many dangerous moments, but with great siyata d'Shmaya, he made it safely to Grosswardein and spent Pesach with his father. Immediately after, his father advised him to escape to Romania and he was thus able to save himself from the Nazis.

Years later, he would reflect on how the importance he placed on the mitzvah of "Ve'higadeta le'vincha" had saved his life.

The metaphor of the story should not be lost on us. If only we would realize that this is the most crucial night for fathers and sons; it is the night that children in danger can be saved. For those sons who have yet to perceive the beauty of Torah, tonight is the night that we can change all that.

With the proper love and attention, there is no telling how much we can accomplish.

Something Important to Say

Rav Shimshon Pincus once met a colleague who had just come back from a fund-raising trip in America. The fellow was somewhat dejected since he had been unable to gather the necessary funds for his yeshivah. Rav Shimshon told him that if he really believes in what he is doing, and is truly confident that it is beneficial for the donor to give him money, then he would be more successful. In fact, he insisted, there was no way he would ever fail. Rav Shimshon then gave an example to prove his point.

"One time, when I was in Los Angeles, someone showed me a New York Times article from 1942, where the Vaad Hatzalah advertised that for $50, one could save Jews in Europe. Imagine that you had read that article, and, unlike American Jewry in 1942, you knew what was happening in the war. You knew that every Jew there wasn't safe, and that he would, in all probability, be killed, unless you were able to get him out of the inferno — soon. And for $50 you would be able to save those people. When you went knocking on doors, you would not leave without a significant donation. You would beg and implore every person to give you the necessary funding. You'd know the value of every $50.

"Indeed, if you really believed that it is beneficial for every person to give the money — so that he could take part in this precious mitzvah of saving lives — you would not leave without a check. Failure would not be an option.

"That," he said, "is the key to raising money for those who are learning. You must really believe that the person who is giving the money is receiving a benefit by giving the money and joining in the mitzvah of limud Torah."

Rav Shimshon recalled an anecdote to emphasize his message.

"There was a housing office in Ofakim, where there were always very long lines. The woman behind the desk was careful not to let anyone cut the line.

"One day, I saw her father walking near our home, when suddenly, he collapsed. Before anyone had a chance to revive him, he passed away. I quickly ran to the woman's office to inform her of the tragic news. As usual, there was a long line, but I walked right

up to the front. She immediately snapped at me that I was to wait in the back of the line like everybody else. But I told her that I have to talk to her about something very important. Again, she told me that I should go to the back of the line. I leaned forward and asked her if she knew where her father was. She did not understand the question, and I repeated it. 'Do you know where your father is?' I broke the news to her gently, and she began to cry. Of course, she apologized for trying to send me away.

"Can you imagine if I would have waited in line to tell her this news? What an absurd thought that is. I knew I had something very important to say to her, and I wasn't about to let anything stand in my way."

Although Rav Pincus used this story to encourage a fund-raiser, this is the way a parent must approach the Seder. We have something very, very important to tell our children. We have the traditions and legacies that our parents passed down to us, and we need to convey the lessons to our progeny.

Initially, we may be met with resistance. Our children may not want to hear what we have to say. They may tell us to "wait in line," by stating, "I have so many important things in my life. I have school and my social life and my other interests."

Yet, tonight we cannot be pushed away. We must let our children know how important this message is: Do you know where your Father is? Do you know where the Almighty is in your life?

When they see how serious we are about it, they will stop pushing us away. They will listen to everything we have to say, and will be eternally grateful to us for sharing this message.

Extraordinary Lives

Mr. Richard Bernstein, Michigan Supreme Court Justice-elect, is an extremely accomplished man; perhaps his most noteworthy accomplishment — and the reason he is such an inspiring individual — is what he has done with his life despite his disability. Richard Bernstein is blind. In spite of the difficulties he faces, Richard has used athletics as a motivational tool to help him grow and achieve. He has run in 18 marathons and a triathlon.

Before the last marathon, he was badly injured by a passing cyclist and spent 10 weeks in the hospital and in a rehab facility. Many people wondered if he would ever be able to compete again. But those people do not know Richard. They don't understand his perseverance and commitment. They don't realize that he believes in something greater than his own abilities and strengths.

He believes in Hashem.

Richard himself describes the challenge of swimming as a blind person, competing with hundreds of others, being kicked in the face and pushed downward, struggling to find his way to the top so he can catch his breath when he can't see anything... and the only thing that is saving him is the rope that is tethered to him as his guide. In life, too, we try to swim along with the crowd, but inevitably, we are pushed down, and we struggle to find our way to the top so we can simply catch our breath. If it were not for the fact that we are tethered to our Guide, Hashem, we would never be able to survive.

At a recent dinner for Ohel Family Services, Mr. Bernstein gave a riveting speech, pulsating with emunah and perspective on life. He told the story of a religious woman, a young mother, who called him up in tears. She had prayed for a long time to have a child, and finally, she was blessed with a boy, but the child had many disabilities. She asked Mr. Bernstein: Would her child ever have friends? Would her child ever be able to walk and talk normally? Would her child ever get a job? Would her child be able to make it on his own, after she is no longer there to protect him? Yes, she wanted to know the answers to all of these questions. "To sum it up," she said, "will my child ever be an ordinary child?"

Richard was quiet for a moment and then he answered her. "No, your child will not be an ordinary child. Because you and your child were not brought to this earth to be merely ordinary. Rather, you were brought here to be extraordinary. You were brought to this earth to lead extraordinary lives: lives of challenge, but lives of excitement, drama, purpose, meaning, and connection to Hashem."

This message must propel us to realize that we, too, have not been brought here to lead ordinary lives. Every individual, family, and community faces its own challenges, which are meant to inspire us to find meaning and purpose in our lives, and to strengthen our connection with Hashem.

This is a message we want to convey to our children tonight — and every night.

לְפִיכָךְ אֲנַחְנוּ חַיָּבִים לְהוֹדוֹת, לְהַלֵּל, לְשַׁבֵּחַ, לְפָאֵר, לְרוֹמֵם, לְהַדֵּר, לְבָרֵךְ, לְעַלֵּה, וּלְקַלֵּס, לְמִי שֶׁעָשָׂה לַאֲבוֹתֵינוּ וְלָנוּ אֶת כָּל הַנִּסִּים הָאֵלּוּ, הוֹצִיאָנוּ מֵעַבְדוּת לְחֵרוּת, מִיָּגוֹן לְשִׂמְחָה, וּמֵאֵבֶל לְיוֹם טוֹב, וּמֵאֲפֵלָה לְאוֹר גָּדוֹל, וּמִשִּׁעְבּוּד לִגְאֻלָּה. וְנֹאמַר לְפָנָיו שִׁירָה חֲדָשָׁה, הַלְלוּיָהּ.

הַלְלוּיָהּ הַלְלוּ עַבְדֵי יהוה, הַלְלוּ אֶת שֵׁם יהוה. יְהִי שֵׁם יהוה מְבֹרָךְ, מֵעַתָּה וְעַד עוֹלָם. מִמִּזְרַח שֶׁמֶשׁ עַד מְבוֹאוֹ, מְהֻלָּל שֵׁם יהוה. רָם עַל כָּל גּוֹיִם יהוה, עַל הַשָּׁמַיִם כְּבוֹדוֹ. מִי כַּיהוה אֱלֹהֵינוּ, הַמַּגְבִּיהִי לָשָׁבֶת. הַמַּשְׁפִּילִי לִרְאוֹת, בַּשָּׁמַיִם וּבָאָרֶץ. מְקִימִי מֵעָפָר דָּל, מֵאַשְׁפֹּת יָרִים אֶבְיוֹן. לְהוֹשִׁיבִי עִם נְדִיבִים, עִם נְדִיבֵי עַמּוֹ. מוֹשִׁיבִי עֲקֶרֶת הַבַּיִת, אֵם הַבָּנִים שְׂמֵחָה; הַלְלוּיָהּ.[1]

לְפִיכָךְ
Therefore...

מֵעַבְדוּת לְחֵרוּת
From servitude to redemption...

◄§ Free to Be Free

Pesach is referred to as *z'man cheiruseinu*, the time of our freedom. Freedom has many definitions. A famous non-Jewish personality defined freedom as "another word for nothing left to lose." Having lived a reckless, irresponsible life, she died at the age of 30.

What is our definition of freedom?

It says in *Pirkei Avos* (6:2), "*Ein lecha ben chorin ella mi she'oseik be'salmud Torah* — You can have no freer man than one who

Therefore it is our duty to thank, praise, pay tribute, glorify, exalt, honor, bless, extol, and acclaim Him Who performed all these miracles for our fathers and for us. He brought us forth from slavery to freedom, from grief to joy, from mourning to festivity, from darkness to great light, and from servitude to redemption. Let us, therefore, recite a new song before Him! Halleluyah!

Halleluyah! Praise, you servants of HASHEM, praise the Name of HASHEM. Blessed is the Name of HASHEM from now and forever. From the rising of the sun to its setting, HASHEM's Name is praised. High above all nations is HASHEM, above the heavens is His glory. Who is like HASHEM, our God, Who is enthroned on high, yet lowers Himself to look upon heaven and earth? He raises the destitute from the dust; from the trash heaps He lifts the needy — to seat them with nobles, with nobles of His people. He transforms the barren wife into a glad mother of children. Halleluyah![1]

---

1. *Tehillim* 113.

---

engages in the study of Torah." All other pursuits do not give a person freedom. Rather, they shackle the individual to his desires. He is not free at all. Only one who toils in Torah is a free person.

The Vizhnitzer Rebbe, the *Yeshuos Moshe*, had a clever twist to the expression *z'man cheiruseinu*, the time of our freedom. He said, "*Zolst bafrie'en di tziet* — We must free up our time," and maximize our ability to learn and do mitzvos. Only then can each of us become a true *ben chorin*, a true free man.

> *A young man was enrolled in a Vizhnitzer yeshivah, but that was the extent of his affiliation. Instead of attending classes or learning with a chavrusa, he would spend his time on the streets, getting into all sorts of trouble. He also wasted his time with the latest technology. This aggravated his parents and his teachers to no end. They searched for a solution, but they came up empty.*

בְּצֵאת יִשְׂרָאֵל מִמִּצְרָיִם, בֵּית יַעֲקֹב מֵעַם לֹעֵז. הָיְתָה יְהוּדָה לְקָדְשׁוֹ, יִשְׂרָאֵל מַמְשְׁלוֹתָיו. הַיָּם רָאָה וַיָּנֹס, הַיַּרְדֵּן יִסֹּב לְאָחוֹר. הֶהָרִים רָקְדוּ כְאֵילִים, גְּבָעוֹת כִּבְנֵי צֹאן. מַה לְּךָ הַיָּם כִּי תָנוּס, הַיַּרְדֵּן תִּסֹּב לְאָחוֹר. הֶהָרִים תִּרְקְדוּ כְאֵילִים, גְּבָעוֹת כִּבְנֵי צֹאן. מִלִּפְנֵי אָדוֹן חוּלִי אָרֶץ, מִלִּפְנֵי אֱלוֹהַּ יַעֲקֹב. הַהֹפְכִי הַצּוּר אֲגַם מָיִם, חַלָּמִישׁ לְמַעְיְנוֹ מָיִם.[1]

Left with no other recourse, they enlisted the help of the Vizhnitzer Rebbe. They were certain that he would scold the young man and threaten him with expulsion if his behavior did not improve drastically.

When the boy was summoned to the Rebbe, he knew what awaited him, and did not want to face the rebuke he was about to receive. He entered the inner chamber of the Rebbe against his will. But when he came out, he was wearing a huge smile across his face. His parents were shocked. What had happened? Why could he possibly be smiling?

He told them that the Rebbe had given him a Minchas Chinuch and instructed him to review three specific chapters. He told him that in three days, he was going to test him on those chapters. Sure enough, three days later, he went back to the Rebbe, and they spent a lot of time discussing what he had learned. Once more, he walked out with a big smile on his face, beaming with pride and a feeling of satisfaction. He continued to learn with the Rebbe, and before long became one of the stars of the yeshivah.

When the shevatim threw Yosef into the pit, the pasuk says (Bereishis 37:24), "Ve'habor reik ein bo mayim — The pit was empty, no water was in it." Rashi tells us that even though there was no water in the pit, there were snakes and scorpions. The Vizhnitzer Rebbe explained that water is a reference to Torah. When one is void of the Torah, the spiritual snakes and scorpions will fill its place.

And so, he explained his method of drawing the boy closer: "I knew that his mind was filled with other interests because he had not filled it with Torah. But once his spiritual thirst was quenched

When Israel went forth from Egypt, Yaakov's household from a people of alien tongue, Yehudah became His sanctuary, Israel His dominion. The sea saw and fled; the Jordan turned backward.The mountains skipped like rams, and the hills like young lambs. What ails you, O sea, that you flee? O Jordan, that you turn backward? O mountains, that you skip like rams? O hills, like young lambs? Before HASHEM's presence: tremble, O earth, before the presence of the God of Yaakov, Who turns the rock into a pond of water, the flint into a flowing fountain.[1]

---

1. *Tehillim* 114.

---

and he tasted the beauty of Torah, the snakes and scorpions would find other places to go."

We often excuse our lack of Torah study by saying we don't have the time. In truth, our time is trapped by the spiritual snakes and scorpions in our lives. We must free our time if we want to be free. *Zolst bafrie'en di tziet!*

בְּצֵאת יִשְׂרָאֵל
When Israel went forth...

הָיְתָה יְהוּדָה לְקָדְשׁוֹ
Yehudah became His sanctuary...

A Sacrifice for Salvation

Nissan is a month of miracles. *Rav Yisrael of Rizhin* explains that, even now, the month still retains its status. However, if we want those miracles to happen, we must follow in the footsteps of our ancestors. How do we do this?

We say in *Hallel*, "*Hayesah Yehudah le'kadsho* — Yehudah became His sanctuary" (*Tehillim* 114: 2). The *Rosh* explains that Hashem singled out the *shevet* of Yehudah for royalty, because they sanctified His Name by the sea. Led by Nachshon ben Aminadav,

According to all customs the cup is lifted and the matzos covered during the recitation of this blessing. (On Motza'ei Shabbos the phrase in parentheses substitutes for the preceding phrase.)

בָּרוּךְ אַתָּה יהוה אֱלֹהֵינוּ מֶלֶךְ הָעוֹלָם, אֲשֶׁר גְּאָלָנוּ וְגָאַל אֶת אֲבוֹתֵינוּ מִמִּצְרַיִם, וְהִגִּיעָנוּ הַלַּיְלָה הַזֶּה לֶאֱכָל בּוֹ מַצָּה וּמָרוֹר. כֵּן יהוה אֱלֹהֵינוּ וֵאלֹהֵי אֲבוֹתֵינוּ, יַגִּיעֵנוּ לְמוֹעֲדִים וְלִרְגָלִים אֲחֵרִים הַבָּאִים לִקְרָאתֵנוּ לְשָׁלוֹם, שְׂמֵחִים בְּבִנְיַן עִירֶךָ וְשָׂשִׂים בַּעֲבוֹדָתֶךָ, וְנֹאכַל שָׁם מִן הַזְּבָחִים וּמִן הַפְּסָחִים (מִן הַפְּסָחִים וּמִן הַזְּבָחִים) אֲשֶׁר יַגִּיעַ דָּמָם עַל קִיר מִזְבַּחֲךָ לְרָצוֹן. וְנוֹדֶה לְךָ שִׁיר חָדָשׁ עַל גְּאֻלָּתֵנוּ וְעַל פְּדוּת נַפְשֵׁנוּ. בָּרוּךְ אַתָּה יהוה, גָּאַל יִשְׂרָאֵל.

Some have the custom to recite the following declaration of intent.

הִנְנִי מוּכָן וּמְזֻמָּן לְקַיֵּם מִצְוַת כּוֹס שֵׁנִי מֵאַרְבַּע כּוֹסוֹת. לְשֵׁם יִחוּד קֻדְשָׁא בְּרִיךְ הוּא וּשְׁכִינְתֵּיהּ, עַל יְדֵי הַהוּא טָמִיר וְנֶעְלָם, בְּשֵׁם כָּל יִשְׂרָאֵל. וִיהִי נֹעַם אֲדֹנָי אֱלֹהֵינוּ עָלֵינוּ, וּמַעֲשֵׂה יָדֵינוּ כּוֹנְנָה עָלֵינוּ, וּמַעֲשֵׂה יָדֵינוּ כּוֹנְנֵהוּ.

בָּרוּךְ אַתָּה יהוה אֱלֹהֵינוּ מֶלֶךְ הָעוֹלָם, בּוֹרֵא פְּרִי הַגָּפֶן.

The second cup is drunk while leaning on the left side — preferably the entire cup, but at least most of it.

---

their prince, they were the first to jump into the water, and that is when the sea split. The *Reishis Chochmah* maintains that the lesson from *Krias Yam Suf* is that if we are prepared to sacrifice ourselves, then we will merit miracles.

In the mid-1800's, the lawmakers of the Russian village of Pezing forbade circumcisions of converts without specific permission from the czar. As he was well aware that no such permission would ever be forthcoming, the rav, Rav Moshe Leib Gedung, risked his life and circumcised those who wished to come into the fold. But then, disaster struck.

According to all customs the cup is lifted and the matzos covered during the recitation of this blessing. (On Motza'ei Shabbos the phrase in parentheses substitutes for the preceding phrase.)

Blessed are You, HASHEM, our God, King of the universe, Who redeemed us and redeemed our ancestors from Egypt and enabled us to reach this night that we may eat on it matzah and *maror.* So, HASHEM, our God and God of our fathers, bring us also to future holidays and festivals in peace, gladdened in the rebuilding of Your city and joyful at Your service. There we shall eat of the offerings and *pesach* sacrifices (of the *pesach* sacrifices and offerings) whose blood will gain the sides of Your Altar for gracious acceptance. We shall then sing a new song of praise to You for our redemption and for the liberation of our souls. Blessed are You, HASHEM, Who has redeemed Israel.

Some have the custom to recite the following declaration of intent.

Behold, I am prepared and ready to fulfill the mitzvah of the second of the Four Cups. For the sake of the unification of the Holy One, Blessed is He, and His Presence, through Him Who is hidden and inscrutable — [I pray] in the name of all Israel. May the pleasantness of the Lord, our God, be upon us, and may He establish our handiwork for us; our handiwork may He establish.

Blessed are You, HASHEM, our God, King of the universe, Who creates the fruit of the vine.

The second cup is drunk while leaning on the left side — preferably the entire cup, but at least most of it.

Rav Moshe Leib performed a circumcision, but the new convert began to hemorrhage, and the rav was unable to stop the bleeding. A few onlookers began to panic. What could they do? They couldn't go to a regular doctor, as he would report the crime and a full investigation could endanger the entire Jewish community. However, if they didn't do something, the convert would die.

Left with no choice, the mohel bandaged his patient as best he could, and brought him to the Chasam Sofer, Rav Moshe Schreiber. The Chasam Sofer listened carefully to the story, and

רחצה

The hands are washed for matzah and the following blessing is recited.
It is preferable to bring water and a basin to the head of the household
at the Seder table.

בָּרוּךְ אַתָּה יהוה אֱלֹהֵינוּ מֶלֶךְ הָעוֹלָם,
אֲשֶׁר קִדְּשָׁנוּ בְּמִצְוֹתָיו, וְצִוָּנוּ עַל
נְטִילַת יָדָיִם.

מוציא / מצה

Some recite the following before the blessing *hamotzi*.

הִנְנִי מוּכָן וּמְזוּמָּן לְקַיֵּם מִצְוַת אֲכִילַת מַצָּה. לְשֵׁם יִחוּד
קֻדְשָׁא בְּרִיךְ הוּא וּשְׁכִינְתֵּיהּ, עַל יְדֵי הַהוּא טָמִיר וְנֶעְלָם,
בְּשֵׁם כָּל יִשְׂרָאֵל. וִיהִי נְעַם אֲדֹנָי אֱלֹהֵינוּ עָלֵינוּ, וּמַעֲשֵׂה יָדֵינוּ
כּוֹנְנָה עָלֵינוּ, וּמַעֲשֵׂה יָדֵינוּ כּוֹנְנֵהוּ.

gave a shocking response. He told the two of them that they had
no choice but to go to the river and take their own lives. If they did
not, they would be guilty of causing all the inhabitants of the city
to be wiped out in a pogrom for violating the czar's decree.

In an admirable display of emunas chachamim, and with
unbelievable self-sacrifice, the two of them walked to the river,
ready to jump in. But when they arrived, an old man whom they
did not recognize approached and asked them what they were
about to do. After they told him their story, he reached into his
pocket and pulled out a small case. Inside was a medicine that
caused clotting. They wanted to thank him for saving both of their
lives, but when they turned away for a moment, he disappeared.
They looked all around, yet were unable to locate him.

It had to have been Eliyahu HaNavi.

After the rav administered the medicine, the two of them
immediately went back to the Chasam Sofer to tell him the wonderful
news. As they entered his home, it seemed as if he was awaiting their
arrival. When they saw him smile before they even said anything,
they realized that he was well aware of the entire episode.

But there was one thing they did not understand. Why did they
have to go through the process of going to the river to end their

RACHTZAH

The hands are washed for matzah and the following blessing is recited. It is preferable to bring water and a basin to the head of the household at the Seder table.

B lessed are You, HASHEM, our God, King of the universe, Who has sanctified us with His commandments, and has commanded us concerning the washing of the hands.

MOTZI / MATZ AH

Some recite the following before the blessing *hamotzi*.

B ehold, I am prepared and ready to fulfill the mitzvah of eating matzah. For the sake of the unification of the Holy One, Blessed is He, and His Presence, through Him Who is hidden and inscrutable — [I pray] in the name of all Israel. May the pleasantness of the Lord, our God, be upon us, and may He establish our handiwork for us; our handiwork may He establish.

---

lives, before the old man came with the clotting agent? Why didn't Eliyahu give it to them immediately?

The Chasam Sofer answered their question with a compelling thought. In order for Eliyahu to come, the individual must first display mesirus nefesh. If the two of them had not gone to the river, the old man would never have come to save them.

At times, we need a miracle to survive. And there are times when the Almighty will send Eliyahu to help perform that miracle, but first we must show that we are willing to give up everything for Him.

Motzi/Matzah / מצה / מוציא

Healing and Believing

Matzah is referred to in the *Zohar* (2:183) by two esoteric names: *michla de'asvasa*, food of healing, and *michla dimheimnusa*, food of belief. The truth is that the two are dependent upon each other. When one believes, the matzah has a power to heal.

The following two blessings are recited over matzah; the first is recited over matzah as food, and the second for the special mitzvah of eating matzah on the night of Passover. [The latter blessing is to be made with the intention that it also apply to the "sandwich" and the *afikoman*.] The head of the household raises all the matzos on the Seder plate and recites the following blessing:

בָּרוּךְ אַתָּה יהוה אֱלֹהֵינוּ מֶלֶךְ הָעוֹלָם, הַמּוֹצִיא לֶחֶם מִן הָאָרֶץ.

The bottom matzah is put down and the following blessing is recited while the top (whole) matzah and the middle (broken) piece are still raised.

בָּרוּךְ אַתָּה יהוה אֱלֹהֵינוּ מֶלֶךְ הָעוֹלָם, אֲשֶׁר קִדְּשָׁנוּ בְּמִצְוֹתָיו, וְצִוָּנוּ עַל אֲכִילַת מַצָּה.

Each participant is required to eat an amount of matzah equal in volume to an egg. Since it is usually impossible to provide a sufficient amount of matzah from the two matzos for all members of the household, other matzos should be available at the head of the table from which to complete the required amounts. However, each participant should receive a piece from each of the top two matzos. The matzos are to be eaten while reclining on the left side and without delay; they need not be dipped in salt.

In the *sefer Be'er Tzvi*, Rav Tzvi Kintzlicher tells a personal story.

"It was a few days before Pesach, and I became critically ill with an intestinal problem. The top doctors in Klausenberg said that it was urgent that I be operated upon immediately. However, I did not want to be in the hospital over Yom Tov. Instead, I trusted in Hashem that the surgery could wait and I went home. The doctor instructed me to eat only milk, eggs, and orange juice, and certainly not any bread or matzah.

"I adhered to the doctor's orders as much as I could, but I allowed myself a kezayis of matzah on each of the nights of the Seder, which I soaked in boiling milk. Amazingly, on the second night after the Seder, my pains disappeared completely and did not return.

"Immediately after Pesach, I returned to Klausenberg to see the doctor. When he took an X-ray, he was astonished that there was no longer any need for surgery, since my stomach was completely healed. He asked me if I had taken any medicines or involved myself in any remedies. I told him that I had eaten a kezayis of

The following two blessings are recited over matzah; the first is recited over matzah as food, and the second for the special mitzvah of eating matzah on the night of Passover. [The latter blessing is to be made with the intention that it also apply to the "sandwich" and the *afikoman*.] The head of the household raises all the matzos on the Seder plate and recites the following blessing:

B lessed are You, HASHEM, our God, King of the universe, Who brings forth bread from the earth.

The bottom matzah is put down and the following blessing is recited while the top (whole) matzah and the middle (broken) piece are still raised.

B lessed are You, HASHEM, our God, King of the universe, Who has sanctified us with His commandments, and has commanded us concerning the eating of the matzah.

Each participant is required to eat an amount of matzah equal in volume to an egg. Since it is usually impossible to provide a sufficient amount of matzah from the two matzos for all members of the household, other matzos should be available at the head of the table from which to complete the required amounts. However, each participant should receive a piece from each of the top two matzos. The matzos are to be eaten while reclining on the left side and without delay; they need not be dipped in salt.

---

matzah on the first two nights of Pesach. The doctor had no choice but to acknowledge the miraculous power of the matzah. He admitted that the knowledge and wisdom of physicians are like nothing when weighed against the will of Hashem."

There are times when we, too, are cynical, yet we must always remember that the power of the commandments we perform and the effect they have on us are directly dependent upon our belief in that power.

Fulfilling the Mitzvah

Rav Ephraim Oshry, the author of the sefer Mi'maamakim, recounted an unusual shailah that came to him during World War II. The people in the ghetto wanted to make sure that they would have matzos for Pesach. It was nearly impossible to procure the flour needed for the baking of the matzos; the food was rationed

מרור

The head of the household takes a half-egg volume of *maror*, dips it into *charoses*, and gives each participant a like amount.

Some recite the following before *maror*:

הִנְנִי מוּכָן וּמְזוּמָן לְקַיֵּם מִצְוַת אֲכִילַת מָרוֹר. לְשֵׁם יִחוּד קֻדְשָׁא בְּרִיךְ הוּא וּשְׁכִינְתֵּיהּ, עַל יְדֵי הַהוּא טָמִיר וְנֶעְלָם, בְּשֵׁם כָּל יִשְׂרָאֵל. וִיהִי נֹעַם אֲדֹנָי אֱלֹהֵינוּ עָלֵינוּ, וּמַעֲשֵׂה יָדֵינוּ כּוֹנְנָה עָלֵינוּ, וּמַעֲשֵׂה יָדֵינוּ כּוֹנְנֵהוּ.

The following blessing is recited with the intention that it also apply to the *maror* of the "sandwich." The *maror* is eaten without reclining, and without delay.

בָּרוּךְ אַתָּה יהוה אֱלֹהֵינוּ מֶלֶךְ הָעוֹלָם, אֲשֶׁר קִדְּשָׁנוּ בְּמִצְוֹתָיו, וְצִוָּנוּ עַל אֲכִילַת מָרוֹר.

כורך

The bottom (thus far unbroken) matzah is now taken. From it, with the addition of other matzos, each participant receives a half-egg volume of matzah with an equal-volume portion of *maror* (dipped into *charoses* which is shaken off). The following paragraph is recited and the "sandwich" is eaten while reclining.

זֵכֶר לְמִקְדָּשׁ כְּהִלֵּל. כֵּן עָשָׂה הִלֵּל בִּזְמַן שֶׁבֵּית הַמִּקְדָּשׁ הָיָה קַיָּם. הָיָה כּוֹרֵךְ (פֶּסַח) מַצָּה וּמָרוֹר וְאוֹכֵל בְּיַחַד. לְקַיֵּם מַה שֶׁנֶּאֱמַר, עַל מַצּוֹת וּמְרֹרִים יֹאכְלֻהוּ.[1]

---

and they were not given any flour. In fact, the Germans, who were aware that Pesach was on the horizon, wanted to do everything within their power to make sure that the Jews did not have matzos to eat on Pesach. But one Yid would not be deterred.

His name was Avraham.

Every day, Avraham was escorted outside the ghetto walls to work for the Germans. As such, he had access to things that many of the others in the ghetto did not. He decided to get flour for matzah, but wondered how to do so without attracting attention. He came

MAROR

The head of the household takes a half-egg volume of *maror*, dips it into *charoses*, and gives each participant a like amount.

Some recite the following before *maror*:

Behold, I am prepared and ready to fulfill the mitzvah of eating maror. For the sake of the unification of the Holy One, Blessed is He, and His Presence, through Him Who is hidden and inscrutable — [I pray] in the name of all Israel. May the pleasantness of the Lord, our God, be upon us, and may He establish our handiwork for us; our handiwork may He establish.

The following blessing is recited with the intention that it also apply to the *maror* of the "sandwich." The *maror* is eaten without reclining, and without delay.

Blessed are You, HASHEM, our God, King of the universe, Who has sanctified us with His commandments, and has commanded us concerning the eating of maror.

KOREICH

The bottom (thus far unbroken) matzah is now taken. From it, with the addition of other matzos, each participant receives a half-egg volume of matzah with an equal-volume portion of *maror* (dipped into *charoses* which is shaken off). The following paragraph is recited and the "sandwich" is eaten while reclining.

In remembrance of the Temple we do as Hillel did in Temple times: He would combine (the *pesach*-offering,) matzah and maror in a sandwich and eat them together, to fulfill what it says [in the Torah]: They shall eat it with matzos and bitter herbs.[1]

---

1. *Bamidbar* 9:11.

---

up with a method of smuggling small amounts around his body.

He did this for two months. The people in the ghetto finally had enough flour, and he was about to stop the smuggling operation. But then, someone asked him to smuggle a bit more, just one more day's worth.

He gladly agreed. However, this time, as he was about to enter the ghetto, one of the Germans decided to search him. Sure enough, he discovered the flour on Avraham's body.

שלחן עורך

The meal should be eaten in a combination of joy and solemnity, for the meal, too, is part of the Seder service. While it is desirable that *zemiros* and discussion of the laws and events of Pesach be part of the meal, extraneous conversation should be avoided. It should be remembered that the *afikoman* must be eaten while there is still some appetite for it. In fact, if one is so sated that he must literally force himself to eat it, he is not credited with the performance of the mitzvah of *afikoman*. Therefore, it is unwise to eat more than a moderate amount during the meal.

צפון

From the *afikoman* matzah (and from additional matzos to make up the required amount) a half-egg volume portion — according to some, a full egg's volume portion — is given to each participant. It should be eaten before midnight, while reclining, without delay, and uninterruptedly. Nothing may be eaten or drunk after the *afikoman* (with the exception of water and the like) except for the last two Seder cups of wine.

Some recite the following before eating the *afikoman:*

הִנְנִי מוּכָן וּמְזוּמָן לְקַיֵּם מִצְוַת אֲכִילַת אֲפִיקוֹמָן. לְשֵׁם יִחוּד
קֻדְשָׁא בְּרִיךְ הוּא וּשְׁכִינְתֵּיהּ, עַל יְדֵי הַהוּא טָמִיר וְנֶעְלָם,
בְּשֵׁם כָּל יִשְׂרָאֵל. וִיהִי נֹעַם אֲדֹנָי אֱלֹהֵינוּ עָלֵינוּ, וּמַעֲשֵׂה יָדֵינוּ
כּוֹנְנָה עָלֵינוּ, וּמַעֲשֵׂה יָדֵינוּ כּוֹנְנֵהוּ:

Avraham was brutally beaten. He awoke in a bed, having lost all of his teeth, his eyes swollen shut. And, despite his condition, a shailah occurred to him: one that would not wait until he felt better.

He hobbled to the rav's house and told him what had happened, crying as he did so. Yet his tears were not about what had happened to him, but about his worry that, without teeth, he would not be yotzei the mitzvah of eating matzah.

Tzafun / צפון

The Cost of Anger

One cannot stress enough the importance of keeping calm and not getting angry before and during the Seder. Whether it means

SHULCHAN OREICH

The meal should be eaten in a combination of joy and solemnity, for the meal, too, is part of the Seder service. While it is desirable that *zemiros* and discussion of the laws and events of Pesach be part of the meal, extraneous conversation should be avoided. It should be remembered that the *afikoman* must be eaten while there is still some appetite for it. In fact, if one is so sated that he must literally force himself to eat it, he is not credited with the performance of the mitzvah of *afikoman*. Therefore, it is unwise to eat more than a moderate amount during the meal.

TZAFUN

From the *afikoman* matzah (and from additional matzos to make up the required amount) a half-egg volume portion — according to some, a full egg's volume portion — is given to each participant. It should be eaten before midnight, while reclining, without delay, and uninterruptedly. Nothing may be eaten or drunk after the *afikoman* (with the exception of water and the like) except for the last two Seder cups of wine.

Some recite the following before eating the *afikoman:*

Behold, I am prepared and ready to fulfill the mitzvah of eating the *afikoman*. For the sake of the unification of the Holy One, Blessed is He, and His Presence, through Him Who is hidden and inscrutable — [I pray] in the name of all Israel. May the pleasantness of the Lord, our God, be upon us, and may He establish our handiwork for us; our handiwork may He establish.

---

being sensitive to a stranger, a spouse, or even one's own child, staying away from *kaas* is part and parcel of fulfilling the mitzvos of the Yom Tov. The *Bnei Yissaschar* writes in *Derech Pikudecha* that since one who gets angry is considered as though he has served an idol (see *Mishneh Torah, Hilchos Dei'os* 2:3), it is possible that he may not be included in a *chaburah* of Yidden who are eating the *korban pesach* together. Perhaps we can take this further, and say that one who gets angry may not be allowed to eat the *afikoman*, since it is in place of the *korban pesach*.

A few stories put this in perspective.

The Tolna Rebbe, Rav Yochanan Twersky, was extremely careful to fulfill many stringencies connected to Pesach. He was especially particular not to eat gebrokts, not to allow any of the matzah to come in contact with liquid, as per the custom of his ancestors of the Chernobyl dynasty. One year, on the yahrtzeit of Rav Aharon of Karlin (the 19th of Nissan, the third day of Chol HaMoed), he conducted a special gathering.

Among those in attendance was a fellow who ate gebrokts. When this gentleman was served a bowl of soup, he took his matzah and broke it into his bowl. As soon as those around him saw what he was doing, they screamed at him and scolded him for his unacceptable behavior. The fellow was so embarrassed that he stopped eating.

The Rebbe did not want to make a bigger scene and risk embarrassing him any further, so at first he kept quiet. Then suddenly, he asked if he could have another bowl of soup. Immediately, a few people jumped up to run into the kitchen to fetch him a bowl. But before they had a chance to do so, he motioned that they should sit down. Instead, he called out to the end of the table where the embarrassed fellow was sitting. "Would I be able to have the rest of your bowl?" To the shock of everyone present, he took the rest of the bowl and ate the soup, wet matzah and all.

When he finished, he looked at those who were staring in bewilderment and explained, "When you screamed at that fellow, there was a strong complaint in Heaven against my family and me for not stopping him from being shamed in public. When I ate his bowl of soup and he was appeased, the complaint was lifted.

"Although customs are important, they are still just customs. But embarrassing another Jew is like murdering him. You tell me which one is more important."

Rav Binyamin Rabinowitz, of the Eidah HaChareidis of Yerushalayim, was very particular to eat the afikoman before chatzos. One year, the discussions during Maggid carried on longer than usual and his family washed for Motzi/Matzah a mere 20 minutes before chatzos. Two of his grandchildren went into the kitchen and informed their grandmother that she should serve the meal very quickly, so they would be able to eat the afikoman on time.

When Rav Binyamin realized what they had done, he instructed them to go back to their places. He then called them over and explained, "You made my rebbetzin feel bad. Do you know that she spent so much time making sure that everything was tasty and delicious, and just perfect? Now, you caused her pain by making her rush the meal. It is a davar pashut that all the stringencies of the Seder are worth nothing when compared to the krechtz of one Jew."

❖

When he conducted his Seder each year, the Tolna Rebbe reached exalted heights, and that was the one time a year in which he wore the yarmulke of the Rebbe, Rav Zishe.

One year, in the middle of the Seder, he noticed a young boy walk into the room holding a bottle of beer — which was genuine chametz. While everyone in the room wondered what to do, the Rebbe approached the child and gently instructed him to put the bottle down. With everyone watching, he told the young boy to get a bucket to place over the bottle, as is dictated by Chazal: One who finds chametz on Pesach must cover it with a vessel (Pesachim 6a). Next, the Rebbe told him to get a white towel to place on top of the bucket, to cover it lichvod Yom Tov. Then he thanked the boy for giving him the opportunity to fulfill the dictum of Chazal.

The stakes are high and there's much pressure, but we must do everything in our power to ensure that we do not get angry.

The Reward for Self-Control

In the village of Yaniv, near the city of Pinsk, lived a fellow named Yaakov who served as a shammas in the shul. He set up the tables, swept and mopped and dusted, and made sure the shul was properly heated in the winter. He would collect the siddurim and Chumashim after davening, and when necessary, distribute them beforehand.

One Erev Yom Kippur, the village inhabitants had already concluded their seudah hamafsekes, and people began to arrive for Kol Nidrei. Yaakov stood in front of the bookcase where all the machzorim were stored, and handed one to each person who came forward. It was self-understood that the more prestigious people received theirs first. However, with a large amount of people standing there, Yaakov could not focus on who was standing before him, and he inadvertently handed a machzor to Reb Zelig the shoemaker before giving one to Reb Moshe the gvir.

Unfortunately, Reb Moshe was obsessed with his own honor and he lost himself. Even though the holiest day of the year was about to begin, he could not control his anger. To the astonishment

בּרך

The third cup is poured and *Bircas HaMazon* (Grace After Meals) is recited. According to some customs, the Cup of Eliyahu is poured at this point.

שִׁיר הַמַּעֲלוֹת בְּשׁוּב יהוה אֶת שִׁיבַת צִיּוֹן, הָיִינוּ כְּחֹלְמִים. אָז יִמָּלֵא שְׂחוֹק פִּינוּ, וּלְשׁוֹנֵנוּ רִנָּה; אָז יֹאמְרוּ בַגּוֹיִם: הִגְדִּיל יהוה לַעֲשׂוֹת עִם אֵלֶּה. הִגְדִּיל יהוה לַעֲשׂוֹת עִמָּנוּ, הָיִינוּ שְׂמֵחִים. שׁוּבָה יהוה אֶת שְׁבִיתֵנוּ, כַּאֲפִיקִים בַּנֶּגֶב. הַזֹּרְעִים בְּדִמְעָה, בְּרִנָּה יִקְצֹרוּ. הָלוֹךְ יֵלֵךְ וּבָכֹה נֹשֵׂא מֶשֶׁךְ הַזָּרַע; בֹּא יָבֹא בְרִנָּה, נֹשֵׂא אֲלֻמֹּתָיו.[1]

---

of everyone present, he smacked Yaakov across the face for his "terrible transgression."

The people in shul gasped. What shocking behavior! They looked at Yaakov and waited to see how he would respond, but they waited for nothing. Although his face was bright red with shame, he walked toward the back of the shul and parked himself among the poor and indigent of the community.

When the poor people asked him why he had placed himself at the back of the shul, he explained that he was in a state of excommunication. They did not understand what he was talking about. Why would Yaakov have been excommunicated? He was beloved by everyone.

Yaakov explained, "If, because of me, a Jew could become so angry at the most exalted moments of the year, then I must accept upon myself a niduy, an excommunication."

The people who witnessed the scene were in awe of the remarkable self-control and humility displayed by Yaakov. But they were not the only ones.

His behavior caused quite a commotion in Heaven. The Heavenly Court decided to reward Yaakov and his wife with a very special child, one who would light up the world with his holiness and his Torah.

BAREICH

The third cup is poured and *Bircas HaMazon* (Grace After Meals) is recited. According to some customs, the Cup of Eliyahu is poured at this point.

A song of Ascents. When HASHEM brings back the exiles to Zion, we will have been like dreamers. Then our mouth will be filled with laughter, and our tongue with glad song. Then will it be said among the nations: HASHEM has done great things for these. HASHEM has done great things for us, and we rejoiced. Restore our captives, HASHEM, like streams in the dry land. Those who sow in tears shall reap in joy. Though the farmer bears the measure of seed to the field in tears, he shall come home with joy, bearing his sheaves.[1]

---
1. *Tehillim* 126.

One year later, Yaakov and his wife were blessed with a child, whom they named Aharon. He would grow up to become Rav Aharon HaGadol, a primary disciple of the Mezritcher Maggid and the founder of the Karliner Chassidus.

Bareich / ברך

Opening the door for, and pouring the Cup of, Eliyahu

◆§ He's Really Here

The *Divrei Chaim of Sanz* would recount a riveting thought from the *Rama MiPano*, one of the great Italian Kabbalists. The Gemara in *Arachin* (13a) says that in the times of the *Beis HaMikdash*, there were always six sheep that were already checked, waiting to be offered as the twice-a-day *korban tamid*.

After the destruction of the second *Beis HaMikdash*, those earmarked sheep were brought to the desert. Every day, Eliyahu

HaNavi goes to the marketplace to purchase female sheep and brings them to the desert to mate with the males and give birth to new sheep. Then, he sacrifices two sheep for the *korban tamid*. When Pesach arrives, Eliyahu sacrifices the *korban pesach* and brings a part of it to the *tzaddikim* of every generation. They are deemed *menuyin*, those designated for the *korban*. Since there are *tzaddikim* who live outside of Eretz Yisrael, Eliyahu brings them the *avira* of Eretz Yisrael, so that it is considered as if they are eating the *korban pesach* in Eretz Yisrael and Yerushalayim.

The *Sanzer* adds that even if one is not worthy of having Eliyahu bring him a portion of the *korban pesach*, if we believe that *tzaddikim* eat from this *korban* and attach ourselves to these *tzaddikim*, it is considered as though we are eating from it.

The *Sanzer* continues that he is not merely referring to the metaphysical concept, but to the actual reality of *tzaddikim* eating the *korban: ah shtik korban pesach*! And if one questions how we can eat of the *korban* if we are *temei'ei meis*, this is not a problem for two possible reasons. First of all, "*tumah hutrah be'tzibbur* — impurity is permitted in a communal setting." Another explanation would be that Eliyahu brings the ashes of the *parah adumah* along with him and purifies those who are *tamei* before he gives them a *kezayis*.

The *Satmar Rav* related this thought from the *Sanzer* and concluded that those who were present saw the *Sanzer* eat the *afikoman* with gusto, as if he were eating the *korban pesach*.

With this thought, the *Satmar Rav* conveyed an inspiring message. In *Ha Lachma Anya,* we declare, "*Kol dichfin yeisei ve'yeichol* — Whoever is hungry, let him come and eat." We sit down at the Seder in the middle of this long Exile, with no Kohen to offer the *korban pesach* for us. Nevertheless, if someone wants: "*Kol ditzrich yesei ve'yifsach* — Whoever is in need, let him partake of the *pesach*." There is nothing that stops our will. The passage continues: "*Hashata hacha* — Now, we are here," and only those with a genuine need and will can eat, but "*le'shanah hab'ah be'ara de'Yisrael* — next year may we be in the Land of Israel." At that time, everyone will be able to partake of the *korban pesach*.

When I shared this thought with others, it was often met with some skepticism; some dismissed it as a "*Chassidishe maaseh*." However, it is important to note the obvious: Eliyahu HaNavi comes to every Seder! Is that also to be dismissed as some far-fetched story? In truth, we must strengthen our *emunas chachamaim;* by attaching ourselves to *tzaddikim,* we can glean from their *kedushah* and connect to their exalted souls.

> *Rav Avrohom Blumenkrantz, a rav from Far Rockaway whose Pesach book has become a staple in many Jewish homes, was blessed with a very large family. One of his children is my brother-in-law. He described the magnificent atmosphere in his home on Pesach. At Shefoch Chamas'cha, the Blumenkrantz children would walk toward the door, the men on one side and the women on the other. Rav Avrohom would open the door and welcome Eliyahu with such genuine warmth, that his loud proclamation, "Baruch haba, Eliyahu HaNavi! Welcome, Eliyahu HaNavi!" left no doubt as to Eliyahu's presence. He then "escorted" him through the row of children toward the Pesach table. After Shefoch Chamas'cha, Rav Avrohom would walk toward the door, and then "walk" Eliyahu out the door. There were even times that Rav Avrohom would follow him a few more steps down the block, all the while calling out, "Gut Yom Tov, Eliyahu!" One could sense the joy and thrill.*

In some homes, people shake the table a bit to show the children that Eliyahu has come to drink from the *Kos shel Eliyahu.* But I would humbly suggest that we teach our children to believe things even if we can't actually see them.

After all, one day soon, he will be here.

Don't You See Him?

For some, Eliyahu has already arrived.

> *Lisa burst through the door with a smile from ear to ear, holding onto her most recent project: a painted kos shel Eliyahu. "Mommy, Mommy, can we use it for Passover?" Lisa was 5 years old and was attending Hebrew School only because her friend was going and Lisa wanted to go, as well. Thus far, her parents, Alan and Sherry Lustman, had managed to temper her enthusiasm for her Jewish studies. They had not anticipated that she would be coming home with anything more than some harmless Chanukah cookies and "Dip the Apple in the Honey" songs. They certainly had not imagined anything like this.*
>
> *Their daughter was getting caught up in the fanaticism of the Orthodox lifestyle, and it was starting to make their lives*

הִנְנִי מוּכָן וּמְווּמָן לְקַיֵּם מִצְוַת עֲשֵׂה שֶׁל בִּרְכַּת הַמָּזוֹן, כַּכָּתוּב, וְאָכַלְתָּ
וְשָׂבָעְתָּ, וּבֵרַכְתָּ אֶת ה' אֱלֹהֶיךָ עַל הָאָרֶץ הַטֹּבָה אֲשֶׁר נָתַן לָךְ.

---

complicated. There was a disturbing argument about the family's
lack of observance of the dietary laws, about which their daughter
had learned. Alan was content with his lifestyle and was not
interested in having his routine altered in any way.

Sherry pretended to be extremely excited about the plastic
painted cup that her daughter had designated for use as Eliyahu's
cup. She ooohhhed and aaahhhed over her daughter's work of
art, and assured her that they would most certainly use it for their
Seder. The only problem was that her husband was not interested
in having a Seder to begin with, let alone allowing their daughter
to become emotionally involved in another religious experience.
He was fine with the upbringing he had. The marginal knowledge
of Hebrew and Jewish concepts had not diminished the quality of
his life, and that was the education and nurturing he wished for his
child. Sherry knew he would be less than thrilled, but she had to
acknowledge her daughter's wishes and adjust accordingly.

As predicted, Alan was not the least bit happy about celebrating
the Seder in any shape or form, but as his daughter listened from
a distance to the conversation he and his wife were having, he
could not help but be moved by her innocent desire for a Seder.
So he agreed, though he worried that Lisa would expect the same
ceremony year after year. Sherry immediately told their daughter
that they would, in fact, be displaying her cup at the Seder, and
Lisa's smile was almost too wide for her tiny face to hold.

The day finally arrived. Alan donned a skullcap for the ceremonial
Seder meal. When urged by his wife to conduct himself in animated
fashion, he again began to question the notion of going through
with this outward show. Perhaps he should not have agreed to it in
the first place. But once more, he was won over by his daughter's
sweet smile and innocence. Alan pretended to care about the Four
Questions and listened as Lisa sang the first line of Dayeinu. Alan
ate some lettuce and actually did not mind the crisp, crunchy taste
of the matzah. The meal was delicious and — as the hour was
getting late — he told his wife and daughter that he was going to
sleep.

Behold, I am prepared and ready to fulfill the mitzvah of Grace After Meals, as it is stated: "And you shall eat and you shall be satisfied and you shall bless HASHEM, your God, for the good land that He gave you."

"But what about the Cup of Eliyahu?" Lisa looked at her mother anxiously.

Alan was quickly losing his patience. In his mind, he had gone beyond the call of duty. He had played the Pesach game, and now he was tired and wanted to go to sleep. To him, Eliyahu was no more of a reality than the tooth fairy. Allowing his child to think otherwise was fine as long as he did not have to play along. He was disgusted and fed up. "That's it. I'm going upstairs." Then, on his way out of the dining room, to his daughter's horror, Alan grabbed the cup of Eliyahu and threw it to the floor.

It was nearly 1 in the morning, and Alan had been twisting and turning since getting into bed. He felt guilty about what had happened earlier that evening and wanted to check on his little girl. But when Alan looked into his daughter's bedroom, he was surprised to see that her bed was empty. Slowly, he walked downstairs to see where she had fallen asleep. But as he reached the bottom of the stairs and walked into the living room, his heart nearly broke.

There she stood, her little face pressed up against the window, precious tears streaming down her face. Alan could not help but cry. His daughter looked up toward him. "What's wrong, Lisa? Why are you up?"

Lisa didn't answer; she just pointed out the window. "What are you looking at? Why don't you go back to sleep?"

One last time, Lisa looked back at her father. "Daddy, don't you see him? He's waiting right by the door for us to open it for him …" Lisa turned back toward her father and buried her head in his strong grasp. Shaking his head in disbelief, he stared out the window and could not help but wonder if his daughter really did see him.

This moving episode not only conveys the purity of faith and trust that small children possess, but also mirrors our beliefs. If only we would be hopeful of his arrival and await his coming, we would recognize that he is indeed standing there just outside, all alone, waiting …

If three or more males, aged 13 or older, participated in the meal, the leader is required to formally invite the others to join him in the recitation of Grace After Meals. Following is the *Zimun*, or formal invitation.

The leader begins:

רַבּוֹתַי נְבָרֵךְ.

The group responds:

יְהִי שֵׁם יהוה מְבֹרָךְ מֵעַתָּה וְעַד עוֹלָם.

The leader continues:

יְהִי שֵׁם יהוה מְבֹרָךְ מֵעַתָּה וְעַד עוֹלָם.

If 10 men join in the *Zimun*, אֱלֹהֵינוּ, *our God* (in parentheses), is included.

בִּרְשׁוּת מָרָנָן וְרַבָּנָן וְרַבּוֹתַי, נְבָרֵךְ [אֱלֹהֵינוּ] שֶׁאָכַלְנוּ מִשֶּׁלּוֹ.

The group responds:

בָּרוּךְ [אֱלֹהֵינוּ] שֶׁאָכַלְנוּ מִשֶּׁלּוֹ וּבְטוּבוֹ חָיִינוּ.

The leader continues:

בָּרוּךְ [אֱלֹהֵינוּ] שֶׁאָכַלְנוּ מִשֶּׁלּוֹ וּבְטוּבוֹ חָיִינוּ.

The following line is recited if 10 men join in the *Zimun*.

בָּרוּךְ הוּא וּבָרוּךְ שְׁמוֹ.

בָּרוּךְ אַתָּה יהוה אֱלֹהֵינוּ מֶלֶךְ הָעוֹלָם, הַזָּן אֶת הָעוֹלָם כֻּלּוֹ, בְּטוּבוֹ, בְּחֵן בְּחֶסֶד וּבְרַחֲמִים, הוּא נֹתֵן לֶחֶם לְכָל בָּשָׂר, כִּי לְעוֹלָם חַסְדּוֹ. וּבְטוּבוֹ הַגָּדוֹל, תָּמִיד לֹא חָסַר לָנוּ, וְאַל יֶחְסַר לָנוּ מָזוֹן לְעוֹלָם וָעֶד. בַּעֲבוּר שְׁמוֹ הַגָּדוֹל, כִּי הוּא אֵל זָן וּמְפַרְנֵס לַכֹּל, וּמֵטִיב לַכֹּל, וּמֵכִין מָזוֹן לְכָל בְּרִיּוֹתָיו אֲשֶׁר בָּרָא. בָּרוּךְ אַתָּה יהוה, הַזָּן אֶת הַכֹּל.

נוֹדֶה לְךָ יהוה אֱלֹהֵינוּ, עַל שֶׁהִנְחַלְתָּ לַאֲבוֹתֵינוּ אֶרֶץ חֶמְדָּה טוֹבָה וּרְחָבָה. וְעַל שֶׁהוֹצֵאתָנוּ יהוה אֱלֹהֵינוּ מֵאֶרֶץ מִצְרַיִם, וּפְדִיתָנוּ מִבֵּית עֲבָדִים,

If three or more males, aged 13 or older, participated in the meal, the leader is required to formally invite the others to join him in the recitation of Grace After Meals. Following is the *Zimun,* or formal invitation.

The leader begins:

Gentlemen, let us bless.

The group responds:

Blessed is the Name of HASHEM from this moment and forever!

The leader continues:

Blessed is the Name of HASHEM from this moment and forever!

If 10 men join in the *Zimun,* אֱלֹהֵינוּ, *our God* (in parentheses), is included.

With the permission of the distinguished people present, let us bless [our God] for we have eaten from what is His.

The group responds:

Blessed is He [our God] of Whose we have eaten and through Whose goodness we live.

The leader continues:

Blessed is He [our God] of Whose we have eaten and through Whose goodness we live.

The following line is recited if 10 men join in the *Zimun.*

Blessed is He and Blessed is His Name.

Blessed are You, HASHEM, our God, King of the universe, Who nourishes the entire world; in His goodness, with grace, with lovingkindness, and with mercy. He gives nourishment to all flesh, for His lovingkindness is eternal. And through His great goodness, nourishment was never lacking to us, and may it never be lacking to us forever. For the sake of His Great Name, because He is God Who nourishes and sustains all, and benefits all, and He prepares food for all of His creatures which He has created. Blessed are You, HASHEM, Who nourishes all.

We thank You, HASHEM, our God, because You have given to our forefathers as a heritage a desirable, good, and spacious land; because You removed us, HASHEM, our God, from the land of Egypt and You redeemed us from the house of bondage;

וְעַל בְּרִיתְךָ שֶׁחָתַמְתָּ בִּבְשָׂרֵנוּ, וְעַל תּוֹרָתְךָ
שֶׁלִּמַּדְתָּנוּ, וְעַל חֻקֶּיךָ שֶׁהוֹדַעְתָּנוּ, וְעַל חַיִּים חֵן
וָחֶסֶד שֶׁחוֹנַנְתָּנוּ, וְעַל אֲכִילַת מָזוֹן שֶׁאַתָּה זָן
וּמְפַרְנֵס אוֹתָנוּ תָּמִיד, בְּכָל יוֹם וּבְכָל עֵת וּבְכָל שָׁעָה.

וְעַל הַכֹּל יהוה אֱלֹהֵינוּ, אֲנַחְנוּ מוֹדִים לָךְ
וּמְבָרְכִים אוֹתָךְ, יִתְבָּרַךְ שִׁמְךָ בְּפִי כָּל
חַי תָּמִיד לְעוֹלָם וָעֶד. כַּכָּתוּב, וְאָכַלְתָּ וְשָׂבָעְתָּ,
וּבֵרַכְתָּ אֶת יהוה אֱלֹהֶיךָ, עַל הָאָרֶץ הַטֹּבָה אֲשֶׁר
נָתַן לָךְ.[1] בָּרוּךְ אַתָּה יהוה, עַל הָאָרֶץ וְעַל הַמָּזוֹן.

רַחֵם (נָא) יהוה אֱלֹהֵינוּ עַל יִשְׂרָאֵל עַמֶּךָ,
וְעַל יְרוּשָׁלַיִם עִירֶךָ, וְעַל צִיּוֹן מִשְׁכַּן
כְּבוֹדֶךָ, וְעַל מַלְכוּת בֵּית דָּוִד מְשִׁיחֶךָ, וְעַל הַבַּיִת
הַגָּדוֹל וְהַקָּדוֹשׁ שֶׁנִּקְרָא שִׁמְךָ עָלָיו. אֱלֹהֵינוּ
אָבִינוּ, רְעֵנוּ זוּנֵנוּ פַּרְנְסֵנוּ וְכַלְכְּלֵנוּ וְהַרְוִיחֵנוּ,
וְהַרְוַח לָנוּ יהוה אֱלֹהֵינוּ מְהֵרָה מִכָּל צָרוֹתֵינוּ.
וְנָא אַל תַּצְרִיכֵנוּ, יהוה אֱלֹהֵינוּ, לֹא לִידֵי מַתְּנַת
בָּשָׂר וָדָם, וְלֹא לִידֵי הַלְוָאָתָם, כִּי אִם לְיָדְךָ
הַמְּלֵאָה הַפְּתוּחָה הַקְּדוֹשָׁה וְהָרְחָבָה, שֶׁלֹּא נֵבוֹשׁ
וְלֹא נִכָּלֵם לְעוֹלָם וָעֶד.

On Shabbos add the following paragraph.

רְצֵה וְהַחֲלִיצֵנוּ יהוה אֱלֹהֵינוּ בְּמִצְוֹתֶיךָ, וּבְמִצְוַת
יוֹם הַשְּׁבִיעִי הַשַּׁבָּת הַגָּדוֹל וְהַקָּדוֹשׁ הַזֶּה, כִּי
יוֹם זֶה גָּדוֹל וְקָדוֹשׁ הוּא לְפָנֶיךָ, לִשְׁבָּת בּוֹ וְלָנוּחַ בּוֹ
בְּאַהֲבָה כְּמִצְוַת רְצוֹנֶךָ, וּבִרְצוֹנְךָ הָנִיחַ לָנוּ יהוה אֱלֹהֵינוּ,
שֶׁלֹּא תְהֵא צָרָה וְיָגוֹן וַאֲנָחָה בְּיוֹם מְנוּחָתֵנוּ, וְהַרְאֵנוּ
יהוה אֱלֹהֵינוּ בְּנֶחָמַת צִיּוֹן עִירֶךָ, וּבְבִנְיַן יְרוּשָׁלַיִם עִיר
קָדְשֶׁךָ, כִּי אַתָּה הוּא בַּעַל הַיְשׁוּעוֹת וּבַעַל הַנֶּחָמוֹת.

for Your covenant which You sealed in our flesh; for Your Torah that You taught us and for Your statutes that You made known to us; for life, grace, and lovingkindness which You granted us; and for the provision of food with which You nourish and sustain us constantly, in every day, in every season and in every hour.

For all, HASHEM, our God, we thank You and bless You. May Your Name be blessed continuously by the mouth of all the living, continuously for all eternity. As it is written: "And you shall eat and you shall be satisfied, and you shall bless HASHEM, your God, for the good land which He gave you."[1] Blessed are You, HASHEM, for the land and for the food.

Have mercy (we beg You) HASHEM, our God, on Your people Israel, on Your city Jerusalem, on Zion the resting place of Your Glory, on the monarchy of the house of David, Your anointed, and on the great and holy House upon which Your Name is called. Our God, our Father — tend us, nourish us, sustain us, support us, relieve us; HASHEM, our God, grant us speedy relief from all our troubles. Please, HASHEM, our God, make us not needful of the gifts of human hands nor of their loans, but only of Your Hand that is full, open, holy, and generous, that we not feel inner shame nor be humiliated for ever and ever.

On Shabbos add the following paragraph.

May it please You to strengthen us, HASHEM, our God — through Your commandments, and through the commandment of the seventh day, this great and holy Sabbath. For this day is great and holy before You to rest on it and be content on it in love, as ordained by Your will. May it be Your will, HASHEM, our God, that there be no distress, grief, or lament on this day of our contentment. And show us, HASHEM, our God, the consolation of Zion, Your city, and the rebuilding of Jerusalem, city of Your holiness, for You are the Master of salvations and Master of consolations.

---

1. *Devarim* 8:10.

[203] **TOUCHED BY OUR STORY**

אֱלֹהֵינוּ וֵאלֹהֵי אֲבוֹתֵינוּ, יַעֲלֶה, וְיָבֹא, וְיַגִּיעַ, וְיֵרָאֶה, וְיֵרָצֶה, וְיִשָּׁמַע, וְיִפָּקֵד, וְיִזָּכֵר זִכְרוֹנֵנוּ וּפִקְדוֹנֵנוּ, וְזִכְרוֹן אֲבוֹתֵינוּ, וְזִכְרוֹן מָשִׁיחַ בֶּן דָּוִד עַבְדֶּךָ, וְזִכְרוֹן יְרוּשָׁלַיִם עִיר קָדְשֶׁךָ, וְזִכְרוֹן כָּל עַמְּךָ בֵּית יִשְׂרָאֵל לְפָנֶיךָ, לִפְלֵיטָה לְטוֹבָה לְחֵן וּלְחֶסֶד וּלְרַחֲמִים, לְחַיִּים וּלְשָׁלוֹם, בְּיוֹם חַג הַמַּצּוֹת הַזֶּה. זָכְרֵנוּ יהוה אֱלֹהֵינוּ בּוֹ לְטוֹבָה, וּפָקְדֵנוּ בוֹ לִבְרָכָה, וְהוֹשִׁיעֵנוּ בוֹ לְחַיִּים (טוֹבִים). וּבִדְבַר יְשׁוּעָה וְרַחֲמִים, חוּס וְחָנֵּנוּ וְרַחֵם עָלֵינוּ וְהוֹשִׁיעֵנוּ, כִּי אֵלֶיךָ עֵינֵינוּ, כִּי אֵל (מֶלֶךְ) חַנּוּן וְרַחוּם אָתָּה.

וּבְנֵה יְרוּשָׁלַיִם עִיר הַקֹּדֶשׁ בִּמְהֵרָה בְיָמֵינוּ. בָּרוּךְ אַתָּה יהוה, בּוֹנֵה (בְרַחֲמָיו) יְרוּשָׁלָיִם. אָמֵן.

בָּרוּךְ אַתָּה יהוה אֱלֹהֵינוּ מֶלֶךְ הָעוֹלָם, הָאֵל אָבִינוּ מַלְכֵּנוּ אַדִּירֵנוּ בּוֹרְאֵנוּ גּוֹאֲלֵנוּ יוֹצְרֵנוּ קְדוֹשֵׁנוּ קְדוֹשׁ יַעֲקֹב, רוֹעֵנוּ רוֹעֵה יִשְׂרָאֵל, הַמֶּלֶךְ הַטּוֹב וְהַמֵּטִיב לַכֹּל, שֶׁבְּכָל יוֹם וָיוֹם הוּא הֵטִיב, הוּא מֵטִיב, הוּא יֵיטִיב לָנוּ. הוּא גְמָלָנוּ הוּא גוֹמְלֵנוּ הוּא יִגְמְלֵנוּ לָעַד, לְחֵן וּלְחֶסֶד וּלְרַחֲמִים וּלְרֶוַח הַצָּלָה וְהַצְלָחָה, בְּרָכָה וִישׁוּעָה נֶחָמָה פַּרְנָסָה וְכַלְכָּלָה וְרַחֲמִים וְחַיִּים וְשָׁלוֹם וְכָל טוֹב, וּמִכָּל טוּב לְעוֹלָם אַל יְחַסְּרֵנוּ.

הָרַחֲמָן הוּא יִמְלוֹךְ עָלֵינוּ לְעוֹלָם וָעֶד. הָרַחֲמָן הוּא יִתְבָּרַךְ בַּשָּׁמַיִם וּבָאָרֶץ. הָרַחֲמָן הוּא יִשְׁתַּבַּח לְדוֹר דּוֹרִים, וְיִתְפָּאַר בָּנוּ לָעַד

Our God and God of our fathers, may there rise, come, reach, be noted, be favored, be heard, be considered, and be remembered before You — the remembrance and consideration of ourselves; the remembrance of our fathers; the remembrance of Mashiach, son of David, Your servant; the remembrance of Jerusalem, Your holy city; and the remembrance of Your entire people, the House of Israel — for deliverance, for well-being, for grace, for lovingkindness, and for mercy, for life and for peace on this day of the Festival of Matzos. Remember us on it, HASHEM, our God, for goodness; consider us on it for blessing; and help us on it for (good) life. In the matter of salvation and mercy, have pity, show grace, and be merciful upon us and help us, for our eyes are turned to You; for You are the Almighty (King), the gracious, and compassionate.

Rebuild Jerusalem, the Holy City, soon in our days. Blessed are You, HASHEM, Who rebuilds Jerusalem (in His mercy). Amen.

Blessed are You, HASHEM, our God, King of the universe, the Almighty, our Father, our King, our Sovereign, our Creator, our Redeemer, our Maker, our Holy One, Holy One of Yaakov, our Shepherd, the Shepherd of Israel, the good and beneficent King. For every single day He did good, does good, and will do good to us. He was bountiful with us, is bountiful with us, and will forever be bountiful with us — with grace and with lovingkindness and with mercy, with relief, salvation, success, blessing, help, consolation, sustenance, support, mercy, life, peace, and all good; and of all good things may He never deprive us.

The compassionate One! May He reign over us forever. The compassionate One! May He be blessed in heaven and on earth. The compassionate One! May He be praised throughout all generations,

וּלְנֶצַח נְצָחִים, וְיִתְהַדַּר בָּנוּ לָעַד וּלְעוֹלְמֵי עוֹלָמִים. הָרַחֲמָן הוּא יְפַרְנְסֵנוּ בְּכָבוֹד. הָרַחֲמָן הוּא יִשְׁבּוֹר עֻלֵּנוּ מֵעַל צַוָּארֵנוּ, וְהוּא יוֹלִיכֵנוּ קוֹמְמִיּוּת לְאַרְצֵנוּ. הָרַחֲמָן הוּא יִשְׁלַח לָנוּ בְּרָכָה מְרֻבָּה בַּבַּיִת הַזֶּה, וְעַל שֻׁלְחָן זֶה שֶׁאָכַלְנוּ עָלָיו. הָרַחֲמָן הוּא יִשְׁלַח לָנוּ אֶת אֵלִיָּהוּ הַנָּבִיא זָכוּר לַטּוֹב, וִיבַשֶּׂר לָנוּ בְּשׂוֹרוֹת טוֹבוֹת יְשׁוּעוֹת וְנֶחָמוֹת.

The Talmud (*Berachos* 46a) gives a rather lengthy text of the blessing that a guest inserts here for the host. It is quoted with minor variations in *Shulchan Aruch* (*Orach Chaim* 201) and many authorities are at a loss to explain why the prescribed text has fallen into disuse in favor of the briefer version commonly used. The text found in *Shulchan Aruch* is:

יְהִי רָצוֹן שֶׁלֹּא יֵבוֹשׁ וְלֹא יִכָּלֵם בַּעַל הַבַּיִת הַזֶּה, לֹא בָּעוֹלָם הַזֶּה, וְלֹא בָּעוֹלָם הַבָּא, וְיַצְלִיחַ בְּכָל נְכָסָיו, וְיִהְיוּ נְכָסָיו מֻצְלָחִים וּקְרוֹבִים לָעִיר, וְאַל יִשְׁלוֹט שָׂטָן בְּמַעֲשֵׂה יָדָיו, וְאַל יִזְדַּקֵּק לְפָנָיו שׁוּם דְּבַר חֵטְא וְהִרְהוּר עָוֹן, מֵעַתָּה וְעַד עוֹלָם.

הָרַחֲמָן הוּא יְבָרֵךְ

Guests recite the following.
Children at their parents' table add words in parentheses.

אֶת [אָבִי מוֹרִי] בַּעַל הַבַּיִת הַזֶּה,
וְאֶת [אִמִּי מוֹרָתִי] בַּעֲלַת הַבַּיִת הַזֶּה,

Those eating at their own table recite the following,
adding the appropriate parenthesized phrases:

אוֹתִי [וְאֶת אִשְׁתִּי / וְאֶת בַּעֲלִי. וְאֶת זַרְעִי]
וְאֶת כָּל אֲשֶׁר לִי.

All guests recite the following:

אוֹתָם וְאֶת בֵּיתָם וְאֶת זַרְעָם וְאֶת כָּל אֲשֶׁר לָהֶם.

All continue here:

אוֹתָנוּ וְאֶת כָּל אֲשֶׁר לָנוּ, כְּמוֹ שֶׁנִּתְבָּרְכוּ אֲבוֹתֵינוּ אַבְרָהָם יִצְחָק וְיַעֲקֹב בַּכֹּל מִכֹּל כֹּל, כֵּן יְבָרֵךְ אוֹתָנוּ כֻּלָּנוּ יַחַד בִּבְרָכָה שְׁלֵמָה, וְנֹאמַר, אָמֵן.

may He be glorified through us forever to the ultimate ends, and be honored through us to the inscrutable everlasting. The compassionate One! May He sustain us in honor. The compassionate One! May He break the yoke of oppression from our necks and guide us erect to our Land. The compassionate One! May He send us abundant blessing to this house and upon this table at which we have eaten. The compassionate One! May He send us Eliyahu HaNavi—may he be remembered for good — to proclaim to us good tidings, salvations, and consolations.

The Talmud (*Berachos* 46a) gives a rather lengthy text of the blessing that a guest inserts here for the host. It is quoted with minor variations in *Shulchan Aruch* (*Orach Chaim* 201) and many authorities are at a loss to explain why the prescribed text has fallen into disuse in favor of the briefer version commonly used. The text found in *Shulchan Aruch* is:

May it be God's will that his host not be shamed nor humiliated in this world or in the World to Come. May he be successful in all his dealings. May his dealings be successful and conveniently close at hand. May no evil impediment reign over his handiwork, and may no semblance of sin or iniquitous thought attach itself to him from this time and forever.

The compassionate One! May He bless

Guests recite the following.
Children at their parents' table add words in parentheses.

(my father, my teacher) the master of this house, and (my mother, my teacher) lady of this house,

Those eating at their own table recite the following,
adding the appropriate parenthesized phrases:

me (my wife/husband and family) and all that is mine,

All guests recite the following:

them, their house, their family, and all that is theirs,

All continue here:

ours and all that is ours — just as our forefathers Avraham, Yitzchak, and Yaakov were blessed in everything, from everything, with everything. So may He bless all of us together, with a perfect blessing. And let us say: Amen!

בַּמָּרוֹם יְלַמְּדוּ עֲלֵיהֶם וְעָלֵינוּ זְכוּת, שֶׁתְּהֵא לְמִשְׁמֶרֶת שָׁלוֹם. וְנִשָּׂא בְרָכָה מֵאֵת יהוה, וּצְדָקָה מֵאֱלֹהֵי יִשְׁעֵנוּ, וְנִמְצָא חֵן וְשֵׂכֶל טוֹב בְּעֵינֵי אֱלֹהִים וְאָדָם.[1]

On Shabbos add the following sentence:

הָרַחֲמָן הוּא יַנְחִילֵנוּ יוֹם שֶׁכֻּלּוֹ שַׁבָּת וּמְנוּחָה לְחַיֵּי הָעוֹלָמִים..

The words in parentheses are added on the two Seder nights in some communities.

הָרַחֲמָן הוּא יַנְחִילֵנוּ יוֹם שֶׁכֻּלּוֹ טוֹב (יוֹם שֶׁכֻּלּוֹ אָרוּךְ, יוֹם שֶׁצַּדִּיקִים יוֹשְׁבִים וְעַטְרוֹתֵיהֶם בְּרָאשֵׁיהֶם וְנֶהֱנִים מִזִּיו הַשְּׁכִינָה, וִיהִי חֶלְקֵנוּ עִמָּהֶם).

הָרַחֲמָן הוּא יְזַכֵּנוּ לִימוֹת הַמָּשִׁיחַ וּלְחַיֵּי הָעוֹלָם הַבָּא. מִגְדּוֹל יְשׁוּעוֹת מַלְכּוֹ וְעֹשֶׂה חֶסֶד לִמְשִׁיחוֹ לְדָוִד וּלְזַרְעוֹ עַד עוֹלָם.[2] עֹשֶׂה שָׁלוֹם בִּמְרוֹמָיו, הוּא יַעֲשֶׂה שָׁלוֹם עָלֵינוּ וְעַל כָּל יִשְׂרָאֵל. וְאִמְרוּ, אָמֵן.

יְראוּ אֶת יהוה קְדֹשָׁיו, כִּי אֵין מַחְסוֹר לִירֵאָיו. כְּפִירִים רָשׁוּ וְרָעֵבוּ, וְדֹרְשֵׁי יהוה לֹא יַחְסְרוּ כָל טוֹב. הוֹדוּ לַיהוה כִּי טוֹב, כִּי לְעוֹלָם חַסְדּוֹ.[3] פּוֹתֵחַ אֶת יָדֶךָ, וּמַשְׂבִּיעַ לְכָל חַי רָצוֹן.[4] בָּרוּךְ הַגֶּבֶר אֲשֶׁר יִבְטַח בַּיהוה, וְהָיָה יהוה מִבְטַחוֹ.[5] נַעַר הָיִיתִי גַּם זָקַנְתִּי, וְלֹא רָאִיתִי צַדִּיק נֶעֱזָב, וְזַרְעוֹ מְבַקֶּשׁ לָחֶם.[6]

On high, may merit be pleaded upon them and upon us, for a safeguard of peace. May we receive a blessing from HASHEM and just kindness from the God of our salvation, and find favor and good understanding in the eyes of God and man.[1]

On Shabbos add the following sentence:

The compassionate One! May He cause us to inherit the day which will be completely a Shabbos and rest day for eternal life.

The words in parentheses are added on the two Seder nights in some communities.

The compassionate One! May He cause us to inherit that day which is altogether good (that everlasting day, the day when the just will sit with crowns on their heads, enjoying the reflection of God's majesty — and may our portion be with them!).

The compassionate One! May He make us worthy of the days of Mashiach and the life of the World to Come. He Who is a tower of salvations to His king and shows lovingkindness for His anointed, to David and his descendants forever.[2] He Who makes peace in His heavenly heights, may He make harmony for us and for all Israel. Say: Amen!

Fear HASHEM, His holy ones, for those who fear Him feel no deprivation. Young lions may feel want and hunger, but those who seek HASHEM will not lack any good. Give thanks to God for He is good; His lovingkindness is eternal.[3] You open up Your hand and satisfy the desire of every living thing.[4] Blessed is the man who trusts in HASHEM, and HASHEM will be his trust.[5] I was a youth and also have aged, and I have not seen a righteous man forsaken, with his children begging for bread.[6]

---

1. Cf. *Mishlei* 3:4. 2. *II Shmuel* 22:51. 3. *Tehillim* 34:10-11. 4. Ibid. 145:16. 5. *Yirmiyah* 17:7. 6. *Tehillim* 37:25.

יהוה עֹז לְעַמּוֹ יִתֵּן, יהוה יְבָרֵךְ אֶת עַמּוֹ בַשָׁלוֹם.[1]

Upon completion of *Bircas HaMazon* the blessing over wine is recited and the third cup is drunk while reclining on the left side. It is preferable to drink the entire cup, but at the very least, most of the cup should be drained.

Some recite the following before the third cup:

הִנְנִי מוּכָן וּמְזוּמָּן לְקַיֵּם מִצְוַת כּוֹס שְׁלִישִׁי שֶׁל אַרְבַּע כּוֹסוֹת. לְשֵׁם יְחוּד קֻדְשָׁא בְּרִיךְ הוּא וּשְׁכִינְתֵּיה, עַל יְדֵי הַהוּא טָמִיר וְנֶעְלָם, בְּשֵׁם כָּל יִשְׂרָאֵל. וִיהִי נֹעַם אֲדֹנָי אֱלֹהֵינוּ עָלֵינוּ, וּמַעֲשֵׂה יָדֵינוּ כּוֹנְנָה עָלֵינוּ, וּמַעֲשֵׂה יָדֵינוּ כּוֹנְנֵהוּ.

בָּרוּךְ אַתָּה יהוה אֱלֹהֵינוּ מֶלֶךְ הָעוֹלָם, בּוֹרֵא פְּרִי הַגָּפֶן.

The fourth cup is poured. According to most customs, the Cup of Eliyahu is poured at this point, after which the door is opened in accordance with the verse, *"It is a guarded night."* Then the following paragraph is recited.

שְׁפֹךְ חֲמָתְךָ אֶל הַגּוֹיִם אֲשֶׁר לֹא יְדָעוּךָ וְעַל מַמְלָכוֹת אֲשֶׁר בְּשִׁמְךָ לֹא קָרָאוּ. כִּי אָכַל אֶת יַעֲקֹב וְאֶת נָוֵהוּ הֵשַׁמּוּ. שְׁפָךְ עֲלֵיהֶם זַעְמֶךָ וַחֲרוֹן אַפְּךָ יַשִּׂיגֵם. תִּרְדֹּף בְּאַף וְתַשְׁמִידֵם מִתַּחַת שְׁמֵי יהוה.

הלל

The door is closed and the recitation of the *Haggadah* is continued.

לֹא לָנוּ יהוה, לֹא לָנוּ; כִּי לְשִׁמְךָ תֵּן כָּבוֹד, עַל חַסְדְּךָ עַל אֲמִתֶּךָ. לָמָה יֹאמְרוּ הַגּוֹיִם, אַיֵּה נָא אֱלֹהֵיהֶם. וֵאלֹהֵינוּ בַשָׁמָיִם, כֹּל אֲשֶׁר חָפֵץ עָשָׂה. עֲצַבֵּיהֶם כֶּסֶף וְזָהָב, מַעֲשֵׂה יְדֵי אָדָם. פֶּה לָהֶם וְלֹא יְדַבֵּרוּ, עֵינַיִם לָהֶם וְלֹא יִרְאוּ. אָזְנַיִם לָהֶם וְלֹא יִשְׁמָעוּ, אַף לָהֶם וְלֹא יְרִיחוּן.

HASHEM will give might to His nation; HASHEM will bless His nation with peace.[1]

Upon completion of *Bircas HaMazon* the blessing over wine is recited and the third cup is drunk while reclining on the left side. It is preferable to drink the entire cup, but at the very least, most of the cup should be drained.

Some recite the following before the third cup:

Behold, I am prepared and ready to fulfill the mitzvah of the third of the Four Cups. For the sake of the unification of the Holy One, Blessed is He, and His Presence, through Him Who is hidden and inscrutable — [I pray] in the name of all Israel. May the pleasantness of the Lord, our God, be upon us, and may He establish our handiwork for us; our handiwork may He establish.

Blessed are You, HASHEM, our God, King of the universe, Who creates the fruit of the vine.

The fourth cup is poured. According to most customs, the Cup of Eliyahu is poured at this point, after which the door is opened in accordance with the verse, *"It is a guarded night."* Then the following paragraph is recited.

Pour Your wrath upon the nations that do not recognize You and upon the kingdoms that do not invoke Your Name. For they have devoured Yaakov and destroyed His habitation. Pour Your anger upon them and let Your fiery wrath overtake them. Pursue them with wrath and annihilate them from beneath the heavens of HASHEM.

HALLEL

The door is closed and the recitation of the *Haggadah* is continued.

Not for our sake, O Lord, not for our sake, but for Your Name's sake give glory, for the sake of Your kindness and Your truth! Why should the nations say, "Where is their God now?" Our God is in the heavens; whatever He pleases, He does! Their idols are silver and gold, the handiwork of man. They have a mouth, but cannot speak; they have eyes, but cannot see; they have ears, but cannot hear; they have a nose,

---

1. *Tehillim* 29:11.

יְדֵיהֶם וְלֹא יְמִישׁוּן, רַגְלֵיהֶם וְלֹא יְהַלֵּכוּ, לֹא יֶהְגּוּ
בִּגְרוֹנָם. כְּמוֹהֶם יִהְיוּ עֹשֵׂיהֶם, כֹּל אֲשֶׁר בֹּטֵחַ
בָּהֶם. יִשְׂרָאֵל בְּטַח בַּיהוה, עֶזְרָם וּמָגִנָּם הוּא.
בֵּית אַהֲרֹן בִּטְחוּ בַיהוה, עֶזְרָם וּמָגִנָּם הוּא. יִרְאֵי
יהוה בִּטְחוּ בַיהוה, עֶזְרָם וּמָגִנָּם הוּא.

יהוה זְכָרָנוּ יְבָרֵךְ; יְבָרֵךְ אֶת בֵּית יִשְׂרָאֵל,
יְבָרֵךְ אֶת בֵּית אַהֲרֹן. יְבָרֵךְ יִרְאֵי יהוה,
הַקְּטַנִּים עִם הַגְּדֹלִים. יֹסֵף יהוה עֲלֵיכֶם, עֲלֵיכֶם
וְעַל בְּנֵיכֶם. בְּרוּכִים אַתֶּם לַיהוה, עֹשֵׂה שָׁמַיִם
וָאָרֶץ. הַשָּׁמַיִם שָׁמַיִם לַיהוה, וְהָאָרֶץ נָתַן לִבְנֵי
אָדָם. לֹא הַמֵּתִים יְהַלְלוּ יָהּ, וְלֹא כָּל יֹרְדֵי
דוּמָה. וַאֲנַחְנוּ נְבָרֵךְ יָהּ, מֵעַתָּה וְעַד עוֹלָם;
הַלְלוּיָהּ.[1]

אָהַבְתִּי כִּי יִשְׁמַע יהוה, אֶת קוֹלִי תַּחֲנוּנָי.
כִּי הִטָּה אָזְנוֹ לִי, וּבְיָמַי אֶקְרָא.
אֲפָפוּנִי חֶבְלֵי מָוֶת, וּמְצָרֵי שְׁאוֹל מְצָאוּנִי;
צָרָה וְיָגוֹן אֶמְצָא. וּבְשֵׁם יהוה אֶקְרָא: אָנָּה
יהוה מַלְּטָה נַפְשִׁי. חַנּוּן יהוה וְצַדִּיק, וֵאלֹהֵינוּ
מְרַחֵם. שֹׁמֵר פְּתָאיִם יהוה, דַּלּוֹתִי וְלִי
יְהוֹשִׁיעַ. שׁוּבִי נַפְשִׁי לִמְנוּחָיְכִי, כִּי יהוה גָּמַל
עָלָיְכִי. כִּי חִלַּצְתָּ נַפְשִׁי מִמָּוֶת; אֶת עֵינִי מִן
דִּמְעָה, אֶת רַגְלִי מִדֶּחִי. אֶתְהַלֵּךְ לִפְנֵי יהוה,
בְּאַרְצוֹת הַחַיִּים. הֶאֱמַנְתִּי כִּי אֲדַבֵּר, אֲנִי
עָנִיתִי מְאֹד. אֲנִי אָמַרְתִּי בְחָפְזִי, כָּל הָאָדָם
כֹּזֵב.

but cannot smell; their hands — they cannot feel; their feet — they cannot walk; nor can they utter a sound with their throat. Those who make them should become like them, whoever trusts in them! O Israel! Trust in HASHEM; He is their help and their shield! House of Aharon! Trust in HASHEM! He is their help and their shield! You who fear HASHEM — trust in HASHEM, He is their help and their shield!

HASHEM Who has remembered us will bless — He will bless the House of Israel; He will bless the House of Aharon; He will bless those who fear HASHEM, the small as well as the great. May HASHEM increase upon you, upon you and your children! You are blessed of HASHEM, Maker of heaven and earth. As for the heaven — the heaven is HASHEM's, but the earth He has given to mankind. Neither the dead can praise HASHEM, nor any who descend into silence; but we will bless God henceforth and for-ever. Halleluyah![1]

I love [Him], for HASHEM hears my voice, my suppli-cations. For He has inclined His ear to me, all my days I will call upon Him. The ropes of death encompassed me; the confines of the grave have found me; trouble and sorrow have I found. Then I called upon the Name of HASHEM: "Please, HASHEM, save my soul." Gracious is HASHEM and righteous, our God is merciful. The Lord protects the simple; I was brought low but He saved me. Return to your rest, my soul, for HASHEM has been kind to you. You delivered my soul from death, my eyes from tears, and my feet from stumbling. I shall walk before the Lord in the lands of the living. I kept faith although I say: "I suffer exceedingly." I said in my haste: "All mankind is deceitful."

---

1. *Tehillim* 115.

מָה אָשִׁיב לַיהוה, כָּל תַּגְמוּלוֹהִי עָלָי. כּוֹס יְשׁוּעוֹת אֶשָּׂא, וּבְשֵׁם יהוה אֶקְרָא. נְדָרַי לַיהוה אֲשַׁלֵּם, נֶגְדָה נָּא לְכָל עַמּוֹ. יָקָר בְּעֵינֵי יהוה, הַמָּוְתָה לַחֲסִידָיו. אָנָּה יהוה כִּי אֲנִי עַבְדֶּךָ; אֲנִי עַבְדְּךָ בֶּן אֲמָתֶךָ, פִּתַּחְתָּ לְמוֹסֵרָי. לְךָ אֶזְבַּח זֶבַח תּוֹדָה, וּבְשֵׁם יהוה אֶקְרָא. נְדָרַי לַיהוה אֲשַׁלֵּם, נֶגְדָה נָּא לְכָל עַמּוֹ. בְּחַצְרוֹת בֵּית יהוה, בְּתוֹכֵכִי יְרוּשָׁלָיִם; הַלְלוּיָהּ.[1]

הַלְלוּ אֶת יהוה, כָּל גּוֹיִם; שַׁבְּחוּהוּ כָּל הָאֻמִּים. כִּי גָבַר עָלֵינוּ חַסְדּוֹ, וֶאֱמֶת יהוה לְעוֹלָם; הַלְלוּיָהּ.[2]

הוֹדוּ לַיהוה כִּי טוֹב,	כִּי לְעוֹלָם חַסְדּוֹ.
יֹאמַר נָא יִשְׂרָאֵל,	כִּי לְעוֹלָם חַסְדּוֹ.
יֹאמְרוּ נָא בֵית אַהֲרֹן,	כִּי לְעוֹלָם חַסְדּוֹ.
יֹאמְרוּ נָא יִרְאֵי יהוה,	כִּי לְעוֹלָם חַסְדּוֹ.

מִן הַמֵּצַר קָרָאתִי יָּהּ, עָנָנִי בַמֶּרְחָב יָהּ. יהוה לִי לֹא אִירָא, מַה יַּעֲשֶׂה לִי אָדָם. יהוה לִי בְּעֹזְרָי, וַאֲנִי אֶרְאֶה בְשֹׂנְאָי. טוֹב לַחֲסוֹת בַּיהוה, מִבְּטֹחַ בָּאָדָם. טוֹב לַחֲסוֹת בַּיהוה, מִבְּטֹחַ בִּנְדִיבִים. כָּל גּוֹיִם סְבָבוּנִי, בְּשֵׁם יהוה כִּי אֲמִילַם. סַבּוּנִי גַם סְבָבוּנִי, בְּשֵׁם יהוה כִּי אֲמִילַם. סַבּוּנִי כִדְבֹרִים, דֹּעֲכוּ כְּאֵשׁ קוֹצִים; בְּשֵׁם יהוה כִּי אֲמִילַם. דָּחֹה דְחִיתַנִי לִנְפֹּל, וַיהוה עֲזָרָנִי.

---

1. *Tehillim* 116.
2. Ibid. 117.

How can I repay HASHEM for all His kindness to me? I will raise the cup of salvations and invoke the Name of HASHEM. My vows to HASHEM I will pay in the presence of His entire people. Precious in the eyes of HASHEM is the death of His devout ones. Please, HASHEM — for I am Your servant, I am Your servant, son of Your handmaid — You have released my bonds. To You I sacrifice thanksgiving offerings, and the Name of HASHEM I will invoke. My vows to HASHEM I will pay in the presence of His entire people; in the courtyards of the House of HASHEM, in your midst, O Jerusalem, Halleluyah![1]

Praise HASHEM, all you nations; praise Him all you peoples! For His kindness to us was overwhelming, and the truth of HASHEM is eternal, Halleluyah![2]

Give thanks to HASHEM for He is good;

His kindness endures forever!

Let Israel say: His kindness endures forever!

Let the House of Aharon say:

His kindness endures forever!

Let those who fear HASHEM say:

His kindness endures forever!

From the straits did I call to God; God answered me with expansiveness. HASHEM is with me; I have no fear; how can man affect me? HASHEM is for me through my helpers; therefore I can face my foes. It is better to take refuge in HASHEM than to rely on man. It is better to take refuge in HASHEM than to rely on princes. All the nations encompass me; but in the Name of HASHEM I cut them down! They encompass me; they swarm around me; but in the Name of HASHEM I cut them down! They swarm around me like bees, but they are extinguished as a fire does thorns; in the Name of HASHEM I cut them down! You pushed me hard that I might fall, but HASHEM assisted me.

עָזִּי וְזִמְרָת יָהּ, וַיְהִי לִי לִישׁוּעָה. קוֹל רִנָּה
וִישׁוּעָה בְּאָהֳלֵי צַדִּיקִים, יְמִין יהוה עֹשָׂה חָיִל.
יְמִין יהוה רוֹמֵמָה, יְמִין יהוה עֹשָׂה חָיִל. לֹא
אָמוּת כִּי אֶחְיֶה, וַאֲסַפֵּר מַעֲשֵׂי יָהּ. יַסֹּר יִסְּרַנִּי
יָּהּ, וְלַמָּוֶת לֹא נְתָנָנִי. פִּתְחוּ לִי שַׁעֲרֵי צֶדֶק,
אָבֹא בָם אוֹדֶה יָהּ. זֶה הַשַּׁעַר לַיהוה, צַדִּיקִים
יָבֹאוּ בוֹ. אוֹדְךָ כִּי עֲנִיתָנִי, וַתְּהִי לִי לִישׁוּעָה.
אוֹדְךָ כִּי עֲנִיתָנִי, וַתְּהִי לִי לִישׁוּעָה. אֶבֶן מָאֲסוּ
הַבּוֹנִים, הָיְתָה לְרֹאשׁ פִּנָּה. אֶבֶן מָאֲסוּ הַבּוֹנִים,
הָיְתָה לְרֹאשׁ פִּנָּה. מֵאֵת יהוה הָיְתָה זֹּאת,
הִיא נִפְלָאת בְּעֵינֵינוּ. מֵאֵת יהוה הָיְתָה זֹּאת,
הִיא נִפְלָאת בְּעֵינֵינוּ. זֶה הַיּוֹם עָשָׂה יהוה,
נָגִילָה וְנִשְׂמְחָה בוֹ. זֶה הַיּוֹם עָשָׂה יהוה, נָגִילָה
וְנִשְׂמְחָה בוֹ.

אָנָּא יהוה, הוֹשִׁיעָה נָּא.

אָנָּא יהוה, הוֹשִׁיעָה נָּא.

אָנָּא יהוה, הַצְלִיחָה נָּא.

אָנָּא יהוה, הַצְלִיחָה נָּא.

בָּרוּךְ הַבָּא בְּשֵׁם יהוה, בֵּרַכְנוּכֶם מִבֵּית
יהוה. בָּרוּךְ הַבָּא בְּשֵׁם יהוה, בֵּרַכְנוּכֶם
מִבֵּית יהוה. אֵל יהוה וַיָּאֶר לָנוּ, אִסְרוּ חַג
בַּעֲבֹתִים עַד קַרְנוֹת הַמִּזְבֵּחַ. אֵל יהוה וַיָּאֶר
לָנוּ, אִסְרוּ חַג בַּעֲבֹתִים עַד קַרְנוֹת הַמִּזְבֵּחַ.
אֵלִי אַתָּה וְאוֹדֶךָּ, אֱלֹהַי אֲרוֹמְמֶךָּ. אֵלִי אַתָּה
וְאוֹדֶךָּ, אֱלֹהַי אֲרוֹמְמֶךָּ. הוֹדוּ לַיהוה כִּי טוֹב,

My strength and song is God; He became my salvation. The sound of rejoicing and salvation is in the tents of the righteous: "The right hand of HASHEM does valiantly! The right hand of HASHEM is raised triumphantly! The right hand of HASHEM does valiantly!" I shall not die! I shall live and relate the deeds of God. God chastened me exceedingly but He did not let me die. Open for me the gates of righteousness, I will enter them and thank God. This is the gate of HASHEM; the righteous shall enter through it. I thank You for You answered me and became my salvation! I thank You for You answered me and became my salvation! The stone which the builders despised has become the cornerstone! The stone which the builders despised has become the cornerstone! This has emanated from HASHEM; it is wondrous in our eyes! This has emanated from HASHEM; it is wondrous in our eyes! This is the day HASHEM has made; we will rejoice and be glad in Him! This is the day HASHEM has made; we will rejoice and be glad in Him!

O HASHEM, please save us!
O HASHEM, please save us!
O HASHEM, please make us prosper!
O HASHEM, please make us prosper!

Blessed be he who comes in the Name of HASHEM; we bless you from the House of HASHEM. Blessed be he who comes in the Name of HASHEM; we bless you from the House of HASHEM. HASHEM is God and He illuminated for us; bind the festival offering with cords to the corners of the Altar. HASHEM is God and He illuminated for us; bind the festival offering with cords to the corners of the Altar. You are my God and I shall thank You; my God and I shall exalt You. You are my God, and I shall thank You; my God and I shall exalt You. Give thanks to HASHEM, for He is good;

כִּי לְעוֹלָם חַסְדּוֹ. הוֹדוּ לַיהוה כִּי טוֹב, כִּי לְעוֹלָם
חַסְדּוֹ.[1]

יְהַלְלוּךָ יהוה אֱלֹהֵינוּ כָּל מַעֲשֶׂיךָ, וַחֲסִידֶיךָ
צַדִּיקִים עוֹשֵׂי רְצוֹנֶךָ, וְכָל עַמְּךָ
בֵּית יִשְׂרָאֵל בְּרִנָּה יוֹדוּ וִיבָרְכוּ וִישַׁבְּחוּ וִיפָאֲרוּ
וִירוֹמְמוּ וְיַעֲרִיצוּ וְיַקְדִּישׁוּ וְיַמְלִיכוּ אֶת שִׁמְךָ
מַלְכֵּנוּ. כִּי לְךָ טוֹב לְהוֹדוֹת וּלְשִׁמְךָ נָאֶה לְזַמֵּר,
כִּי מֵעוֹלָם וְעַד עוֹלָם אַתָּה אֵל.

הוֹדוּ לַיהוה כִּי טוֹב,   כִּי לְעוֹלָם חַסְדּוֹ.

הוֹדוּ לֵאלֹהֵי הָאֱלֹהִים,   כִּי לְעוֹלָם חַסְדּוֹ.

הוֹדוּ לַאֲדֹנֵי הָאֲדֹנִים,   כִּי לְעוֹלָם חַסְדּוֹ.

לְעֹשֵׂה נִפְלָאוֹת גְּדֹלוֹת לְבַדּוֹ,   כִּי לְעוֹלָם חַסְדּוֹ.

לְעֹשֵׂה הַשָּׁמַיִם בִּתְבוּנָה,   כִּי לְעוֹלָם חַסְדּוֹ.

לְרֹקַע הָאָרֶץ עַל הַמָּיִם,   כִּי לְעוֹלָם חַסְדּוֹ.

לְעֹשֵׂה אוֹרִים גְּדֹלִים,   כִּי לְעוֹלָם חַסְדּוֹ.

אֶת הַשֶּׁמֶשׁ לְמֶמְשֶׁלֶת בַּיּוֹם,   כִּי לְעוֹלָם חַסְדּוֹ.

אֶת הַיָּרֵחַ וְכוֹכָבִים לְמֶמְשְׁלוֹת בַּלָּיְלָה,

כִּי לְעוֹלָם חַסְדּוֹ.

לְמַכֵּה מִצְרַיִם בִּבְכוֹרֵיהֶם,   כִּי לְעוֹלָם חַסְדּוֹ.

וַיּוֹצֵא יִשְׂרָאֵל מִתּוֹכָם,   כִּי לְעוֹלָם חַסְדּוֹ.

בְּיָד חֲזָקָה וּבִזְרוֹעַ נְטוּיָה,   כִּי לְעוֹלָם חַסְדּוֹ.

---

1. *Tehillim* 118.

His kindness endures forever! Give thanks to HASHEM, for He is good; His kindness endures forever![1]

They shall praise You, HASHEM our God, for all Your works, along with Your pious followers, the righteous, who do Your will, and Your entire people, the House of Israel, with joy will thank, bless, praise, glorify, exalt, revere, sanctify, and coronate Your Name, our King! For to You it is fitting to give thanks, and unto Your Name it is proper to sing praises, for from eternity to eternity You are God.

Give thanks to HASHEM, for He is good;
His kindness endures forever!
Give thanks to the God of gods;
His kindness endures forever!
Give thanks to the Master of masters;
His kindness endures forever!
To Him Who alone does great wonders;
His kindness endures forever!
To Him Who makes the heaven with understanding;
His kindness endures forever!
To Him Who stretched out the earth over the waters;
His kindness endures forever!
To Him Who makes great luminaries;
His kindness endures forever!
The sun for the reign of the day;
His kindness endures forever!
The moon and the stars for the reign of the night;
His kindness endures forever!
To Him Who struck the Egyptians through
their firstborn;   His kindness endures forever!
And took Israel out from their midst;
His kindness endures forever!
With strong hand and outstretched arm;
His kindness endures forever!

TOUCHED BY OUR STORY

לִגְזֵר יַם סוּף לִגְזָרִים,   כִּי לְעוֹלָם חַסְדּוֹ.

וְהֶעֱבִיר יִשְׂרָאֵל בְּתוֹכוֹ,   כִּי לְעוֹלָם חַסְדּוֹ.

וְנִעֵר פַּרְעֹה וְחֵילוֹ בְיַם סוּף,   כִּי לְעוֹלָם חַסְדּוֹ.

לְמוֹלִיךְ עַמּוֹ בַּמִּדְבָּר,   כִּי לְעוֹלָם חַסְדּוֹ.

לְמַכֵּה מְלָכִים גְּדֹלִים,   כִּי לְעוֹלָם חַסְדּוֹ.

וַיַּהֲרֹג מְלָכִים אַדִּירִים,   כִּי לְעוֹלָם חַסְדּוֹ.

לְסִיחוֹן מֶלֶךְ הָאֱמֹרִי,   כִּי לְעוֹלָם חַסְדּוֹ.

וּלְעוֹג מֶלֶךְ הַבָּשָׁן,   כִּי לְעוֹלָם חַסְדּוֹ.

וְנָתַן אַרְצָם לְנַחֲלָה,   כִּי לְעוֹלָם חַסְדּוֹ.

נַחֲלָה לְיִשְׂרָאֵל עַבְדּוֹ,   כִּי לְעוֹלָם חַסְדּוֹ.

שֶׁבְּשִׁפְלֵנוּ זָכַר לָנוּ,   כִּי לְעוֹלָם חַסְדּוֹ.

וַיִּפְרְקֵנוּ מִצָּרֵינוּ,   כִּי לְעוֹלָם חַסְדּוֹ.

נֹתֵן לֶחֶם לְכָל בָּשָׂר,   כִּי לְעוֹלָם חַסְדּוֹ.

הוֹדוּ לְאֵל הַשָּׁמָיִם,   כִּי לְעוֹלָם חַסְדּוֹ.[1]

נִשְׁמַת כָּל חַי תְּבָרֵךְ אֶת שִׁמְךָ יהוה אֱלֹהֵינוּ, וְרוּחַ כָּל בָּשָׂר תְּפָאֵר וּתְרוֹמֵם זִכְרְךָ מַלְכֵּנוּ תָּמִיד. מִן הָעוֹלָם וְעַד הָעוֹלָם אַתָּה אֵל, וּמִבַּלְעָדֶיךָ אֵין לָנוּ מֶלֶךְ גּוֹאֵל וּמוֹשִׁיעַ. פּוֹדֶה וּמַצִּיל וּמְפַרְנֵס וּמְרַחֵם, בְּכָל עֵת צָרָה וְצוּקָה, אֵין לָנוּ מֶלֶךְ אֶלָּא אָתָּה. אֱלֹהֵי הָרִאשׁוֹנִים וְהָאַחֲרוֹנִים, אֱלוֹהַּ כָּל בְּרִיּוֹת, אֲדוֹן כָּל תּוֹלָדוֹת, הַמְהֻלָּל בְּרֹב הַתִּשְׁבָּחוֹת,

---

1. *Tehillim* 136.

To Him Who divided the Sea of Reeds into parts;
His kindness endures forever!
And caused Israel to pass through it;
His kindness endures forever!
And threw Pharaoh and his army into the Sea of Reeds;
His kindness endures forever!
To Him Who led His people through the Wilderness;
His kindness endures forever!
To Him Who smote great kings;
His kindness endures forever!
And slew mighty kings;
His kindness endures forever!
Sichon, king of the Emorites;
His kindness endures forever!
And Og, king of Bashan;
His kindness endures forever!
And gave their land as an inheritance;
His kindness endures forever!
An inheritance to Israel His servant;
His kindness endures forever!
Who remembered us in our lowliness;
His kindness endures forever!
And released us from our foes;
His kindness endures forever!
He gives food to all living creatures;
His kindness endures forever!
Give thanks to God of heaven;
His kindness endures forever![1]

The soul of every living being shall bless Your Name, HASHEM our God; the spirit of all flesh shall always glorify and exalt Your remembrance, our King. From eternity to eternity You are God, and except for You we have no king, redeemer or helper. O Rescuer, and Redeemer, Sustainer, and Merciful One in every time of trouble and distress. We have no king but You — God of the first and of the last, God of all creatures, Master of all generations, Who

הַמְנַהֵג עוֹלָמוֹ בְּחֶסֶד וּבְרִיּוֹתָיו בְּרַחֲמִים.
וַיהוה לֹא יָנוּם וְלֹא יִישָׁן. הַמְעוֹרֵר יְשֵׁנִים,
וְהַמֵּקִיץ נִרְדָּמִים, וְהַמֵּשִׂיחַ אִלְּמִים, וְהַמַּתִּיר
אֲסוּרִים, וְהַסּוֹמֵךְ נוֹפְלִים, וְהַזּוֹקֵף כְּפוּפִים.
לְךָ לְבַדְּךָ אֲנַחְנוּ מוֹדִים. אִלּוּ פִינוּ מָלֵא
שִׁירָה כַיָּם, וּלְשׁוֹנֵנוּ רִנָּה כַּהֲמוֹן גַּלָּיו,
וְשִׂפְתוֹתֵינוּ שֶׁבַח כְּמֶרְחֲבֵי רָקִיעַ, וְעֵינֵינוּ
מְאִירוֹת כַּשֶּׁמֶשׁ וְכַיָּרֵחַ, וְיָדֵינוּ פְרוּשׂוֹת
כְּנִשְׁרֵי שָׁמַיִם, וְרַגְלֵינוּ קַלּוֹת כָּאַיָּלוֹת, אֵין
אֲנַחְנוּ מַסְפִּיקִים לְהוֹדוֹת לְךָ, יהוה אֱלֹהֵינוּ
וֵאלֹהֵי אֲבוֹתֵינוּ, וּלְבָרֵךְ אֶת שְׁמֶךָ עַל אַחַת
מֵאֶלֶף אֶלֶף אַלְפֵי אֲלָפִים וְרִבֵּי רְבָבוֹת פְּעָמִים
הַטּוֹבוֹת שֶׁעָשִׂיתָ עִם אֲבוֹתֵינוּ וְעִמָּנוּ.
מִמִּצְרַיִם גְּאַלְתָּנוּ יהוה אֱלֹהֵינוּ, וּמִבֵּית
עֲבָדִים פְּדִיתָנוּ. בְּרָעָב זַנְתָּנוּ, וּבְשָׂבָע
כִּלְכַּלְתָּנוּ, מֵחֶרֶב הִצַּלְתָּנוּ, וּמִדֶּבֶר מִלַּטְתָּנוּ,
וּמֵחֳלָיִם רָעִים וְנֶאֱמָנִים דִּלִּיתָנוּ. עַד הֵנָּה
עֲזָרוּנוּ רַחֲמֶיךָ, וְלֹא עֲזָבוּנוּ חֲסָדֶיךָ. וְאַל
תִּטְּשֵׁנוּ יהוה אֱלֹהֵינוּ לָנֶצַח. עַל כֵּן אֵבָרִים
שֶׁפִּלַּגְתָּ בָּנוּ, וְרוּחַ וּנְשָׁמָה שֶׁנָּפַחְתָּ בְּאַפֵּינוּ,
וְלָשׁוֹן אֲשֶׁר שַׂמְתָּ בְּפִינוּ, הֵן הֵם יוֹדוּ
וִיבָרְכוּ וִישַׁבְּחוּ וִיפָאֲרוּ וִירוֹמְמוּ וְיַעֲרִיצוּ
וְיַקְדִּישׁוּ וְיַמְלִיכוּ אֶת שִׁמְךָ מַלְכֵּנוּ. כִּי כָל
פֶּה לְךָ יוֹדֶה, וְכָל לָשׁוֹן לְךָ תִשָּׁבַע,
וְכָל בֶּרֶךְ לְךָ תִכְרַע, וְכָל קוֹמָה לְפָנֶיךָ
תִשְׁתַּחֲוֶה, וְכָל לְבָבוֹת יִירָאוּךָ, וְכָל קֶרֶב
וּכְלָיוֹת יְזַמְּרוּ לִשְׁמֶךָ, כַּדָּבָר שֶׁכָּתוּב: כָּל

is extolled through a multitude of praises, Who guides His world with kindness and His creatures with mercy. HASHEM neither slumbers nor sleeps; He rouses the sleepers and awakens the slumberers; He makes the mute speak and releases the bound; He supports the falling and raises erect the bowed down. To You alone we give thanks.

Were our mouth as full of song as the sea, and our tongue as full of jubilation as its multitude of waves, and our lips as full of praise as the breadth of the heavens, and our eyes as brilliant as the sun and the moon, and our hands as outspread in prayer as eagles of the sky and our feet as swift as deer — we still could not sufficiently thank You, HASHEM our God and God of our fathers, and bless Your Name for even one of the thousands upon thousands, and myriads upon myriads of favors [miracles and wonders], that You performed for our ancestors and for us. You redeemed us from Egypt, HASHEM our God, and liberated us from the house of bondage. In famine You nourished us and in plenty You supported us. From the sword You saved us; from the plague You let us escape; and You spared us from severe and enduring diseases. Until now Your mercy has helped us and Your kindness has not forsaken us; do not abandon us, HASHEM our God, to the ultimate end. Therefore, the limbs which You have set within us, and the spirit and soul which You breathed into our nostrils, and the tongue which You have placed in our mouth — they shall thank and bless, praise and glorify, exalt, be devoted to, sanctify, and do homage to Your Name, our King forever. For every mouth shall offer thanks to You; every tongue shall vow allegiance to You; every knee shall bend to You; all who stand erect shall bow before You; all hearts shall fear You; and all men's innermost feelings and thoughts shall sing praises to Your Name, as it is written: "All my

עַצְמוֹתַי תֹּאמַרְנָה, יהוה מִי כָמְוֹךָ, מַצִּיל עָנִי מֵחָזָק מִמֶּנּוּ, וְעָנִי וְאֶבְיוֹן מִגֹּזְלוֹ.[1] מִי יִדְמֶה לָךְ, וּמִי יִשְׁוֶה לָךְ, וּמִי יַעֲרָךְ לָךְ. הָאֵל הַגָּדוֹל הַגִּבּוֹר וְהַנּוֹרָא, אֵל עֶלְיוֹן, קֹנֵה שָׁמַיִם וָאָרֶץ. נְהַלֶּלְךָ וּנְשַׁבֵּחֲךָ וּנְפָאֶרְךָ וּנְבָרֵךְ אֶת שֵׁם קָדְשֶׁךָ, כָּאָמוּר: לְדָוִד, בָּרְכִי נַפְשִׁי אֶת יהוה, וְכָל קְרָבַי אֶת שֵׁם קָדְשׁוֹ.[2]

הָאֵל בְּתַעֲצֻמוֹת עֻזֶּךָ, הַגָּדוֹל בִּכְבוֹד שְׁמֶךָ, הַגִּבּוֹר לָנֶצַח וְהַנּוֹרָא בְּנוֹרְאוֹתֶיךָ. הַמֶּלֶךְ הַיּוֹשֵׁב עַל כִּסֵּא רָם וְנִשָּׂא.

שׁוֹכֵן עַד מָרוֹם וְקָדוֹשׁ שְׁמוֹ. וְכָתוּב: רַנְּנוּ צַדִּיקִים בַּיהוה לַיְשָׁרִים נָאוָה תְהִלָּה.[3] בְּפִי יְשָׁרִים תִּתְהַלָּל. וּבְדִבְרֵי צַדִּיקִים תִּתְבָּרַךְ. וּבִלְשׁוֹן חֲסִידִים תִּתְרוֹמָם. וּבְקֶרֶב קְדוֹשִׁים תִּתְקַדָּשׁ.

וּבְמַקְהֲלוֹת רִבְבוֹת עַמְּךָ בֵּית יִשְׂרָאֵל, בְּרִנָּה יִתְפָּאֵר שִׁמְךָ מַלְכֵּנוּ בְּכָל דּוֹר וָדוֹר. שֶׁכֵּן חוֹבַת כָּל הַיְצוּרִים, לְפָנֶיךָ יהוה אֱלֹהֵינוּ וֵאלֹהֵי אֲבוֹתֵינוּ, לְהוֹדוֹת לְהַלֵּל לְשַׁבֵּחַ לְפָאֵר לְרוֹמֵם לְהַדֵּר לְבָרֵךְ לְעַלֵּה וּלְקַלֵּס, עַל כָּל דִּבְרֵי שִׁירוֹת וְתִשְׁבְּחוֹת דָּוִד בֶּן יִשַׁי עַבְדְּךָ מְשִׁיחֶךָ.

יִשְׁתַּבַּח שִׁמְךָ לָעַד, מַלְכֵּנוּ, הָאֵל הַמֶּלֶךְ הַגָּדוֹל וְהַקָּדוֹשׁ, בַּשָּׁמַיִם וּבָאָרֶץ. כִּי לְךָ נָאֶה, יהוה אֱלֹהֵינוּ וֵאלֹהֵי אֲבוֹתֵינוּ, שִׁיר וּשְׁבָחָה, הַלֵּל וְזִמְרָה, עֹז וּמֶמְשָׁלָה, נֶצַח גְּדֻלָּה

bones declare: 'HASHEM, who is like You?' You save the poor man from one stronger than him, the poor and needy from one who would rob him."[1] Who may be likened to You? Who is equal to You? Who can be compared to You? O great, mighty, and awesome God, supreme God, Maker of heaven and earth. We shall praise, acclaim, and glorify You and bless Your holy Name, as it is said:"A psalm of David: Bless HASHEM, O my soul, and let my whole inner being bless His holy Name!"[2]

O God, in the omnipotence of Your strength, great in the honor of Your Name, powerful forever and awesome through Your awesome deeds, O King enthroned upon a high and lofty throne!

He Who abides forever, exalted and holy is His Name. And it is written: "Rejoice in HASHEM, you righteous; for the upright, His praise is pleasant."[3] By the mouth of the upright You shall be praised; by the words of the righteous You shall be praised; by the tongue of the pious You shall be exalted; and amid the holy You shall be sanctified.

And in the assemblies of the myriads of Your people, the House of Israel, with jubilation shall Your Name, our King, be glorified in every generation. For such is the duty of all creatures — before You, HASHEM, our God, and God of our fathers, to thank, praise, laud, glorify, exalt, adore, bless, raise high, and sing praises — even beyond all expressions of the songs and praises of David the son of Jesse, Your servant, Your anointed.

May Your Name be praised forever, our King, the God, and King Who is great and holy in heaven and on earth; for to You, HASHEM, our God, and the God of our fathers, it is fitting to render song and praise, *hallel* and hymns, power and dominion,

---

1. *Tehillim* 35:10. 2. Ibid. 103:1. 3. Ibid. 33:1.

וּגְבוּרָה, תְּהִלָּה וְתִפְאֶרֶת, קְדֻשָּׁה וּמַלְכוּת, בְּרָכוֹת וְהוֹדָאוֹת מֵעַתָּה וְעַד עוֹלָם. בָּרוּךְ אַתָּה יהוה, אֵל מֶלֶךְ גָּדוֹל בַּתִּשְׁבָּחוֹת, אֵל הַהוֹדָאוֹת, אֲדוֹן הַנִּפְלָאוֹת, הַבּוֹחֵר בְּשִׁירֵי זִמְרָה, מֶלֶךְ אֵל חֵי הָעוֹלָמִים.

The blessing over wine is recited and the fourth cup is drunk while reclining to the left side. It is preferable that the entire cup be drunk.
Some recite the following before the fourth cup:

הִנְנִי מוּכָן וּמְזֻמָּן לְקַיֵּם מִצְוַת כּוֹס רְבִיעִי שֶׁל אַרְבַּע כּוֹסוֹת. לְשֵׁם יִחוּד קֻדְשָׁא בְּרִיךְ הוּא וּשְׁכִינְתֵּיהּ, עַל יְדֵי הַהוּא טָמִיר וְנֶעְלָם, בְּשֵׁם כָּל יִשְׂרָאֵל. וִיהִי נֹעַם אֲדֹנָי אֱלֹהֵינוּ עָלֵינוּ, וּמַעֲשֵׂה יָדֵינוּ כּוֹנְנָה עָלֵינוּ, וּמַעֲשֵׂה יָדֵינוּ כּוֹנְנֵהוּ.

בָּרוּךְ אַתָּה יהוה אֱלֹהֵינוּ מֶלֶךְ הָעוֹלָם, בּוֹרֵא פְּרִי הַגָּפֶן.

After drinking the fourth cup, the concluding blessing is recited.
On Shabbos include the passage in parentheses.

בָּרוּךְ אַתָּה יהוה אֱלֹהֵינוּ מֶלֶךְ הָעוֹלָם, עַל הַגֶּפֶן וְעַל פְּרִי הַגָּפֶן, וְעַל תְּנוּבַת הַשָּׂדֶה, וְעַל אֶרֶץ חֶמְדָּה טוֹבָה וּרְחָבָה, שֶׁרָצִיתָ וְהִנְחַלְתָּ לַאֲבוֹתֵינוּ, לֶאֱכוֹל מִפִּרְיָהּ וְלִשְׂבּוֹעַ מִטּוּבָהּ. רַחֵם (נָא) יהוה אֱלֹהֵינוּ עַל יִשְׂרָאֵל עַמֶּךְ, וְעַל יְרוּשָׁלַיִם עִירֶךָ, וְעַל צִיּוֹן מִשְׁכַּן כְּבוֹדֶךָ, וְעַל מִזְבְּחֶךָ וְעַל הֵיכָלֶךָ. וּבְנֵה יְרוּשָׁלַיִם עִיר הַקֹּדֶשׁ בִּמְהֵרָה בְיָמֵינוּ, וְהַעֲלֵנוּ לְתוֹכָהּ, וְשַׂמְּחֵנוּ בְּבִנְיָנָהּ, וְנֹאכַל מִפִּרְיָהּ, וְנִשְׂבַּע מִטּוּבָהּ, וּנְבָרֶכְךָ עָלֶיהָ בִּקְדֻשָּׁה וּבְטָהֳרָה [וּרְצֵה וְהַחֲלִיצֵנוּ בְּיוֹם הַשַּׁבָּת הַזֶּה]. וְשַׂמְּחֵנוּ בְּיוֹם חַג הַמַּצּוֹת הַזֶּה. כִּי אַתָּה יהוה טוֹב וּמֵטִיב לַכֹּל, וְנוֹדֶה לְּךָ עַל הָאָרֶץ וְעַל פְּרִי הַגָּפֶן. בָּרוּךְ אַתָּה יהוה, עַל הָאָרֶץ וְעַל פְּרִי הַגָּפֶן.

victory, greatness and might, praise and glory, holi-
ness and sovereignty, blessings and thanksgivings
from now and forever. Blessed are You, HASHEM,
God, King, great in praises, God of thanksgivings,
Master of wonders, Who favors songs of praise —
King, God, Life of all worlds.

The blessing over wine is recited and the fourth cup is drunk while
reclining to the left side. It is preferable that the entire cup be drunk.

Some recite the following before the fourth cup:

Behold, I am prepared and ready to fulfill the mitzvah of the
fourth of the Four Cups. For the sake of the unification of the
Holy One, Blessed is He, and His Presence, through Him Who is
hidden and inscrutable — [I pray] in the name of all Israel. May
the pleasantness of the Lord, our God, be upon us, and may He
establish our handiwork for us; our handiwork may He establish.

Blessed are You, HASHEM, our God, King of the
universe, Who creates the fruit of the vine.

After drinking the fourth cup, the concluding blessing is recited.
On Sabbos include the passage in parentheses.

Blessed are You, HASHEM, our God, King of the
universe, for the vine and the fruit of the vine,
and for the produce of the field. For the desirable,
good, and spacious land that You were pleased to
give our forefathers as a heritage, to eat of its fruit
and to be satisfied with its goodness. Have mercy,
(we beg You,) HASHEM, our God, on Israel Your
people; on Jerusalem, Your city; on Zion, resting
place of Your glory; Your Altar, and Your Temple.
Rebuild Jerusalem the city of holiness, speedily in
our days. Bring us up into it and gladden us in
its rebuilding, and let us eat from its fruit and be
satisfied with its goodness and bless You upon it
in holiness and purity. (Favor us and strengthen
us on this Shabbos day) and grant us happiness
on this Festival of Matzos; for You, HASHEM, are
good and do good to all, and we thank You for the
land and for the fruit of the vine. Blessed are You,
HASHEM, for the land and for the fruit of the vine.

נרצה

חֲסַל סִדּוּר פֶּסַח כְּהִלְכָתוֹ, כְּכָל מִשְׁפָּטוֹ וְחֻקָּתוֹ. כַּאֲשֶׁר זָכִינוּ לְסַדֵּר אוֹתוֹ, כֵּן נִזְכֶּה לַעֲשׂוֹתוֹ. זָךְ שׁוֹכֵן מְעוֹנָה, קוֹמֵם קְהַל עֲדַת מִי מָנָה. בְּקָרוֹב נַהֵל נִטְעֵי כַנָּה, פְּדוּיִם לְצִיּוֹן בְּרִנָּה.

לְשָׁנָה הַבָּאָה בִּירוּשָׁלָיִם.

Nirtzah / נרצה

לְשָׁנָה הַבָּאָה בִּירוּשָׁלָיִם
Next Year In Jerusalem.

This Year in Jerusalem

Yeshivah had just ended and I walked home carrying my laptop, briefcase, and some interesting Haggados that I had shown to some of the boys in my class. The day had gone well, but with Pesach cleaning and all that comes with it, I was slightly tired and looking forward to a restful lunch break. My wife had prepared an onion-cheese omelet and I was eager to eat, as I had skipped breakfast that morning. I walked through the door and spoke for a few moments with my wife, before we sat down to eat lunch together.

I had noticed that a meshulach was coming out of one of the neighbors' houses and knew that he was coming my way. I recognized him, as he had probably called at my house for several years in a row. Sure enough, a few minutes after I sat down to eat, the doorbell rang. I got up and went to answer the door. I invited the man in and offered him a seat and something to drink.

He was collecting for Machon Rus, a fine institution for physically disabled children. His brochure included heartrending pictures of young boys and girls who were struggling to walk or even sit on their own. Some were unable to feed themselves. Each photograph told the story of another challenge, another struggle. I opened my checkbook and wrote out a check. As I handed it to

NIRTZAH

The Seder is now concluded in accordance with its laws, with all its ordinances and statutes. Just as we were privileged to arrange it, so may we merit to perform it. O Pure One, Who dwells on high, raise up the countless congregation, soon guide the offshoots of Your plants, redeemed to Zion with glad song.

NEXT YEAR IN JERUSALEM

him, he began sharing a vort on the Haggadah with me. He struck me as the type of person who had a wealth of Torah thoughts at the tip of his tongue. Though I listened, I must admit that I was itching to get back to my omelet. Eventually, he finished his thought, placed the check in his pocket, and wished me well.

We were still sitting at my dining-room table, when he turned to me and said, "Im yirtzeh Hashem, I will see you soon in Yerushalayim." I nodded, smiled, and mumbled that I hoped to see him, as well. However, he persisted. "You know that Mashiach is coming soon." Again I nodded, expressing the wish that I had for Mashiach to finally come.

At this point, the elderly Jew held onto my hand with a firm grip. He stared deeply into my eyes and did not say a word. Finally, after a moment of silence, he declared, "You know, last week I went down to Komemiyus and bought a sheep for a korban pesach." I waited for the smile to appear on his face, but none came. I went numb.

Did I hear correctly? I asked him if he really had a sheep walking around his courtyard, and he promised me he did. It was incredible! Many people have spoken about Mashiach, but this man went and did something to prove his faith. Trying to relate, I asked him if I could participate together with my family in his chaburah for the korban pesach. He looked down at his fingers and began to count, as if he were calculating if he could, in fact, afford to take on an extra family. He then looked up and asked, "How many gedolim [adults] and how many ketanim [children]? For the adults I can promise a kezayis, but the children are only partaking because of chinuch purposes, and for that they don't need to receive a kezayis."

On the first night recite the following.
On the second night continue on page 232.

וּבְכֵן וַיְהִי בַּחֲצִי הַלַּיְלָה.

אָז רוֹב נִסִּים הִפְלֵאתָ בַּלַּיְלָה,
בְּרֹאשׁ אַשְׁמוֹרֶת זֶה הַלַּיְלָה,
גֵּר צֶדֶק נִצַּחְתּוֹ כְּנֶחֱלַק לוֹ לַיְלָה,
וַיְהִי בַּחֲצִי הַלַּיְלָה.

דַּנְתָּ מֶלֶךְ גְּרָר בַּחֲלוֹם הַלַּיְלָה,
הִפְחַדְתָּ אֲרַמִּי בְּאֶמֶשׁ לַיְלָה,
וַיָּשַׂר יִשְׂרָאֵל לְמַלְאָךְ וַיּוּכַל לוֹ לַיְלָה,
וַיְהִי בַּחֲצִי הַלַּיְלָה.

זֶרַע בְּכוֹרֵי פַתְרוֹס מָחַצְתָּ בַּחֲצִי הַלַּיְלָה,
חֵילָם לֹא מָצְאוּ בְּקוּמָם בַּלַּיְלָה,
טִיסַת נְגִיד חֲרֹשֶׁת סִלִּיתָ בְּכוֹכְבֵי לַיְלָה,
וַיְהִי בַּחֲצִי הַלַּיְלָה.

יָעַץ מְחָרֵף לְנוֹפֵף אִוּוּי הוֹבַשְׁתָּ פְגָרָיו בַּלַּיְלָה,
כָּרַע בֵּל וּמַצָּבוֹ בְּאִישׁוֹן לַיְלָה,
לְאִישׁ חֲמוּדוֹת נִגְלָה רָז חֲזוֹת לַיְלָה,
וַיְהִי בַּחֲצִי הַלַּיְלָה.

מִשְׁתַּכֵּר בִּכְלֵי קֹדֶשׁ נֶהֱרַג בּוֹ בַּלַּיְלָה,
נוֹשַׁע מִבּוֹר אֲרָיוֹת פּוֹתֵר בְּעִתּוּתֵי לַיְלָה,
שִׂנְאָה נָטַר אֲגָגִי וְכָתַב סְפָרִים בַּלַּיְלָה,
וַיְהִי בַּחֲצִי הַלַּיְלָה.

On the first night recite the following.
On the second night continue on page 232.

It came to pass at midnight.

Y ou have, of old, performed many wonders
by night.
At the head of the watches of this night.
To the righteous convert (Avraham)
You gave triumph by dividing for him the night.
It came to pass at midnight.
You judged the king of Gerar (Avimelech),
in a dream by night.
You frightened the Aramean (Lavan),
in the dark of night.
Yisrael (Yaakov) fought with an angel
and overcame him by night.
It came to pass at midnight.
Egypt's firstborn You crushed at midnight.
Their host they found not upon arising at night.
The army of the prince of Charoshes (Sisera)
You swept away with stars of the night.
It came to pass at midnight.
The blasphemer (Sancheriv) planned to raise
his hand against Jerusalem —
but You withered his corpses by night.
Bel was overturned with its pedestal,
in the darkness of night.
To the man of Your delights (Daniel)
was revealed the mystery of the visions of night.
It came to pass at midnight.
He (Belshazzar) who caroused from the holy
vessels
was killed that very night.
From the lions' den was rescued he (Daniel)
who interpreted the "terrors" of the night.
The Agagite (Haman) nursed hatred
and wrote decrees at night.
It came to pass at midnight.

עוֹרַרְתָּ נִצְחֲךָ עָלָיו בְּנֶדֶד שְׁנַת לַיְלָה,

פּוּרָה תִדְרוֹךְ לְשׁוֹמֵר מַה מִלַּיְלָה,

צָרַח כַּשּׁוֹמֵר וְשָׂח אָתָא בְקֶר וְגַם לַיְלָה,

וַיְהִי בַּחֲצִי הַלַּיְלָה.

קָרֵב יוֹם אֲשֶׁר הוּא לֹא יוֹם וְלֹא לַיְלָה,

רָם הוֹדַע כִּי לְךָ הַיּוֹם אַף לְךָ הַלַּיְלָה,

שׁוֹמְרִים הַפְקֵד לְעִירְךָ כָּל הַיּוֹם וְכָל הַלַּיְלָה,

תָּאִיר כְּאוֹר יוֹם חֶשְׁכַּת לַיְלָה,

וַיְהִי בַּחֲצִי הַלַּיְלָה.

On the second night recite the following.
On the first night continue on page 236.

וּבְכֵן וַאֲמַרְתֶּם זֶבַח פֶּסַח:

אֹמֶץ גְּבוּרוֹתֶיךָ הִפְלֵאתָ בַּפֶּסַח.

בְּרֹאשׁ כָּל מוֹעֲדוֹת נִשֵּׂאתָ פֶּסַח.

גִּלֵּיתָ לְאֶזְרָחִי חֲצוֹת לֵיל פֶּסַח.

וַאֲמַרְתֶּם זֶבַח פֶּסַח.

Again, I waited for the smile. But for this fellow, the subject was no laughing matter. Walking him to the door, I wished him a kosher Pesach. He responded that he looked forward to seeing me in Yerushalayim soon.

For some reason, I felt that it would not be too much longer until we would indeed meet in Yerushalayim.

וַאֲמַרְתֶּם זֶבַח פֶּסַח
You shall say: This is the feast of Pesach.

❧ A Matzah-less Pesach

In the story of Purim, Queen Esther pleaded with Mordechai to encourage the Jewish people to fast for her for three days, hoping that

You began Your triumph over him
when You disturbed (Acheshveirosh's) sleep at night.
Trample the winepress to help those who ask the
watchman, "What of the   long night?"
He will shout, like a watchman, and say:
"Morning shall come   after night."
      It came to pass at midnight.
Hasten the day (of Meshiach),
that is neither day   nor night.
Most High — make known that Yours
are day   and night.
Appoint guards for Your city,
all the day and all   the night.
Brighten like the light of day the darkness of night.
      It came to pass at midnight.

On the second night recite the following.
On the first night continue on page 236.

And you shall say: This is the feast of Pesach.

Yᴏᴜ displayed wondrously Your mighty powers
          on Pesach.
Above all festivals You elevated   Pesach.
To the Oriental (Avraham) You revealed
the future midnight   of Pesach.
  And you shall say: This is the feast of Pesach.

---

this would prevent their annihilation. In fact, we make mention of this in the liturgy of *Va'Amartem Zevach Pesach* at the end of the Seder. In this passage, we mention the events that happened on Pesach in the history of the Jewish people, including: "*Kahal kinsah Hadassah tzom le'shaleish be'Pesach* — Hadassah [Esther] gathered a congregation for a three-day fast on Pesach." Esther instructed Mordechai to declare a three-day fast, on the first three days of Pesach, and he followed what she said, as the Gemara (*Megillah* 15a) tells us. And the *pasuk* (*Esther* 4:17) says: "*Va'yaavor Mordechai* — Mordechai transgressed," which indicates that he told the people to disregard the mitzvos of the first day of Pesach and to fast instead. That year, the Jews did not eat matzah, they did not drink the four cups of wine,

בְּפֶֽסַח.	**דְּ**לָתָיו דָּפַֽקְתָּ כְּחֹם הַיּוֹם
בְּפֶֽסַח.	**הִ**סְעִיד נוֹצְצִים עֻגוֹת מַצּוֹת
פֶּֽסַח.	**וְ**אֶל הַבָּקָר רָץ זֵֽכֶר לְשׁוֹר עֵֽרֶךְ
	וַאֲמַרְתֶּם זֶֽבַח פֶּֽסַח.
בְּפֶֽסַח.	**זֹ**עֲמוּ סְדוֹמִים וְלוֹהֲטוּ בָּאֵשׁ
פֶּֽסַח.	**חֻ**לַּץ לוֹט מֵהֶם וּמַצּוֹת אָפָה בְּקֵץ
בְּפֶֽסַח.	**טִ**אטֵֽאתָ אַדְמַת מוֹף וְנוֹף בְּעָבְרְךָ
	וַאֲמַרְתֶּם זֶֽבַח פֶּֽסַח.
פֶּֽסַח.	**יָ**הּ רֹאשׁ כָּל אוֹן מָחַֽצְתָּ בְּלֵיל שִׁמּוּר
פֶּֽסַח.	**כַּ**בִּיר עַל בֵּן בְּכוֹר פָּסַֽחְתָּ בְּדַם
בְּפֶֽסַח.	**לְ**בִלְתִּי תֵּת מַשְׁחִית לָבֹא בִּפְתָחַי
	וַאֲמַרְתֶּם זֶֽבַח פֶּֽסַח.
פֶּֽסַח.	**מְ**סֻגֶּֽרֶת סֻגָּֽרָה בְּעִתּֽוֹתֵי
פֶּֽסַח.	**נִ**שְׁמְדָה מִדְיָן בִּצְלִיל שְׂעוֹרֵי עֹֽמֶר
פֶּֽסַח.	**שֹׂ**רְפוּ מִשְׁמַנֵּי פּוּל וְלוּד בִּיקַד יְקוֹד
	וַאֲמַרְתֶּם זֶֽבַח פֶּֽסַח.
פֶּֽסַח.	**ע**וֹד הַיּוֹם בְּנֹב לַעֲמוֹד עַד גָּעָה עוֹנַת
בְּפֶֽסַח.	**פַּ**ס יַד כָּתְבָה לְקַעֲקֵֽעַ צוּל
בְּפֶֽסַח.	**צָ**פֹה הַצָּפִית עָרוֹךְ הַשֻּׁלְחָן

---

they did not dip vegetables in salt water, and they did not eat *maror*.

The question arises: Why did they not delay the fast for a few days, until the days of Chol HaMoed? They had almost 12 months until the day that Haman's diabolical plan was to be set in motion; another few days would not have made a difference. Why did Esther insist that the fast be observed specifically on the days when the Jewish people would have to forgo observing these very important commandments?

At his door You knocked in the heat of the day
on Pesach;
He satiated the angels with matzah-cakes on Pesach.
And he ran to the herd —
symbolic of the sacrificial beast   of Pesach.
  And you shall say: This is the feast of Pesach.

The Sodomites provoked (God)
and were devoured by fire   on Pesach;
Lot was withdrawn from them —
he had baked matzos at the time   of Pesach.
You swept clean the soil of Mof and Nof (in Egypt)
when You passed through   on Pesach.
  And you shall say: This is the feast of Pesach.

God, You crushed every firstborn of On (in Egypt)
on the watchful night   of Pesach.
But Master — Your own firstborn,
You skipped by merit of the blood   of Pesach,
Not to allow the Destroyer to enter my doors
on Pesach.
  And you shall say: This is the feast   of Pesach.

The beleaguered (Yericho) was besieged on Pesach.
Midyan was destroyed with a barley cake,
from the Omer   of Pesach.
The mighty nobles of Pul and Lud (Ashur) were
consumed in a great conflagration   on Pesach.
  And you shall say: This is the feast of Pesach.

He (Sancheiriv) would have stood that day at Nov,
but for the advent   of Pesach.
A hand inscribed the destruction of Zul (Bavel)
on Pesach.
As the watch was set, and the royal table decked
on Pesach.

The *Tiferes Shlomo of Radomsk* explains that her plan was enacted precisely with this in mind. Esther's sole intention was to nullify this decree. She knew that the Jewish people are able to accomplish amazing things on the nights that they perform

וַאֲמַרְתֶּם זֶבַח פֶּסַח.

קָהָל כִּנְּסָה הֲדַסָּה צוֹם לְשַׁלֵּשׁ   בַּפֶּסַח.
רֹאשׁ מִבֵּית רָשָׁע מָחַצְתָּ בְּעֵץ חֲמִשִּׁים   בַּפֶּסַח.
שְׁתֵּי אֵלֶּה רֶגַע תָּבִיא לְעוּצִית   בַּפֶּסַח.
תָּעֹז יָדְךָ וְתָרוּם יְמִינְךָ כְּלֵיל הִתְקַדֵּשׁ חַג פֶּסַח.
וַאֲמַרְתֶּם זֶבַח פֶּסַח.

On both nights continue here:

כִּי לוֹ נָאֶה, כִּי לוֹ יָאֶה:

אַדִּיר בִּמְלוּכָה, בָּחוּר כַּהֲלָכָה, גְּדוּדָיו יֹאמְרוּ
לוֹ, לְךָ וּלְךָ, לְךָ כִּי לְךָ, לְךָ אַף לְךָ, לְךָ
יהוה הַמַּמְלָכָה, כִּי לוֹ נָאֶה, כִּי לוֹ יָאֶה.

דָּגוּל בִּמְלוּכָה, הָדוּר כַּהֲלָכָה, וָתִיקָיו יֹאמְרוּ לוֹ,
לְךָ וּלְךָ, לְךָ כִּי לְךָ, לְךָ אַף לְךָ, לְךָ יהוה הַמַּמְלָכָה,
כִּי לוֹ נָאֶה, כִּי לוֹ יָאֶה.

זַכַּאי בִּמְלוּכָה, חָסִין כַּהֲלָכָה, טַפְסְרָיו יֹאמְרוּ
לוֹ, לְךָ וּלְךָ, לְךָ כִּי לְךָ, לְךָ אַף לְךָ, לְךָ יהוה
הַמַּמְלָכָה, כִּי לוֹ נָאֶה, כִּי לוֹ יָאֶה.

---

these commandments. On this night, when we eat the matzah and *maror* and tell over the story of our Exodus from Egypt, we reach the highest of levels and become closer to the Almighty. Esther understood that the mitzvos of the Seder are possible only through the Jewish people.

Thus, she devised a plan. She decided that we must disregard these commandments just this one time. It was as if she wanted the Almighty to know what it would be like if the Jewish people would be destroyed, when the mitzvos would no longer be performed. This created a great commotion in the Heavens. On that night, the night of Pesach, a great amount of love was stirred in the heart of the Almighty for His people.

And you shall say: This is the feast of Pesach.
Hadassah (Esther) gathered a congregation
for a three-day fast   on Pesach.
You caused the head of the evil clan (Haman)
to be hanged on a 50-cubit gallows   on Pesach.
Doubly, will You bring in an instant
upon Utzis (Edom)   on Pesach.
Let Your hand be strong, and Your right arm exalted,
as on that night when You hallowed the festival
                                             of Pesach.
And you shall say: This is the feast of Pesach.

On both nights continue here:

To Him praise is due!
To Him praise is fitting!

Mighty in majesty, perfectly distinguished, His companies of angels say to Him: Yours and only Yours; Yours, yes Yours; Yours, surely Yours; Yours, HASHEM, is the sovereignty. To Him praise is due! To Him praise is fitting!
Supreme in kingship, perfectly glorious, His faithful say to Him: Yours and only Yours; Yours, yes Yours; Yours, surely Yours; Yours, HASHEM, is the sovereignty. To Him praise is due! To Him praise is fitting!
Pure in kingship, perfectly mighty, His angels say to Him: Yours and only Yours; Yours, yes Yours; Yours, surely Yours; Yours, HASHEM, is the sovereignty. To Him praise is due! To Him praise is fitting!

The steps of salvation were set in motion.
We end the poem of *Va'Amartem Zevach Pesach* with the words: "*Ta'oz yadcha ve'sarum yemincha ke'leil hiskadeish chag Pesach* — Let Your hand be strong, and Your right arm exalted, as on that night when You hallowed the festival of Pesach." We daven that Hashem should bring the Final Redemption, and His strength should be obvious as in Mitzrayim.
May the steps of salvation toward that *Geulah* be set in motion, as well.

יָחִיד בִּמְלוּכָה, כַּבִּיר כַּהֲלָכָה, לִמּוּדָיו יֹאמְרוּ
לוֹ, לְךָ וּלְךָ, לְךָ כִּי לְךָ, לְךָ אַף לְךָ, לְךָ יהוה
הַמַּמְלָכָה, כִּי לוֹ נָאֶה, כִּי לוֹ יָאֶה.

מוֹשֵׁל בִּמְלוּכָה, נוֹרָא כַּהֲלָכָה, סְבִיבָיו יֹאמְרוּ
לוֹ, לְךָ וּלְךָ, לְךָ כִּי לְךָ, לְךָ אַף לְךָ, לְךָ יהוה
הַמַּמְלָכָה, כִּי לוֹ נָאֶה, כִּי לוֹ יָאֶה.

עָנָיו בִּמְלוּכָה, פּוֹדֶה כַּהֲלָכָה, צַדִּיקָיו יֹאמְרוּ לוֹ,
לְךָ וּלְךָ, לְךָ כִּי לְךָ, לְךָ אַף לְךָ, לְךָ יהוה הַמַּמְלָכָה,
כִּי לוֹ נָאֶה, כִּי לוֹ יָאֶה.

קָדוֹשׁ בִּמְלוּכָה, רַחוּם כַּהֲלָכָה, שִׁנְאַנָּיו יֹאמְרוּ
לוֹ, לְךָ וּלְךָ, לְךָ כִּי לְךָ, לְךָ אַף לְךָ, לְךָ יהוה
הַמַּמְלָכָה, כִּי לוֹ נָאֶה, כִּי לוֹ יָאֶה.

תַּקִּיף בִּמְלוּכָה, תּוֹמֵךְ כַּהֲלָכָה, תְּמִימָיו יֹאמְרוּ
לוֹ, לְךָ וּלְךָ, לְךָ כִּי לְךָ, לְךָ אַף לְךָ, לְךָ יהוה
הַמַּמְלָכָה, כִּי לוֹ נָאֶה, כִּי לוֹ יָאֶה.

אַדִּיר הוּא יִבְנֶה בֵיתוֹ בְּקָרוֹב, בִּמְהֵרָה,
בִּמְהֵרָה, בְּיָמֵינוּ בְּקָרוֹב. אֵל
בְּנֵה, אֵל בְּנֵה, בְּנֵה בֵיתְךָ בְּקָרוֹב.

בָּחוּר הוּא. גָּדוֹל הוּא. דָּגוּל הוּא. יִבְנֶה בֵיתוֹ
בְּקָרוֹב, בִּמְהֵרָה, בִּמְהֵרָה, בְּיָמֵינוּ בְּקָרוֹב. אֵל
בְּנֵה, אֵל בְּנֵה, בְּנֵה בֵיתְךָ בְּקָרוֹב.

הָדוּר הוּא. וָתִיק הוּא. זַכַּאי הוּא. חָסִיד הוּא.
יִבְנֶה בֵיתוֹ בְּקָרוֹב, בִּמְהֵרָה, בִּמְהֵרָה, בְּיָמֵינוּ
בְּקָרוֹב. אֵל בְּנֵה, אֵל בְּנֵה, בְּנֵה בֵיתְךָ בְּקָרוֹב.

טָהוֹר הוּא. יָחִיד הוּא. כַּבִּיר הוּא. לָמוּד הוּא.

Alone in kingship, perfectly omnipotent, His scholars say to Him: Yours and only Yours; Yours, yes Yours; Yours, surely Yours; Yours, HASHEM, is the sovereignty. To Him praise is due! To Him praise is fitting!

Commanding in kingship, perfectly wondrous, His surrounding (angels) say to Him: Yours and only Yours; Yours, yes Yours; Yours, surely Yours; Yours, HASHEM, is the sovereignty. To Him praise is due! To Him praise is fitting!

Humble in kingship, perfectly the Redeemer, His righteous say to Him: Yours and only Yours; Yours, yes Yours; Yours, surely Yours; Yours, HASHEM, is the sovereignty. To Him praise is due! To Him praise is fitting!

Holy in kingship, perfectly merciful, His troops of angels say to Him: Yours and only Yours; Yours, yes Yours; Yours, surely Yours; Yours, HASHEM, is the sovereignty. To Him praise is due! To Him praise is fitting.

Almighty in kingship, perfectly sustaining, His perfect ones say to Him: Yours and only Yours; Yours, yes Yours; Yours, surely Yours; Yours, HASHEM, is the sovereignty. To Him praise is due! To Him praise is fitting!

He is most mighty. May He soon rebuild His House, speedily, yes speedily, in our days, soon. God, rebuild, God, rebuild, rebuild Your House soon! He is distinguished, He is great, He is exalted. May He soon rebuild His House, speedily, yes speedily, in our days, soon. God, rebuild, God, rebuild, rebuild Your House soon! He is all glorious, He is faithful, He is faultless, He is righteous. May He soon rebuild His House, speedily, yes speedily, in our days, soon. God, rebuild, God, rebuild, rebuild Your House soon! He is pure, He is unique, He is powerful, He is all-wise,

מֶלֶךְ הוּא. נוֹרָא הוּא. סַגִּיב הוּא. עִזּוּז הוּא. פּוֹדֶה הוּא. צַדִּיק הוּא. יִבְנֶה בֵיתוֹ בְּקָרוֹב, בִּמְהֵרָה, בִּמְהֵרָה, בְּיָמֵינוּ בְּקָרוֹב. אֵל בְּנֵה, אֵל בְּנֵה, בְּנֵה בֵיתְךָ בְּקָרוֹב.

קָדוֹשׁ הוּא. רַחוּם הוּא. שַׁדַּי הוּא. תַּקִּיף הוּא. יִבְנֶה בֵיתוֹ בְּקָרוֹב, בִּמְהֵרָה, בִּמְהֵרָה, בְּיָמֵינוּ בְּקָרוֹב. אֵל בְּנֵה, אֵל בְּנֵה, בְּנֵה בֵיתְךָ בְּקָרוֹב.

אֶחָד מִי יוֹדֵעַ? אֶחָד אֲנִי יוֹדֵעַ. אֶחָד אֱלֹהֵינוּ שֶׁבַּשָּׁמַיִם וּבָאָרֶץ.

שְׁנַיִם מִי יוֹדֵעַ? שְׁנַיִם אֲנִי יוֹדֵעַ. שְׁנֵי לֻחוֹת הַבְּרִית, אֶחָד אֱלֹהֵינוּ שֶׁבַּשָּׁמַיִם וּבָאָרֶץ.

שְׁלֹשָׁה מִי יוֹדֵעַ? שְׁלֹשָׁה אֲנִי יוֹדֵעַ. שְׁלֹשָׁה אָבוֹת, שְׁנֵי לֻחוֹת הַבְּרִית, אֶחָד אֱלֹהֵינוּ שֶׁבַּשָּׁמַיִם וּבָאָרֶץ.

אַרְבַּע מִי יוֹדֵעַ? אַרְבַּע אֲנִי יוֹדֵעַ. אַרְבַּע אִמָּהוֹת, שְׁלֹשָׁה אָבוֹת, שְׁנֵי לֻחוֹת הַבְּרִית, אֶחָד אֱלֹהֵינוּ שֶׁבַּשָּׁמַיִם וּבָאָרֶץ.

אֶחָד מִי יוֹדֵעַ
Who knows one?

◆§ All for One

After Adam sinned when he ate from the *Eitz HaDaas*, the ground was also cursed, as Hashem said (*Bereishis* 3:17,18), "*Arurah ha'adamah ba'avurecha … Kotz ve'dardar tatzmiach lach —* Accursed is the ground because of you … Thorns and thistles will grow for you." The *Bnei Yissaschar* notes that there are two verses in the Torah where one letter is enlarged, since that letter changes the meaning of the entire verse.

He is King, He is awesome, He is sublime, He is all-powerful, He is the Redeemer, He is the all-righteous. May He soon rebuild His House, speedily, yes speedily, in our days, soon. God, rebuild, God, rebuild, rebuild Your House soon!

He is holy, He is compassionate, He is Almighty, He is omnipotent. May He soon rebuild His House, speedily, yes speedily, in our days, soon. God, rebuild, God, rebuild, rebuild Your House soon!

Who knows one? I know one: One is our God, in heaven and on earth.

Who knows two? I know two: two are the Tablets of the Covenant; One is our God, in heaven and on earth.

Who knows three? I know three: three are the Patriarchs; two are the Tablets of the Covenant; One is our God, in heaven and on earth.

Who knows four? I know four: four are the Matriarchs; three are the Patriarchs; two are the Tablets of the Covenant; One is our God, in heaven and on earth.

The *pasuk* of *Shema Yisrael* (*Devarim* 6:4) ends with an enlarged letter *dalet* in the word *Echad* — One. The letter *reish,* the last letter, in the verse (*Shemos* 34:14), "*Ki lo sishtachaveh le'eil acher* — For you shall not prostrate yourselves to an alien god," is also enlarged. It is as if the Torah is emphasizing the importance of realizing that those two letters are mutually exclusive, since the first two letters in both words are the same. With the *dalet,* the word means "One," and with the *reish,* the word means "other." אֶחָד connotes our belief that Hashem watches over every detail of our lives. אַחֵר conveys a complete subservience to the natural order of the world, with no Providential design. We must do everything within our power to punctuate the *dalet* implication, and stay away from the *reish* connotation.

The difference between the two letters (ד and ר) is nothing more than a *kotz,* a thornlike jutting. In fact, the difference between the

חֲמִשָּׁה מִי יוֹדֵעַ? חֲמִשָּׁה אֲנִי יוֹדֵעַ. חֲמִשָּׁה חֻמְשֵׁי תוֹרָה, אַרְבַּע אִמָּהוֹת, שְׁלֹשָׁה אָבוֹת, שְׁנֵי לֻחוֹת הַבְּרִית, אֶחָד אֱלֹהֵינוּ שֶׁבַּשָּׁמַיִם וּבָאָרֶץ.

שִׁשָּׁה מִי יוֹדֵעַ? שִׁשָּׁה אֲנִי יוֹדֵעַ. שִׁשָּׁה סִדְרֵי מִשְׁנָה, חֲמִשָּׁה חֻמְשֵׁי תוֹרָה, אַרְבַּע אִמָּהוֹת, שְׁלֹשָׁה אָבוֹת, שְׁנֵי לֻחוֹת הַבְּרִית, אֶחָד אֱלֹהֵינוּ שֶׁבַּשָּׁמַיִם וּבָאָרֶץ.

שִׁבְעָה מִי יוֹדֵעַ? שִׁבְעָה אֲנִי יוֹדֵעַ. שִׁבְעָה יְמֵי שַׁבַּתָּא, שִׁשָּׁה סִדְרֵי מִשְׁנָה, חֲמִשָּׁה חֻמְשֵׁי תוֹרָה, אַרְבַּע אִמָּהוֹת, שְׁלֹשָׁה אָבוֹת, שְׁנֵי לֻחוֹת הַבְּרִית, אֶחָד אֱלֹהֵינוּ שֶׁבַּשָּׁמַיִם וּבָאָרֶץ.

שְׁמוֹנָה מִי יוֹדֵעַ? שְׁמוֹנָה אֲנִי יוֹדֵעַ. שְׁמוֹנָה יְמֵי מִילָה, שִׁבְעָה יְמֵי שַׁבַּתָּא, שִׁשָּׁה סִדְרֵי מִשְׁנָה, חֲמִשָּׁה חֻמְשֵׁי תוֹרָה, אַרְבַּע אִמָּהוֹת, שְׁלֹשָׁה אָבוֹת, שְׁנֵי לֻחוֹת הַבְּרִית, אֶחָד אֱלֹהֵינוּ שֶׁבַּשָּׁמַיִם וּבָאָרֶץ.

תִּשְׁעָה מִי יוֹדֵעַ? תִּשְׁעָה אֲנִי יוֹדֵעַ. תִּשְׁעָה יַרְחֵי לֵדָה, שְׁמוֹנָה יְמֵי מִילָה, שִׁבְעָה יְמֵי שַׁבַּתָּא, שִׁשָּׁה סִדְרֵי מִשְׁנָה, חֲמִשָּׁה חֻמְשֵׁי תוֹרָה, אַרְבַּע אִמָּהוֹת, שְׁלֹשָׁה אָבוֹת, שְׁנֵי לֻחוֹת הַבְּרִית, אֶחָד אֱלֹהֵינוּ שֶׁבַּשָּׁמַיִם וּבָאָרֶץ.

---

numerical value of the letter *reish* (200) and *dalet* (4) is 196, the *gematria* of קוֹץ. After Adam sinned and ate from the *Eitz HaDaas*, it became difficult to discern between the two. This is hinted at in the word that follows *kotz* in the above *pasuk*, וְדַרְדַּר, which is made up of the two letters: ד and ר.

Rav Elimelech Biderman, in his *Haggadah Be'er HaChaim*, adds a beautiful footnote. The night of the Seder hints to this conflict, as

Who knows five? I know five: five are the Books of the Torah; four are the Matriarchs; three are the Patriarchs; two are the Tablets of the Covenant; One is our God, in heaven and on earth.

Who knows six? I know six: six are the Orders of the Mishnah; five are the Books of the Torah; four are the Matriarchs; three are the Patriarchs; two are the Tablets of the Covenant; One is our God, in heaven and on earth.

Who knows seven? I know seven: seven are the days of the week; six are the Orders of the Mishnah; five are the Books of the Torah; four are the Matriarchs; three are the Patriarchs; two are the Tablets of the Covenant; One is our God, in heaven and on earth.

Who knows eight? I know eight: eight are the days of circumcision; seven are the days of the week; six are the Orders of the Mishnah; five are the Books of the Torah; four are the Matriarchs; three are the Patriarchs; two are the Tablets of the Covenant; One is our God, in heaven and on earth.

Who knows nine? I know nine: nine are the months of pregnancy; eight are the days of circumcision; seven are the days of the week; six are the Orders of the Mishnah; five are the Books of the Torah; four are the Matriarchs; three are the Patriarchs; two are the Tablets of the Covenant; One is our God, in heaven and on earth.

---

the word סֵדֶר can stand for: סוֹד ד' ר' — the secret of the *dalet* and *reish*. The basis of the night of the Seder is *emunah,* in which we don't confuse the *dalet* and the *reish.*

Our archenemy, Amalek, has made it his lifelong mission to destroy our perception of the Almighty as *Echad,* as he attempts to promulgate the notion that He is, God forbid, *acher.* The Torah writes (*Shemos* 17:16) that the battle against this nation will continue מִדֹּר דֹּר — from generation to generation — which is written without a

עֲשָׂרָה מִי יוֹדֵעַ? עֲשָׂרָה אֲנִי יוֹדֵעַ. עֲשָׂרָה דִבְּרַיָּא,
תִּשְׁעָה יַרְחֵי לֵדָה, שְׁמוֹנָה יְמֵי מִילָה, שִׁבְעָה יְמֵי
שַׁבַּתָּא, שִׁשָּׁה סִדְרֵי מִשְׁנָה, חֲמִשָּׁה חֻמְשֵׁי תוֹרָה,
אַרְבַּע אִמָּהוֹת, שְׁלֹשָׁה אָבוֹת, שְׁנֵי לֻחוֹת הַבְּרִית,
אֶחָד אֱלֹהֵינוּ שֶׁבַּשָּׁמַיִם וּבָאָרֶץ.

אַחַד עָשָׂר מִי יוֹדֵעַ? אַחַד עָשָׂר אֲנִי יוֹדֵעַ. אַחַד
עָשָׂר כּוֹכְבַיָּא, עֲשָׂרָה דִבְּרַיָּא, תִּשְׁעָה יַרְחֵי לֵדָה,
שְׁמוֹנָה יְמֵי מִילָה, שִׁבְעָה יְמֵי שַׁבַּתָּא, שִׁשָּׁה סִדְרֵי
מִשְׁנָה, חֲמִשָּׁה חֻמְשֵׁי תוֹרָה, אַרְבַּע אִמָּהוֹת,
שְׁלֹשָׁה אָבוֹת, שְׁנֵי לֻחוֹת הַבְּרִית, אֶחָד אֱלֹהֵינוּ
שֶׁבַּשָּׁמַיִם וּבָאָרֶץ.

שְׁנֵים עָשָׂר מִי יוֹדֵעַ? שְׁנֵים עָשָׂר אֲנִי יוֹדֵעַ. שְׁנֵים
עָשָׂר שִׁבְטַיָּא, אַחַד עָשָׂר כּוֹכְבַיָּא, עֲשָׂרָה דִבְּרַיָּא,
תִּשְׁעָה יַרְחֵי לֵדָה, שְׁמוֹנָה יְמֵי מִילָה, שִׁבְעָה יְמֵי
שַׁבַּתָּא, שִׁשָּׁה סִדְרֵי מִשְׁנָה, חֲמִשָּׁה חֻמְשֵׁי תוֹרָה,
אַרְבַּע אִמָּהוֹת, שְׁלֹשָׁה אָבוֹת, שְׁנֵי לֻחוֹת הַבְּרִית,
אֶחָד אֱלֹהֵינוּ שֶׁבַּשָּׁמַיִם וּבָאָרֶץ.

---

vau, and leaves us with the *dalet* and *reish* — once again hinting to
the struggle between these two ideologies. one of total belief and
the other of heresy.

At the end of the Seder, we sing the song, *Echad Mi Yodei'a,*
which reminds us over and over, at the end of each stanza, of the
Oneness of God. The *Klausenberger Rebbe* explains that this song
may be understood in the following light. A rich man accumulates a
great deal of wealth, and then makes an accounting of what he has
acquired. After the entire night, we have accumulated great spiritual
wealth. In this song, we detail our acquisitions and accomplishments.
But the greatest one of all is our clarity and understanding that the
Almighty is One.

Nothing is more valuable.

Who knows ten? I know ten: ten are the Ten Commandments; nine are the months of pregnancy; eight are the days of circumcision; seven are the days of the week; six are the Orders of the Mishnah; five are the Books of the Torah; four are the Matriarchs; three are the Patriarchs; two are the Tablets of the Covenant; One is our God, in heaven and on earth.

Who knows eleven? I know eleven: eleven are the stars (in Yosef's dream); ten are the Ten Commandments; nine are the months of pregnancy; eight are the days of circumcision; seven are the days of the week; six are the Orders of the Mishnah; five are the Books of the Torah; four are the Matriarchs; three are the Patriarchs; two are the Tablets of the Covenant; One is our God, in heaven and on earth.

Who knows twelve? I know twelve: twelve are the tribes; eleven are the stars (in Yosef's dream); ten are the Ten Commandments; nine are the months of pregnancy; eight are the days of circumcision; seven are the days of the week; six are the Orders of the Mishnah; five are the Books of the Torah; four are the Matriarchs; three are the Patriarchs; two are the Tablets of the Covenant; One is our God, in heaven and on earth.

What We Can Accomplish

Rav Tuviah Wein told a story in the name of the Chofetz Chaim, which gives us insight into what our efforts can accomplish and how we must never give up. Outside of Vilna was situated a small shtetl, where there lived a small cluster of families. While they were all well-meaning individuals, there were very few learned men among them. Nevertheless, they enjoyed attending a small shiur on Mishnah between Minchah and Maariv.

At the time of our story, they were learning Maseches Yevamos. Those sitting in the shiur listened and tried to follow. Among those in attendance was a Cantonist. Snatched away from his home at

שְׁלֹשָׁה עָשָׂר מִי יוֹדֵעַ? שְׁלֹשָׁה עָשָׂר אֲנִי יוֹדֵעַ.
שְׁלֹשָׁה עָשָׂר מִדַּיָּא, שְׁנֵים עָשָׂר שִׁבְטַיָּא, אַחַד
עָשָׂר כּוֹכְבַיָּא, עֲשָׂרָה דִבְּרַיָּא, תִּשְׁעָה יַרְחֵי לֵדָה,
שְׁמוֹנָה יְמֵי מִילָה, שִׁבְעָה יְמֵי שַׁבַּתָּא, שִׁשָּׁה סִדְרֵי
מִשְׁנָה, חֲמִשָּׁה חֻמְשֵׁי תוֹרָה, אַרְבַּע אִמָּהוֹת,
שְׁלֹשָׁה אָבוֹת, שְׁנֵי לֻחוֹת הַבְּרִית, אֶחָד אֱלֹהֵינוּ
שֶׁבַּשָּׁמַיִם וּבָאָרֶץ.

חַד גַּדְיָא. חַד גַּדְיָא, דְּזַבִּין אַבָּא בִּתְרֵי זוּזֵי,
חַד גַּדְיָא חַד גַּדְיָא.
וְאָתָא שׁוּנְרָא וְאָכְלָה לְגַדְיָא, דְּזַבִּין אַבָּא בִּתְרֵי
זוּזֵי, חַד גַּדְיָא חַד גַּדְיָא.
וְאָתָא כַלְבָּא וְנָשַׁךְ לְשׁוּנְרָא, דְּאָכְלָא לְגַדְיָא,
דְּזַבִּין אַבָּא בִּתְרֵי זוּזֵי, חַד גַּדְיָא חַד גַּדְיָא.
וְאָתָא חוּטְרָא וְהִכָּה לְכַלְבָּא, דְּנָשַׁךְ לְשׁוּנְרָא,

the tender age of 5, he spent the next 38 years of his life under the
influence of the government: first he was brainwashed to forget
his religion, and then he was forced to spend the best years of
his life serving in the czar's army. Unfortunately, the people in the
town were insensitive and they called him Yavan, since he knew
less than the Yevanim, the Greeks. Although this bothered him, he
never said anythingabout it.

As he sat through the shiur, he kept hearing the word yavam
(one who marries his deceased brother's wife). After it was
repeated over and over, he stood up and began to yell. "I don't
know what you people want from me. I was taken away from my
home when I was a small boy, and I didn't have the opportunity
to learn anything. Do you really have to make fun of me? I don't
forgive any of you for your despicable behavior."

The others were shocked at his outburst. He had clearly
mistaken the word Yavan for yavam. He obviously didn't realize
that the one who was giving the class was merely reading and

Who knows thirteen? I know thirteen: thirteen are the attributes of God; twelve are the tribes; eleven are the stars (in Yosef's dream); ten are the Ten Commandments; nine are the months of pregnancy; eight are the days of circumcision; seven are the days of the week; six are the Orders of the Mishnah; five are the Books of the Torah; four are the Matriarchs; three are the Patriarchs; two are the Tablets of the Covenant; One is our God, in heaven and on earth.

A kid, a kid, that father bought for two zuzim, a kid, a kid.

A **cat** then came and devoured the kid that father bought for two zuzim, a kid, a kid.

A **dog** then came and bit the cat, that devoured the kid that father bought for two zuzim, a kid, a kid.

A **stick** then came and beat the dog, that bit the

---

explaining the Mishnah. It was an innocent misunderstanding, and it was unfortunate that he was hurt. They tried to explain the difference: one is יָוֵן and the other is יָבָם; but nothing they said registered. Finally, they asked, "What can we do to make it up to you?"

He looked around at the group and said, "There is only one way you can make it up to me. Teach me the aleph-beis."

And they did. When they finished, they continued to teach him: first siddur, then Chumash, then Mishnah, then Gemara. Like a famished individual, he devoured everything he learned. He learned and learned and never stopped, until he had made up much of the material he had missed and surpassed most of the townspeople in his studies. It was a long and arduous journey.

Eventually, he developed into a great talmid chacham, and became known as the Gaon of Lepnishok.

Indeed, we have accomplished much on this holy night. But there is always more to do ...

דְּאָכְלָה לְגַדְיָא, דְּזַבִּין אַבָּא בִּתְרֵי זוּזֵי, חַד גַּדְיָא חַד גַּדְיָא.

וְאָתָא **נוּרָא** וְשָׂרַף לְחוּטְרָא, דְּהִכָּה לְכַלְבָּא, דְּנָשַׁךְ לְשׁוּנְרָא, דְּאָכְלָה לְגַדְיָא, דְּזַבִּין אַבָּא בִּתְרֵי זוּזֵי, חַד גַּדְיָא חַד גַּדְיָא.

וְאָתָא **מַיָּא** וְכָבָה לְנוּרָא, דְּשָׂרַף לְחוּטְרָא,דְּהִכָּה לְכַלְבָּא, דְּנָשַׁךְ לְשׁוּנְרָא, דְּאָכְלָה לְגַדְיָא, דְּזַבִּין אַבָּא בִּתְרֵי זוּזֵי, חַד גַּדְיָא חַד גַּדְיָא.

וְאָתָא **תוֹרָא** וְשָׁתָה לְמַיָּא, דְּכָבָה לְנוּרָא, דְּשָׂרַף לְחוּטְרָא, דְּהִכָּה לְכַלְבָּא, דְּנָשַׁךְ לְשׁוּנְרָא, דְּאָכְלָה לְגַדְיָא, דְּזַבִּין אַבָּא בִּתְרֵי זוּזֵי, חַד גַּדְיָא חַד גַּדְיָא.

וְאָתָא **הַשּׁוֹחֵט** וְשָׁחַט לְתוֹרָא, דְּשָׁתָא לְמַיָּא, דְּכָבָה לְנוּרָא, דְּשָׂרַף לְחוּטְרָא, דְּהִכָּה לְכַלְבָּא, דְּנָשַׁךְ לְשׁוּנְרָא, דְּאָכְלָה לְגַדְיָא, דְּזַבִּין אַבָּא בִּתְרֵי זוּזֵי, חַד גַּדְיָא חַד גַּדְיָא.

וְאָתָא **מַלְאַךְ הַמָּוֶת** וְשָׁחַט לְשׁוֹחֵט, דְּשָׁחַט לְתוֹרָא, דְּשָׁתָה לְמַיָּא, דְּכָבָה לְנוּרָא, דְּשָׂרַף לְחוּטְרָא, דְּהִכָּה לְכַלְבָּא, דְּנָשַׁךְ לְשׁוּנְרָא, דְּאָכְלָה לְגַדְיָא, דְּזַבִּין אַבָּא בִּתְרֵי זוּזֵי, חַד גַּדְיָא חַד גַּדְיָא.

וְאָתָא **הַקָּדוֹשׁ בָּרוּךְ הוּא** וְשָׁחַט לְמַלְאַךְ הַמָּוֶת, דְּשָׁחַט לְשׁוֹחֵט, דְּשָׁחַט לְתוֹרָא, דְּשָׁתָה לְמַיָּא, דְּכָבָה לְנוּרָא, דְּשָׂרַף לְחוּטְרָא, דְּהִכָּה לְכַלְבָּא, דְּנָשַׁךְ לְשׁוּנְרָא, דְּאָכְלָה לְגַדְיָא, דְּזַבִּין אַבָּא בִּתְרֵי זוּזֵי, חַד גַּדְיָא חַד גַּדְיָא.

Although the *Haggadah* formally ends at this point, one should continue to occupy himself with the story of the Exodus, and the laws of Pesach, until sleep overtakes him.

cat, that devoured the kid that father bought for two zuzim, a kid, a kid.

A fire then came and burnt the stick, that beat the dog, that bit the cat, that devoured the kid that father bought for two zuzim, a kid, a kid.

Water then came and quenched the fire, that burnt the stick, that beat the dog, that bit the cat, that devoured the kid that father bought for two zuzim, a kid, a kid.

An ox then came and drank the water, that quenched the fire, that burnt the stick, that beat the dog, that bit the cat, that devoured the kid that father bought for two zuzim, a kid, a kid.

A slaughterer then came and slaughtered the ox, that drank the water, that quenched the fire, that burnt the stick, that beat the dog, that bit the cat, that devoured the kid that father bought for two zuzim, a kid, a kid.

The angel of death then came and killed the slaughterer, who slaughtered the ox, that drank the water, that quenched the fire, that burnt the stick, that beat the dog, that bit the cat, that devoured the kid that father bought for two zuzim, a kid, a kid.

The Holy One, Blessed is He, then came and slew the angel of death, who killed the slaughterer, who slaughtered the ox, that drank the water, that quenched the fire, that burnt the stick, that beat the dog, that bit the cat, that devoured the kid that father bought for two zuzim, a kid, a kid.

Although the *Haggadah* formally ends at this point, one should continue to occupy himself with the story of the Exodus, and the laws of Pesach, until sleep overtakes him.

‎ שיר השירים / Song of Songs ‏‎

Many have the custom to recite *Shir HaShirim* following the Seder.

פרק א

א שִׁיר הַשִּׁירִים אֲשֶׁר לִשְׁלֹמֹה: ב יִשָּׁקֵנִי מִנְּשִׁיקוֹת פִּיהוּ כִּי־טוֹבִים דֹּדֶיךָ מִיָּיִן: ג לְרֵיחַ שְׁמָנֶיךָ טוֹבִים שֶׁמֶן תּוּרַק שְׁמֶךָ עַל־כֵּן עֲלָמוֹת אֲהֵבוּךָ: ד מָשְׁכֵנִי אַחֲרֶיךָ נָּרוּצָה הֱבִיאַנִי הַמֶּלֶךְ חֲדָרָיו נָגִילָה וְנִשְׂמְחָה בָּךְ נַזְכִּירָה דֹדֶיךָ מִיַּיִן מֵישָׁרִים אֲהֵבוּךָ: ה שְׁחוֹרָה אֲנִי וְנָאוָה בְּנוֹת יְרוּשָׁלָ͏ִם כְּאָהֳלֵי קֵדָר כִּירִיעוֹת שְׁלֹמֹה: ו אַל־תִּרְאֻנִי שֶׁאֲנִי שְׁחַרְחֹרֶת שֶׁשֱּׁזָפַתְנִי הַשָּׁמֶשׁ בְּנֵי אִמִּי נִחֲרוּ־בִי שָׂמֻנִי נֹטֵרָה אֶת־הַכְּרָמִים כַּרְמִי שֶׁלִּי לֹא נָטָרְתִּי: ז הַגִּידָה לִּי שֶׁאָהֲבָה נַפְשִׁי אֵיכָה תִרְעֶה אֵיכָה תַּרְבִּיץ בַּצָּהֳרָיִם שַׁלָּמָה אֶהְיֶה כְּעֹטְיָה עַל עֶדְרֵי חֲבֵרֶיךָ: ח אִם־לֹא תֵדְעִי לָךְ הַיָּפָה בַּנָּשִׁים צְאִי־לָךְ בְּעִקְבֵי הַצֹּאן וּרְעִי אֶת־גְּדִיֹּתַיִךְ עַל מִשְׁכְּנוֹת הָרֹעִים: ט לְסֻסָתִי בְּרִכְבֵי פַרְעֹה דִּמִּיתִיךְ רַעְיָתִי: י נָאווּ לְחָיַיִךְ בַּתֹּרִים צַוָּארֵךְ בַּחֲרוּזִים: יא תּוֹרֵי זָהָב נַעֲשֶׂה־לָּךְ עִם נְקֻדּוֹת הַכָּסֶף: יב עַד־

Shir HaShirim / ‎ שיר השירים ‏

‎ Accepted and Beloved ‏

The Seder is just about over. A night that began with such excitement begins to wind down. Many of the formerly eager children are already sleeping on the couch and elsewhere. It is only natural, as we sit at the table — emotionally and physically exhausted — to wonder if we've lived up to the expectations we had for an unforgettable evening.

With this serving as our backdrop, *Rav Avrohom Tzvi Kluger* writes in his *sefer Asichah BeChukecha*, that *Nirtzah* is the time when Hashem tells His anxious and exhausted children that their *avodah* has been accepted, as the word *nirtzah* means to be accepted. In *Rav Kluger's* words, "Throughout the Seder, it is the father who

שֶׁהַמֶּ֙לֶךְ֙ בִּמְסִבּ֔וֹ נִרְדִּ֖י נָתַ֥ן רֵיחֽוֹ: יג צְר֨וֹר הַמֹּ֤ר ׀ דּוֹדִי֙ לִ֔י בֵּ֥ין
שָׁדַ֖י יָלִֽין: יד אֶשְׁכֹּ֨ל הַכֹּ֤פֶר ׀ דּוֹדִי֙ לִ֔י בְּכַרְמֵ֖י עֵ֥ין גֶּֽדִי: טו הִנָּ֤ךְ
יָפָה֙ רַעְיָתִ֔י הִנָּ֥ךְ יָפָ֖ה עֵינַ֥יִךְ יוֹנִֽים: טז הִנְּךָ֨ יָפֶ֤ה דוֹדִי֙ אַ֣ף נָעִ֔ים
אַף־עַרְשֵׂ֖נוּ רַעֲנָנָֽה: יז קֹר֤וֹת בָּתֵּ֙ינוּ֙ אֲרָזִ֔ים רַהִיטֵ֖נוּ בְּרוֹתִֽים:

פרק ב

א אֲנִי֙ חֲבַצֶּ֣לֶת הַשָּׁר֔וֹן שֽׁוֹשַׁנַּ֖ת הָעֲמָקִֽים: ב כְּשֽׁוֹשַׁנָּה֙ בֵּ֣ין
הַחוֹחִ֔ים כֵּ֥ן רַעְיָתִ֖י בֵּ֥ין הַבָּנֽוֹת: ג כְּתַפּ֙וּחַ֙ בַּעֲצֵ֣י הַיַּ֔עַר
כֵּ֥ן דּוֹדִ֖י בֵּ֣ין הַבָּנִ֑ים בְּצִלּוֹ֙ חִמַּ֣דְתִּי וְיָשַׁ֔בְתִּי וּפִרְי֖וֹ מָת֥וֹק
לְחִכִּֽי: ד הֱבִיאַ֙נִי֙ אֶל־בֵּ֣ית הַיָּ֔יִן וְדִגְל֥וֹ עָלַ֖י אַהֲבָֽה: ה סַמְּכ֙וּנִי֙
בָּֽאֲשִׁישׁ֔וֹת רַפְּד֖וּנִי בַּתַּפּוּחִ֑ים כִּי־חוֹלַ֥ת אַהֲבָ֖ה אָֽנִי:
ו שְׂמֹאלוֹ֙ תַּ֣חַת לְרֹאשִׁ֔י וִֽימִינ֖וֹ תְּחַבְּקֵֽנִי: ז הִשְׁבַּ֙עְתִּי אֶתְכֶ֜ם
בְּנ֤וֹת יְרֽוּשָׁלַ֙͏ִם֙ בִּצְבָא֔וֹת א֖וֹ בְּאַיְל֣וֹת הַשָּׂדֶ֑ה אִם־תָּעִ֣ירוּ ׀
וְאִם־תְּע֣וֹרְר֗וּ אֶת־הָאַהֲבָ֖ה עַ֥ד שֶׁתֶּחְפָּֽץ: ח ק֣וֹל דּוֹדִ֔י הִנֵּה־
זֶ֖ה בָּ֑א מְדַלֵּג֙ עַל־הֶ֣הָרִ֔ים מְקַפֵּ֖ץ עַל־הַגְּבָעֽוֹת: ט דּוֹמֶ֤ה
דוֹדִי֙ לִצְבִ֔י א֖וֹ לְעֹ֣פֶר הָֽאַיָּלִ֑ים הִנֵּה־זֶ֤ה עוֹמֵד֙ אַחַ֣ר כׇּתְלֵ֔נוּ
מַשְׁגִּ֙יחַ֙ מִן־הַֽחַלֹּנ֔וֹת מֵצִ֖יץ מִן־הַֽחֲרַכִּֽים: י עָנָ֥ה דוֹדִ֖י וְאָ֣מַר
לִ֑י ק֥וּמִי לָ֛ךְ רַעְיָתִ֥י יָפָתִ֖י וּלְכִי־לָֽךְ: יא כִּֽי־הִנֵּ֥ה הַסְּתָ֖ו עָבָ֑ר

---

acts as the *chazzan,* calling out the various *simanim* as the children respond. But now, with the children sleeping, the Almighty takes on the role of the *Chazzan* and it is He, so to speak, Who calls out to us, '*Nirtzah.*'"

Rav Kluger also says, "We know how extra careful everyone is about exposure to even a '*mashehu* of *chametz.*' If only people would realize how special it is to benefit from even a '*mashehu* of *Nirtzah.*'" *Rav Kluger* notes that the word *nirtzah* echoes the theme of "*Ki nirtzah avonah* — That her iniquity has been forgiven," which is part of the Almighty's proclamation of "*Nachamu,*" in *Yeshayah* (40:1, 2).

Many people have the custom that immediately following the Seder, they recite the holiest song of all: *Shir HaShirim,* the love story of the Almighty with His people. As we sit in His loving embrace, benefiting from Hashem's acceptance, we are ready to sing our Song of Songs to Him.

הַגֶּשֶׁם חָלַף הָלַךְ לוֹ: יב הַנִּצָּנִים נִרְאוּ בָאָרֶץ עֵת הַזָּמִיר
הִגִּיעַ וְקוֹל הַתּוֹר נִשְׁמַע בְּאַרְצֵנוּ: יג הַתְּאֵנָה חָנְטָה פַגֶּיהָ
וְהַגְּפָנִים סְמָדַר נָתְנוּ רֵיחַ קוּמִי לָךְ רַעְיָתִי יָפָתִי וּלְכִי־לָךְ:
יד יוֹנָתִי בְּחַגְוֵי הַסֶּלַע בְּסֵתֶר הַמַּדְרֵגָה הַרְאִינִי אֶת־מַרְאַיִךְ
הַשְׁמִיעִנִי אֶת־קוֹלֵךְ כִּי־קוֹלֵךְ עָרֵב וּמַרְאֵיךְ נָאוֶה: טו אֶחֱזוּ־
לָנוּ שׁוּעָלִים שׁוּעָלִים קְטַנִּים מְחַבְּלִים כְּרָמִים וּכְרָמֵינוּ
סְמָדַר: טז דּוֹדִי לִי וַאֲנִי לוֹ הָרֹעֶה בַּשּׁוֹשַׁנִּים: יז עַד שֶׁיָּפוּחַ
הַיּוֹם וְנָסוּ הַצְּלָלִים סֹב דְּמֵה־לְךָ דוֹדִי לִצְבִי אוֹ לְעֹפֶר
הָאַיָּלִים עַל־הָרֵי בָתֶר:

פרק ג

א עַל־מִשְׁכָּבִי בַּלֵּילוֹת בִּקַּשְׁתִּי אֵת שֶׁאָהֲבָה נַפְשִׁי בִּקַּשְׁתִּיו
וְלֹא מְצָאתִיו: ב אָקוּמָה נָּא וַאֲסוֹבְבָה בָעִיר בַּשְּׁוָקִים וּבָרְחֹבוֹת
אֲבַקְשָׁה אֵת שֶׁאָהֲבָה נַפְשִׁי בִּקַּשְׁתִּיו וְלֹא מְצָאתִיו: ג מְצָאוּנִי
הַשֹּׁמְרִים הַסֹּבְבִים בָּעִיר אֵת שֶׁאָהֲבָה נַפְשִׁי רְאִיתֶם: ד כִּמְעַט
שֶׁעָבַרְתִּי מֵהֶם עַד שֶׁמָּצָאתִי אֵת שֶׁאָהֲבָה נַפְשִׁי אֲחַזְתִּיו
וְלֹא אַרְפֶּנּוּ עַד־שֶׁהֲבֵיאתִיו אֶל־בֵּית אִמִּי וְאֶל־חֶדֶר הוֹרָתִי:
ה הִשְׁבַּעְתִּי אֶתְכֶם בְּנוֹת יְרוּשָׁלַם בִּצְבָאוֹת אוֹ בְּאַיְלוֹת
הַשָּׂדֶה אִם־תָּעִירוּ | וְאִם־תְּעוֹרְרוּ אֶת־הָאַהֲבָה עַד שֶׁתֶּחְפָּץ:
ו מִי זֹאת עֹלָה מִן־הַמִּדְבָּר כְּתִימְרוֹת עָשָׁן מְקֻטֶּרֶת מֹר
וּלְבוֹנָה מִכֹּל אַבְקַת רוֹכֵל: ז הִנֵּה מִטָּתוֹ שֶׁלִּשְׁלֹמֹה שִׁשִּׁים
גִּבֹּרִים סָבִיב לָהּ מִגִּבֹּרֵי יִשְׂרָאֵל: ח כֻּלָּם אֲחֻזֵי חֶרֶב מְלֻמְּדֵי
מִלְחָמָה אִישׁ חַרְבּוֹ עַל־יְרֵכוֹ מִפַּחַד בַּלֵּילוֹת: ט אַפִּרְיוֹן עָשָׂה
לוֹ הַמֶּלֶךְ שְׁלֹמֹה מֵעֲצֵי הַלְּבָנוֹן: י עַמּוּדָיו עָשָׂה כֶסֶף רְפִידָתוֹ
זָהָב מֶרְכָּבוֹ אַרְגָּמָן תּוֹכוֹ רָצוּף אַהֲבָה מִבְּנוֹת יְרוּשָׁלָם:
יא צְאֶינָה | וּרְאֶינָה בְּנוֹת צִיּוֹן בַּמֶּלֶךְ שְׁלֹמֹה בָּעֲטָרָה שֶׁעִטְּרָה־
לּוֹ אִמּוֹ בְּיוֹם חֲתֻנָּתוֹ וּבְיוֹם שִׂמְחַת לִבּוֹ:

פרק ד

א הִנָּךְ יָפָה רַעְיָתִי הִנָּךְ יָפָה עֵינַיִךְ יוֹנִים מִבַּעַד לְצַמָּתֵךְ
שַׂעְרֵךְ כְּעֵדֶר הָעִזִּים שֶׁגָּלְשׁוּ מֵהַר גִּלְעָד: ב שִׁנַּיִךְ כְּעֵדֶר

הַקְּצוּבוֹת שֶׁעָלוּ מִן־הָרַחְצָה שֶׁכֻּלָּם מַתְאִימוֹת וְשַׁכֻּלָה
אֵין בָּהֶם: גכְּחוּט הַשָּׁנִי שִׂפְתוֹתַיִךְ וּמִדְבָּרֵךְ נָאוֶה כְּפֶלַח
הָרִמּוֹן רַקָּתֵךְ מִבַּעַד לְצַמָּתֵךְ: דכְּמִגְדַּל דָּוִיד צַוָּארֵךְ בָּנוּי
לְתַלְפִּיּוֹת אֶלֶף הַמָּגֵן תָּלוּי עָלָיו כֹּל שִׁלְטֵי הַגִּבֹּרִים: השְׁנֵי
שָׁדַיִךְ כִּשְׁנֵי עֳפָרִים תְּאוֹמֵי צְבִיָּה הָרֹעִים בַּשּׁוֹשַׁנִּים: ועַד
שֶׁיָּפוּחַ הַיּוֹם וְנָסוּ הַצְּלָלִים אֵלֵךְ לִי אֶל־הַר הַמּוֹר וְאֶל־
גִּבְעַת הַלְּבוֹנָה: זכֻּלָּךְ יָפָה רַעְיָתִי וּמוּם אֵין בָּךְ: חאִתִּי
מִלְּבָנוֹן כַּלָּה אִתִּי מִלְּבָנוֹן תָּבוֹאִי תָּשׁוּרִי | מֵרֹאשׁ אֲמָנָה
מֵרֹאשׁ שְׂנִיר וְחֶרְמוֹן מִמְּעֹנוֹת אֲרָיוֹת מֵהַרְרֵי נְמֵרִים:
טלִבַּבְתִּנִי אֲחֹתִי כַלָּה לִבַּבְתִּנִי בְּאַחַת מֵעֵינַיִךְ בְּאַחַד עֲנָק
מִצַּוְּרֹנָיִךְ: ימַה־יָּפוּ דֹדַיִךְ אֲחֹתִי כַלָּה מַה־טֹּבוּ דֹדַיִךְ מִיַּיִן
וְרֵיחַ שְׁמָנַיִךְ מִכָּל־בְּשָׂמִים: יאנֹפֶת תִּטֹּפְנָה שִׂפְתוֹתַיִךְ כַּלָּה
דְּבַשׁ וְחָלָב תַּחַת לְשׁוֹנֵךְ וְרֵיחַ שַׂלְמֹתַיִךְ כְּרֵיחַ לְבָנוֹן: יבגַּן |
נָעוּל אֲחֹתִי כַלָּה גַּל | נָעוּל מַעְיָן חָתוּם: יגשְׁלָחַיִךְ פַּרְדֵּס
רִמּוֹנִים עִם פְּרִי מְגָדִים כְּפָרִים עִם־נְרָדִים: ידנֵרְדְּ | וְכַרְכֹּם
קָנֶה וְקִנָּמוֹן עִם כָּל־עֲצֵי לְבוֹנָה מֹר וַאֲהָלוֹת עִם כָּל־רָאשֵׁי
בְשָׂמִים: טומַעְיַן גַּנִּים בְּאֵר מַיִם חַיִּים וְנֹזְלִים מִן־לְבָנוֹן:
טזעוּרִי צָפוֹן וּבוֹאִי תֵימָן הָפִיחִי גַנִּי יִזְּלוּ בְשָׂמָיו יָבֹא דוֹדִי
לְגַנּוֹ וְיֹאכַל פְּרִי מְגָדָיו:

פרק ה

אבָּאתִי לְגַנִּי אֲחֹתִי כַלָּה אָרִיתִי מוֹרִי עִם־בְּשָׂמִי עִם־
יַעְרִי עִם־דִּבְשִׁי שָׁתִיתִי יֵינִי עִם־חֲלָבִי אִכְלוּ רֵעִים שְׁתוּ
וְשִׁכְרוּ דּוֹדִים: באֲנִי יְשֵׁנָה וְלִבִּי עֵר קוֹל | דּוֹדִי דוֹפֵק פִּתְחִי־
לִי אֲחֹתִי רַעְיָתִי יוֹנָתִי תַמָּתִי שֶׁרֹּאשִׁי נִמְלָא־טָל קְוֻצּוֹתַי
רְסִיסֵי לָיְלָה: גפָּשַׁטְתִּי אֶת־כֻּתָּנְתִּי אֵיכָכָה אֶלְבָּשֶׁנָּה
רָחַצְתִּי אֶת־רַגְלַי אֵיכָכָה אֲטַנְּפֵם: דדּוֹדִי שָׁלַח יָדוֹ מִן־
הַחֹר וּמֵעַי הָמוּ עָלָיו: הקַמְתִּי אֲנִי לִפְתֹּחַ לְדוֹדִי וְיָדַי נָטְפוּ־
מוֹר וְאֶצְבְּעֹתַי מוֹר עֹבֵר עַל כַּפּוֹת הַמַּנְעוּל: ופָּתַחְתִּי אֲנִי
לְדוֹדִי וְדוֹדִי חָמַק עָבָר נַפְשִׁי יָצְאָה בְדַבְּרוֹ בִּקַּשְׁתִּיהוּ וְלֹא
מְצָאתִיהוּ קְרָאתִיו וְלֹא עָנָנִי: זמְצָאֻנִי הַשֹּׁמְרִים הַסֹּבְבִים

בָּעִיר הִכּוּנִי פְצָעוּנִי נָשְׂאוּ אֶת־רְדִידִי מֵעָלַי שֹׁמְרֵי הַחֹמוֹת: ח הִשְׁבַּעְתִּי אֶתְכֶם בְּנוֹת יְרוּשָׁלָ͏ִם אִם־תִּמְצְאוּ אֶת־דּוֹדִי מַה־תַּגִּידוּ לוֹ שֶׁחוֹלַת אַהֲבָה אָנִי: ט מַה־דּוֹדֵךְ מִדּוֹד הַיָּפָה בַּנָּשִׁים מַה־דּוֹדֵךְ מִדּוֹד שֶׁכָּכָה הִשְׁבַּעְתָּנוּ: י דּוֹדִי צַח וְאָדוֹם דָּגוּל מֵרְבָבָה: יא רֹאשׁוֹ כֶּתֶם פָּז קְוֻצּוֹתָיו תַּלְתַּלִּים שְׁחֹרוֹת כָּעוֹרֵב: יב עֵינָיו כְּיוֹנִים עַל־אֲפִיקֵי מָיִם רֹחֲצוֹת בֶּחָלָב יֹשְׁבוֹת עַל־מִלֵּאת: יג לְחָיָו כַּעֲרוּגַת הַבֹּשֶׂם מִגְדְּלוֹת מֶרְקָחִים שִׂפְתוֹתָיו שׁוֹשַׁנִּים נֹטְפוֹת מוֹר עֹבֵר: יד יָדָיו גְּלִילֵי זָהָב מְמֻלָּאִים בַּתַּרְשִׁישׁ מֵעָיו עֶשֶׁת שֵׁן מְעֻלֶּפֶת סַפִּירִים: טו שׁוֹקָיו עַמּוּדֵי שֵׁשׁ מְיֻסָּדִים עַל־אַדְנֵי־פָז מַרְאֵהוּ כַּלְּבָנוֹן בָּחוּר כָּאֲרָזִים: טז חִכּוֹ מַמְתַקִּים וְכֻלּוֹ מַחֲמַדִּים זֶה דוֹדִי וְזֶה רֵעִי בְּנוֹת יְרוּשָׁלָ͏ִם:

פרק ו

א אָנָה הָלַךְ דּוֹדֵךְ הַיָּפָה בַּנָּשִׁים אָנָה פָּנָה דוֹדֵךְ וּנְבַקְשֶׁנּוּ עִמָּךְ: ב דּוֹדִי יָרַד לְגַנּוֹ לַעֲרֻגוֹת הַבֹּשֶׂם לִרְעוֹת בַּגַּנִּים וְלִלְקֹט שׁוֹשַׁנִּים: ג אֲנִי לְדוֹדִי וְדוֹדִי לִי הָרֹעֶה בַּשּׁוֹשַׁנִּים: ד יָפָה אַתְּ רַעְיָתִי כְּתִרְצָה נָאוָה כִּירוּשָׁלָ͏ִם אֲיֻמָּה כַּנִּדְגָּלוֹת: ה הָסֵבִּי עֵינַיִךְ מִנֶּגְדִּי שֶׁהֵם הִרְהִיבֻנִי שַׂעְרֵךְ כְּעֵדֶר הָעִזִּים שֶׁגָּלְשׁוּ מִן־הַגִּלְעָד: ו שִׁנַּיִךְ כְּעֵדֶר הָרְחֵלִים שֶׁעָלוּ מִן־הָרַחְצָה שֶׁכֻּלָּם מַתְאִימוֹת וְשַׁכֻּלָה אֵין בָּהֶם: ז כְּפֶלַח הָרִמּוֹן רַקָּתֵךְ מִבַּעַד לְצַמָּתֵךְ: ח שִׁשִּׁים הֵמָּה מְלָכוֹת וּשְׁמֹנִים פִּילַגְשִׁים וַעֲלָמוֹת אֵין מִסְפָּר: ט אַחַת הִיא יוֹנָתִי תַמָּתִי אַחַת הִיא לְאִמָּהּ בָּרָה הִיא לְיוֹלַדְתָּהּ רָאוּהָ בָנוֹת וַיְאַשְּׁרוּהָ מְלָכוֹת וּפִילַגְשִׁים וַיְהַלְלוּהָ: י מִי־זֹאת הַנִּשְׁקָפָה כְּמוֹ־שָׁחַר יָפָה כַלְּבָנָה בָּרָה כַּחַמָּה אֲיֻמָּה כַּנִּדְגָּלוֹת: יא אֶל־גִּנַּת אֱגוֹז יָרַדְתִּי לִרְאוֹת בְּאִבֵּי הַנָּחַל לִרְאוֹת הֲפָרְחָה הַגֶּפֶן הֵנֵצוּ הָרִמֹּנִים: יב לֹא יָדַעְתִּי נַפְשִׁי שָׂמַתְנִי מַרְכְּבוֹת עַמִּי נָדִיב:

פרק ז

א שׁוּבִי שׁוּבִי הַשּׁוּלַמִּית שׁוּבִי שׁוּבִי וְנֶחֱזֶה־בָּךְ מַה־תֶּחֱזוּ בַּשּׁוּלַמִּית כִּמְחֹלַת הַמַּחֲנָיִם: ב מַה־יָּפוּ פְעָמַיִךְ בַּנְּעָלִים

בַּת־נָדִיב חַמּוּקֵי יְרֵכַ֫יִךְ כְּמ֣וֹ חֲלָאִ֔ים מַעֲשֵׂ֖ה יְדֵ֥י אָמָּֽן:

ג שָׁרְרֵךְ֙ אַגַּ֣ן הַסַּ֔הַר אַל־יֶחְסַ֖ר הַמָּ֑זֶג בִּטְנֵךְ֙ עֲרֵמַ֣ת חִטִּ֔ים סוּגָ֖ה בַּשּׁוֹשַׁנִּֽים: ד שְׁנֵ֥י שָׁדַ֛יִךְ כִּשְׁנֵ֥י עֳפָרִ֖ים תָּאֳמֵ֥י צְבִיָּֽה:

ה צַוָּארֵ֖ךְ כְּמִגְדַּ֣ל הַשֵּׁ֑ן עֵינַ֜יִךְ בְּרֵכ֣וֹת בְּחֶשְׁבּ֗וֹן עַל־שַׁ֙עַר֙ בַּת־רַבִּ֔ים אַפֵּךְ֙ כְּמִגְדַּ֣ל הַלְּבָנ֔וֹן צוֹפֶ֖ה פְּנֵ֥י דַמָּֽשֶׂק: ו רֹאשֵׁ֤ךְ עָלַ֙יִךְ֙ כַּכַּרְמֶ֔ל וְדַלַּ֥ת רֹאשֵׁ֖ךְ כָּאַרְגָּמָ֑ן מֶ֖לֶךְ אָס֥וּר בָּרְהָטִֽים:

ז מַה־יָּפִית֙ וּמַה־נָּעַ֔מְתְּ אַהֲבָ֖ה בַּתַּעֲנוּגִֽים: ח זֹ֤את קֽוֹמָתֵךְ֙ דָּֽמְתָ֣ה לְתָמָ֔ר וְשָׁדַ֖יִךְ לְאַשְׁכֹּלֽוֹת: ט אָמַ֙רְתִּי֙ אֶעֱלֶ֣ה בְתָמָ֔ר אֹֽחֲזָ֖ה בְּסַנְסִנָּ֑יו וְיִֽהְיוּ־נָ֤א שָׁדַ֙יִךְ֙ כְּאֶשְׁכְּל֣וֹת הַגֶּ֔פֶן וְרֵ֥יחַ אַפֵּ֖ךְ כַּתַּפּוּחִֽים: י וְחִכֵּ֕ךְ כְּיֵ֥ין הַטּ֛וֹב הוֹלֵ֥ךְ לְדוֹדִ֖י לְמֵישָׁרִ֑ים דּוֹבֵ֖ב שִׂפְתֵ֥י יְשֵׁנִֽים: יא אֲנִ֣י לְדוֹדִ֔י וְעָלַ֖י תְּשׁוּקָתֽוֹ: יב לְכָ֤ה דוֹדִי֙ נֵצֵ֣א הַשָּׂדֶ֔ה נָלִ֖ינָה בַּכְּפָרִֽים: יג נַשְׁכִּ֙ימָה֙ לַכְּרָמִ֔ים נִרְאֶ֞ה אִם פָּֽרְחָ֤ה הַגֶּ֙פֶן֙ פִּתַּ֣ח הַסְּמָדַ֔ר הֵנֵ֖צוּ הָרִמּוֹנִ֑ים שָׁ֛ם אֶתֵּ֥ן אֶת־דֹּדַ֖י לָֽךְ: יד הַֽדּוּדָאִ֣ים נָֽתְנוּ־רֵ֗יחַ וְעַל־פְּתָחֵ֙ינוּ֙ כָּל־מְגָדִ֔ים חֲדָשִׁ֖ים גַּם־יְשָׁנִ֑ים דּוֹדִ֖י צָפַ֥נְתִּי לָֽךְ:

פרק ח

א מִ֤י יִתֶּנְךָ֙ כְּאָ֣ח לִ֔י יוֹנֵ֖ק שְׁדֵ֣י אִמִּ֑י אֶֽמְצָאֲךָ֤ בַחוּץ֙ אֶשָּׁ֣קְךָ֔ גַּ֖ם לֹא־יָבֻ֥זוּ לִֽי: ב אֶנְהָֽגֲךָ֗ אֲבִֽיאֲךָ֛ אֶל־בֵּ֥ית אִמִּ֖י תְּלַמְּדֵ֑נִי אַשְׁקְךָ֙ מִיַּ֣יִן הָרֶ֔קַח מֵעֲסִ֖יס רִמֹּנִֽי: ג שְׂמֹאלוֹ֙ תַּ֣חַת רֹאשִׁ֔י וִֽימִינ֖וֹ תְּחַבְּקֵֽנִי: ד הִשְׁבַּ֥עְתִּי אֶתְכֶ֖ם בְּנ֣וֹת יְרוּשָׁלִָ֑ם מַה־תָּעִ֧ירוּ | וּֽמַה־תְּעֹֽרְר֛וּ אֶת־הָאַהֲבָ֖ה עַ֥ד שֶׁתֶּחְפָּֽץ: ה מִ֣י זֹ֗את עֹלָה֙ מִן־הַמִּדְבָּ֔ר מִתְרַפֶּ֖קֶת עַל־דּוֹדָ֑הּ תַּ֤חַת הַתַּפּ֙וּחַ֙ עֽוֹרַרְתִּ֔יךָ שָׁ֚מָּה חִבְּלַ֣תְךָ אִמֶּ֔ךָ שָׁ֖מָּה חִבְּלָ֥ה יְלָדַֽתְךָ: ו שִׂימֵ֨נִי כַֽחוֹתָ֜ם עַל־לִבֶּ֗ךָ כַּֽחוֹתָם֙ עַל־זְרוֹעֶ֔ךָ כִּֽי־עַזָּ֤ה כַמָּ֙וֶת֙ אַהֲבָ֔ה קָשָׁ֥ה כִשְׁא֖וֹל קִנְאָ֑ה רְשָׁפֶ֕יהָ רִשְׁפֵּ֕י אֵ֖שׁ שַׁלְהֶבֶתְיָֽה: ז מַ֣יִם רַבִּ֗ים לֹ֤א יֽוּכְלוּ֙ לְכַבּ֣וֹת אֶת־הָֽאַהֲבָ֔ה וּנְהָר֖וֹת לֹ֣א יִשְׁטְפ֑וּהָ אִם־יִתֵּ֨ן אִ֜ישׁ אֶת־כָּל־ה֤וֹן בֵּיתוֹ֙ בָּֽאַהֲבָ֔ה בּ֖וֹז יָב֥וּזוּ לֽוֹ: ח אָח֥וֹת לָ֙נוּ֙ קְטַנָּ֔ה וְשָׁדַ֖יִם אֵ֣ין לָ֑הּ מַֽה־נַּעֲשֶׂה֙ לַאֲחֹתֵ֔נוּ בַּיּ֖וֹם שֶׁיְּדֻבַּר־בָּֽהּ: ט אִם־חוֹמָ֣ה הִ֔יא נִבְנֶ֥ה עָלֶ֖יהָ טִ֣ירַת כָּ֑סֶף וְאִם־דֶּ֣לֶת הִ֔יא נָצ֥וּר עָלֶ֖יהָ ל֥וּחַ אָֽרֶז: י אֲנִ֣י חוֹמָ֔ה וְשָׁדַ֖י כַּמִּגְדָּל֑וֹת אָ֚ז הָיִ֣יתִי

בְּעֵינָיו כְּמוֹצְאֵת שָׁלוֹם: יא כֶּרֶם הָיָה לִשְׁלֹמֹה בְּבַעַל הָמוֹן נָתַן אֶת הַכֶּרֶם לַנֹּטְרִים אִישׁ יָבִא בְּפִרְיוֹ אֶלֶף כָּסֶף: יב כַּרְמִי שֶׁלִּי לְפָנָי הָאֶלֶף לְךָ שְׁלֹמֹה וּמָאתַיִם לְנֹטְרִים אֶת־פִּרְיוֹ: יג הַיּוֹשֶׁבֶת בַּגַּנִּים חֲבֵרִים מַקְשִׁיבִים לְקוֹלֵךְ הַשְׁמִיעִנִי: יד בְּרַח | דּוֹדִי וּדְמֵה־לְךָ לִצְבִי אוֹ לְעֹפֶר הָאַיָּלִים עַל הָרֵי בְשָׂמִים: